Thinking Through Writing

Susan R. Horton is associate professor of English at the University of Massachusetts at Boston. She is the author of *Interpreting Interpreting: Interpreting Dickens's "Dombey"* (also published by Johns Hopkins) and *The Reader in the Dickens World*.

Thinking Through Writing

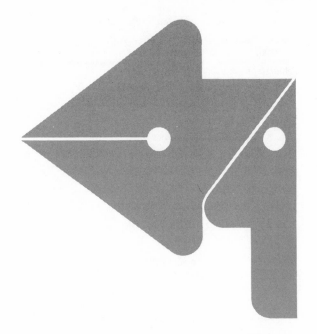

Susan R. Horton

The Johns Hopkins University Press
Baltimore and London

See p. 213 for permission notices.

Copyright © 1982 by The Johns Hopkins University Press
All rights reserved
Printed in the United States of America

Originally published (hardcover and paperback), 1982
Second printing (paperback), 1983
Third printing (paperback), 1983
Fourth printing (paperback), 1986

The Johns Hopkins University Press
701 West 40th Street
Baltimore, Maryland 21211
The Johns Hopkins Press Ltd., London

Library of Congress Cataloging in Publication Data

Horton, Susan R.
  Thinking through writing.

Bibliography: p. 203
  Includes index.
  1. English language—Rhetoric. 2. Concepts.
I. Title
PE1408.H6836   808'.042   81–18628
ISBN 0–8018–2716–7   AACR2
ISBN 0–8018–2717–5 (pbk.)

TOM REED
This one's for you

The more the mind knows, the better it understands its forces and the order of nature; the more it understands its forces or strength, the better it will be able to direct itself and lay down rules for itself; and the more it understands the order of nature, the more easily it will be able to liberate itself from useless things.

Spinoza, De intellectus emendatione

Contents

Acknowledgments

My thanks go first to all the people in my writing classes over the past ten years, especially to those who pushed, questioned, argued with me, and shared the fun and fascination I feel when watching the mind thinking and the hand writing. Gratitude and affection in large measure go also to my friend and colleague Neal Bruss, whose incisive and extensive commentary on an earlier draft of this book was of exactly the kind and quality every writer dreams of, but rarely gets. Thirdly, I want to thank my colleague Ann E. Berthoff, with whom I am convinced no one could share the profession of teacher and fail to be inspired. My thanks go also to Carolyn Q. Wilson and Judith Pinch of the Woodrow Wilson Fellowship Foundation, who not only provided financial support in the form of a Woodrow Wilson Faculty Development Grant but who took a personal interest in my work as well. Finally, I am grateful to the staff of The Johns Hopkins University Press, most notably Bill Sisler and Jane Warth, for exhibiting grace, patience, and ingenuity in seeing the manuscript through to publication.

Thinking Through Writing

1

What Is Writing and Why Do It?

Somehow, writing should be easier than it is, and more fun. In trying to make it so, somehow we all—teachers, students, beginning writers—got off the track and made it, I think, more difficult instead. We started talking about errors and how to stay away from them; about the "rules" of the game—watching for comma faults, making sure we had an "introduction," a "body," a "conclusion," devising "outlines," living in fear we would violate the rules of "unity" and "coherence." Rules are necessary, of course, but we focused so much on the rules we forgot to talk about what the game is: what it is for, how it changes lives and minds, how it works, and even what *it* is. We paid so much attention to avoiding mistakes we forgot the joys that come from saying something new. We talked about "having a thesis statement," but rarely about how one gets one. An idea *is* a thesis statement, and we have not talked much about that at all. Somehow, even those of us who can write pretty well, who have written fine and interesting essays on personal subjects, have felt first puzzled and then betrayed when we discovered that our writing fell apart if we were asked to produce analytical essays for a college course or to subdue lots of data into a readable form. How does one organize all there is to say on a subject like altruism and selfishness—especially when one is trying to fit what one thinks in with what two or three philosophers have to say on the subject? Suddenly, warnings and advice about making sure there is an introduction, body, and conclusion do not seem like much help at all.

That is what this book is for, and it may be thought of as a "Back to Basics" book. But I am talking about the real basics.

Not grammar, but basics like what writing is and is for, how you get an idea, and how and why each idea demands its own kind of organization, how ideas turn into essays, and, even more basic, about how your mind forms ideas in the first place. You can use this book with or without a teacher in front of you. It is designed not to *tell* you what to do or how to write so much as to set things up so that you can discover for yourself how writing works (yours and everybody else's), and, in the process, how your mind works as well. It is a kind of "watch yourself think" book. There are not many answers in it, but there are lots of questions: lots of things to try and explore and discover and play with. Even more than that, this is a book that tries to teach you not just how to answer questions, but how to find questions to ask. As Michel Foucault says in *The Archaeology of Knowledge*, and as Susanne Langer says in *Philosophy in a New Key*, it is our questions—the questions we ask of the world and that are asked of us—that determine what we can see and what we cannot. And for Foucault, the most important part of thinking is learning even to question our questions. ("What made me ask that question," you might ask yourself as a thinking writer.) All of this may sound like a long way from writing with ease, but in this case, the longest road is the shortest way home—and the most fun.

In the next chapter we will talk about the most basic thing of all: what an essay is. But what is "writing"? Simply, writing is how minds think. Just as you can add 2 + 3 in your head, but cannot add 1,827 + 9,369 without paper and pencil, so you can think "What should I have for dinner?" in your head, but not "What is the relationship between American child-raising practices and adolescent rebellion?" or "What conceptions of the world was I given as a child that determine how I think and act now?" or "What factors combined to create the conditions for the onset of World War II?" To think about complex issues and to answer complex questions, we need paper. We push the pen, and the pen pushes us—to harder, more complex ideas than we could ever reach without pen and paper acting as a kind of storage-and-retrieval mechanism for us. (That only means that writing stores ideas for us.) Writing—putting things down on paper—is what allows you to hold onto one idea while you go off and explore some idea that some small, nagging voice in the back of your mind tells you might be related to it. In and because of writing, you can discover how certain things you thought were different might turn out to have things in common; how certain things you thought were alike really turn out to be different. Writing is the mind's way of *thinking beyond* what it can think without an aid like paper and pen. It is also, of course, a way of reaching beyond yourself to other minds, whose only access to yours is provided by those traces of your mind you leave behind, in your writings.

Several things follow from what I have just said. One is that it does no good to think you can "just write the way you talk." An essay—and we will talk about this more in the next chapter— is not just talk written down. It is the product of a special and specialized kind of language and thinking. This book will help you see why and how this is so, and what that means to you as a writer. It also does no good to think you should not start writing until you are quite sure what you have to say. Because essays convey ideas usually too complex to be held in the mind all at once, it makes sense that you can only get to those ideas through and by way of writing. You approach those ideas by steps, on paper. You circle around them, you push toward them. I seriously doubt that anyone ever writes anything really good in one try. Those finished, polished essays you read in books are rarely if ever the product of one try. The words you are reading now are the product of a fifth draft, and were you with me here you could see the scraps and crumpled heaps of earlier tries piled around my desk. I confess this because I am distressed to think about how many beginning writers try to write, find their first drafts unsatisfying, watch themselves begin, stop, and begin again, and conclude they just are not "meant" to be writers.

In the pages that follow, I want to get you to capitalize on what is a very basic human drive, and to see how this drive can be harnessed to produce essays. The smallest baby has a strong drive to know what something is: to name things and, shortly thereafter, to find out where those things came from, what they are for, where they fit into his world. Watch a baby study a toy, a spoon, put it in his mouth, turn it 'round and 'round looking at it from all angles. Watch a toddler ask repeatedly, "What's that?" "What's that?" He wants a name so that he can categorize what he encounters. Adults do the same thing. Scientists, philosophers, thinkers, writers, you, me. To compose is to take seriously this basic tendency of mind. To read is to comprehend someone else's answer to "What's that?" To write an essay is to communicate your "What's that?" process and conclusions to others.

Of course, to name what is there, we first have to *see* it; and this is also a book in exercising the eye: the face's eye and the mind's eye. Getting used to looking closely at "what's there": on the page in front of you, in the textbook you are studying, in the world through which you walk.

It is probably clear by now that this is not a usual kind of writing book, and this is so not only in what it says, but in what it does not say. I do not believe, for instance, that there is any point in spending one paragraph or one page on things like punctuation and spelling. If you are old enough to read this book, you are old enough to take responsibility for those things yourself. Surely you had at least one, and more likely a dozen, teachers who corrected your commas and your spelling and told you the difference between *their* and *there* (not to mention *they're*), and between *affect* and *effect*. If you do not know those distinctions by now, one more person going through them one more time will not help you. The only thing that will is your taking yourself seriously enough, right now, to learn them for yourself. I say this to put the responsibility where it belongs by this point in your life, and to spare us the illusion that good writing has to do primarily with these things. It does not. It has to do with those things I have already begun to talk about: paying close attention as you read, so that when you write about what you have read, you do so with an accurate assessment of what was on the page. This is the "looking closely" I just talked about. Good writing has to do with putting together what is there in a plausible, interesting, and persuasive way.

What this means is that writing well has more to do with attitudes and understanding—understanding what game you are playing and wanting to play it well—than with following rules or just not making mistakes. I may be able to teach you to drive a car by telling you to get in, turn the key, and put in the clutch, shift, push the gas pedal, and steer. But if you want to make the car work better (and not just drive it), you should want to know how a combustion engine works. If you want to make your writing work better—maybe so that you can let it take you on longer and more interesting trips—then you will want to know how writing works. To do this, you will need to become your own paper mechanic, because unfortunately you cannot drive a bad essay into the repair shop and let someone else fix it. And the kind of things that need fixing in a paper are as numerous as those things that need fixing in a car. This book will help you find out just which things in your "machine" need to be tightened up, thrown out, replaced, or repaired. You will carry out the diagnosis and repair work. The problem may be *inspiration* ("I don't have anything to say, and I've read lots of material already"), *intuition* ("I know there's a connection here, but I don't know what it is"), or *articulation* ("I know what I want to say, but I can't get it to come out right"). And then there is always the harder problem ("I have lots of things to say, and I know they are all related, but I can't figure out exactly how yet, and so I can't figure out how to organize my essay").

No one can tell you how to solve these problems—every essay is a whole new challenge anyway—but I can help you to see what kind of problem you have in each instance, and feel in control of the writing process enough so that you will not panic and so that you can come to see your raw materials, your hunches, and your assignments as challenges, or as problems to be solved rather than as dilemmas.

This is part of what I mean by saying that writing is a matter more of attitude than of skill; a matter of defining a problem as finding things to say and getting rid of the common pseudo-problem ("I have to fill up ten pages somehow").

Part of the attitude of the good writer is a willingness to take chances saying something new. It is also a willingness to struggle and wrestle ideas into shape. But writing well also involves getting used to having your antennae out all the time, watching for material you might use in an essay. That material might be hiding anywhere: on the subway, in some book far outside your major field, in some comment your father always made in times of stress. We will practice using metaphors from other worlds—the worlds of machines and of nature, for instance—to force resemblances and to clarify things to ourselves and our readers. I just compared writing an essay with learning the inside of your car. That is an analogy. And pointing to it is thinking about thinking and writing about writing. We will do that too.

We will use materials from lots of different fields: the natural sciences, sociology, history, politics, mathematics. Whenever such material is used, or whenever other people's notions of how the thinking and writing process works are cited, you will find an author's name and page number in parentheses immediately following. If the statement or excerpt or ideas intrigue you, go to the bibliography at the back of this book for a full reference to the source, find the book, and read more of it. As a writer, you should be reading lots of things in lots of different places. People who read a lot may not necessarily be writers, but writers are always people who read a lot. Having a well-stocked mind ensures that you will always have a fund of ideas to write about, and that you will be able to recognize the answer to a question or problem when it crosses your path. As Jerome Bruner tells us in his book *On Knowing*, discovery always favors the well-prepared mind. You should get used to having that well-prepared mind.

In all its particularity, and in the ways it thinks—not only in *what* it thinks but also in the *ways* it thinks—that well-prepared, well-stocked mind of yours works exactly like no other on earth. Sitting with two friends and talking about how we teach writing, I was astounded to notice that each of us was using completely different hand gestures to describe what we do and say in classes. Eileen held her two hands pressed together as if she were praying and then pushed those praying hands in a straight line in front of her: "I just tell students to get on the track and keep on until they get to the end," she said. Neal held his two hands far apart, in a "there's *this*, and then *that*" gesture. My hands seemed to be holding a ball, turning it 'round and 'round to look at all its surfaces. I kept talking about going around behind an idea, to see what it looks like from another angle. Eileen's thinking was linear. Neal's binary. Mine, three-dimensional. Different minds think in different ways, and part of what I hope you will learn by doing the exercises in this book is what kind of mind you have.

That mind you have also needs different things in order to work, and I hope this book gets you in touch with what you need to work and write. Samuel Johnson needed a "purring cat, orange peel and plenty of tea," or nothing would come. Balzac could only write at night and needed plenty of black coffee to do it. Emile Zola needed the opposite: he worked in the daytime, but he pulled all the blinds because he needed artificial light or he could not think or write. Carlyle tried to create a soundproof room. Schiller could not write unless he had a drawer full of rotting apples he could pull out and catch whiffs of to inspire him. Poincaré the mathematician needed black coffee. Stephen Spender needed tea and lots of note slips. W. H. Auden, coffee and tobacco. Kipling could only write with black ink. (You will find these stories in Peter McKellar's *Imagination and Thinking*.) Hart Crane could not write a poem unless he was in a room full of music and noise and people, but he would suddenly rush out of the room, go off and scribble furiously, race back into the room and shout, "Isn't this the *greatest* poem you ever heard?" He knew it was not, of course, and he went off alone later to revise and revise and get it right. But he knew he needed that noise to chase the poem out of its hole, just as a hunter flushes a rabbit out of its hole with water. My favorite story is about the novelist Malcolm Lowry, and I read it in an account written by his doctor, C. G. McNeill, in *American Review 17*. Lowry came to the doctor with huge callouses on the backs of his knuckles, "like an ape," his doctor said, and with varicose veins in his legs. It turned out that Lowry had a severe block against holding a pen in his hands, and could only write standing up (thus the varicose veins), dictating to his wife, and leaning with his knuckles against a lectern (thus the callouses). The doctor's suggestion was that he dictate lying down, or have surgery to correct the veins. Lowry chose the surgery. He knew he could write no way but standing up, with his knuckles pressed against the lectern, dictating to his wife.

The point of all these stories is that no one can tell you exactly what you need to create except you. No one can tell you what kind of mind you have—linear, binary, three-dimensional—except you. But this book will try to make it possible for you to find out what you do need in order to create, and what works best for you. In the pages that follow, you will find almost a hundred questions and exercises designed to get you to discover how writing works and how you work. This book will also allow you to see how other minds think and write, and, in the process, learn something about the moves one can make (theoreticians call them *tropes*) when composing discourse.

It would help if you would keep a writer's journal as you go through the exercises in this book. This should not be anything like a diary of "How I feel today," but instead might be constructed in four parts, according to the description that follows:

1. *A log.*   In this log, you should keep track of how much time you spend in each phase of each writing exercise. How long (and where) did you do your best thinking, reading, and idea gathering? Where and for how long did you do your first brainstorming? How much time did it take you to read the primary materials you needed to read in order to write the essay? How much time passed between the reading phase and the writing phase? Was that enough time? Too much? How much time did you spend on the first draft? On the second? The third? How much time did you spend just sitting? Composing an opening sentence? What did you learn that works best for you? What place is best for you to write in? What should you not repeat the next time? Where do you suspect you wasted or lost time? If some time or place or tactic seemed to be a breakthrough for you, record and remember that in the log. What really got you writing best: Sheer grit? Deadlines? Some people (like Einstein) think better in bed. Try sneaking up on a problem first thing in the morning before you are fully awake. Browse through Arthur Koestler's *The Act of Creation* for accounts of how and why such tactics have worked for other people, and consider if they might work for you.

2. *An idea fund.*   Keep a fund of images that intrigue you, and of ideas that strike you at odd moments—about the relationship between one thing and another; about the causes for something you had not thought of before. About all kinds of connections you make. All kinds of statements you make to yourself that begin "Have you ever noticed that/how. . . ." Collect material for analogies: "This is like that."

3. *A clipping bank.*   Cut out of newspapers, or type copies of, paragraphs that intrigue you either because of their subject matter, their style, or their tone. You may find them helpful as raw material, as models, or as pump primers (do you know what a pump primer is?) when you write.

4. *A self-study.*   Keep a record of the personal strengths, propensities, fears, or suspicions you have about your own relation to your writing. What is there that might work

against your being a good writer? A clear writer? Some people are afraid of being clear because they are afraid they will discover what they really think or believe. Some are afraid they will discover they are not sure what they think or believe. Some are deliberately fuzzy when they write so that they can cover their tracks if their readers disagree with them. If you are subconsciously sabotaging your own efforts, you should find out now how you do that, and why. Some people grew up rewarded for *not* speaking out, and they find that old habit getting in the way of their progress as writers. Think about your relation to the whole enterprise of speaking clearly and speaking out. Some people are stubborn and capable of "worrying" (see the dictionary for the right definition of that word here) an idea forever. Are you one of those people? If so, it would help if you were aware of it. Do you have a fear of coming to conclusions? A fear of being wrong? What are your strengths outside of writing, that may become strengths in writing as well?

If you will keep this journal, if you will read the pages that follow, do the exercises, and listen—especially if you will listen to yourself, you will have a strong sense of what an essay is and how it works; about how your mind works and puts ideas together; about how minds in general take things apart and put them together (that is called *analysis* and *synthesis* in some circles); about how thinking and writing are themselves matters of taking things apart and putting them together in new ways; about how you can do that more efficiently and with results you like. As the book progresses, you will find more and more lists of things: points about writing, lists of strategies to use when you are trying to read difficult material, lists of suggestions for things to do when you are trying to get or shape an idea, lists of procedures to follow when you are writing an essay, and then questions to ask yourself as you edit what you write.

There are almost a hundred suggestions for writing in the book as well, and you are invited to try as many of them as you have time for, or as many as catch your fancy. They are really one hundred different ways into the same thing. My assumption is that at the point of illumination—the point at which you really see what discourse is and how it works—you will not need the book any longer. You will understand the game and its rules and, consequently, be able to play the game well. Or, to put things another way, you might consider these practice exercises and suggestions that follow as one-hundred jump starts to get your motor running on cold mornings. I hope you will be able to get into your car on the 101st morning, drive off with ease, and reach whatever destination you choose.

Below is a series of suggestions for writing exercises designed to get you started on that journey and to let you watch how writing and thinking work for you.

1. To discover for yourself the extent to which good writers lean on their prose to hold onto ideas too complex for them to hold in their minds without writing, try this experiment: get a ballpoint pen that no longer writes. On a sheet of paper that has a sheet of carbon paper and another sheet of paper beneath that, write out a description of any process with which you are very familiar, using the worn-out pen. Notice how easy it is to lose your train of thought when you cannot see what you have written. Notice how easy it is for your sentences to become awkward, and maybe even to disintegrate altogether. Notice how difficult it is to write when you cannot see what you've already written. Think about how much truer this is when you are discussing something more complex than a process you know well. Notice, finally, how important it is for you as a writer, whenever you are "stuck," to pause and reread what you have written so far as a prod and an inspiration to discover what ought to come next.

2. Again, try writing up a process you know well. This time use a working pen, but try to write as rapidly as you can. This time, notice the extent to which no matter how fast you write, your mind is moving faster. Notice how it is that things you did not think you were going to say suddenly begin to enter your consciousness as you are writing. That phenomenon is what I am talking about when I said you push the pen and the pen pushes you.

3. Read carefully the excerpt below, written by the scientist Francis Galton: "When I pronounce one sentence, where is the following one. Certainly not in the field of my consciousness, which is occupied by sentence number one; and nevertheless, I do think of it, and it is ready to appear the next instant, which cannot occur if I do not think of it unconsciously" (in Hadamard, p. 24). In response to these musings of Galton's, Jacques Hadamard the mathmetician says:

It seems to me that we can identify this with what Francis Galton calls the "ante-chamber" of consciousness: "When I am engaged in trying to think anything out, the process of doing so appears to me to be this: The ideas that lie at any moment within my full consciousness seem to attract of their own accord the most appropriate out of a number of other ideas that are lying close at hand, but imperfectly within the range of my consciousness. There seems to be a presence-chamber in my mind where full consciousness holds court, and where two or three ideas are at the same time in audience, and an ante-chamber full of more or less allied ideas, which is situated just beyond the full ken of consciousness. Out of this ante-chamber the ideas most nearly allied to those in the presence-chamber appear to be summoned in a mechanically logical way, and to have their turn of audience" (Hadamard, pp. 24–25).

This description sounds much like the kind of dialectic between the writer and what he or she has written that makes essay writing exciting. This is the process by which we find out how and what we think *in the act of writing*. What we can tap in this way is what William James calls the "fringe-consciousness," what Edward deBono calls "lateral thinking," and Arthur Koestler calls "thinking aside." Simply, we keep ourselves busy so that new ideas can creep up on us. As you watch yourself write, see if this happens to you. In the log section of your writer's journal, consider what you might remember in order to ensure that you will always be alert enough to catch those ideas as they fly by the corner of your mind and consciousness.

2

What Is an Essay, Anyway?

If writing itself is a kind of pushing of the mind, and a kind of storage-and-retrieval mechanism, what is the particular kind of writing we call an *essay*? In college courses people take essay exams. What features do those things have? If we write papers for courses, what must those pieces of writing look like? It is not surprising that people often have misconceptions about what they are to write when they are asked to write an essay. The world is full of writing that resembles, on the surface, an essay. I am convinced much of the writing people do in college that is not well received is not well received because it was written by someone who *thought* he or she was writing an essay, but was really imitating a very different kind of writing: textbook writing, "theme" writing, or newspaper writing, for instance. It makes sense for us to look closely at a sample of each kind to discover what features distinguish an essay from other kinds of writing.

Beginning on page 25, you will find four excerpts of writing. The subject of each one is anthropology, if we assume that anthropology is the study of a culture or cultures, and the study of the relationship of a culture to its artifacts. Read through all four excerpts and, as you do, see if you can answer the following questions. You could use your writer's log as a place in which you compose answers to the questions.

1. For what audience does each piece of writing seem intended?

2. How much does the writer of each piece assume his or her audience knows about the subject, and how much attention

does the writer pay to leading the reader from one point to the next?

3. Which piece or pieces of writing seem broad and relatively superficial, and which seem narrower in scope, but to have more depth?

4. Can you detect traces of that "struggle into consciousness" that we talked about in the last chapter in any or all of these four pieces? Do you see these writers "thinking beyond" to new and more complex ideas than those we carry around in our heads? Where do you see those traces: in which pieces, and in which places in which pieces?

5. Which piece would you call an "essay," and what would you call the other pieces that you would not classify as essays?

The first writing sample you just read is from a textbook, as I am sure you could tell. This kind of writing should never be mistaken for essay writing, and should never be imitated when you are asked to or want to write an essay. Its differences from an essay can be summarized easily:

1. Each of its sentences is a *generalization*: a very large statement that sweeps together a great deal of separate "facts." A sentence such as "Every culture and subculture provides several sets of concepts or categories for perceiving and understanding phenomena" would be called a generalization.

2. Beyond this, you might note that each of the generalizations in the first piece, if they were found in an essay rather than in a textbook, would require support, defense, exemplification. But the textbook writer is assumed to be an authority giving an overview of a field, and thus he or she is allowed to make a general point ("World War II was caused by. . . ," "The main reason for the downfall of the King was . . .") without supporting those points. The essayist is not given that license and is expected to support and defend each generalization, except for the very safe,

obvious, shared assumption. Even at those points, as we shall see, at times the great essayist is the one who challenges exactly those "safe" shared assumptions.

3. The audience for the textbook is assumed to have little or no knowledge of the subject being discussed and is assumed to want only a brief and relatively superficial survey or introduction to a field.

4. This assumption on the part of the textbook writer that his or her audience wants a superficial survey often leads to prose in which every sentence literally brings up a new topic. If the essays you have written are returned to you with comments in the margins like "Develop this point," "How do you know?" "You haven't explained your position," or "Explain," consider whether you might be taking textbook prose as your model rather than essay writing.

5. The style of this prose is fairly clear, using mostly the active voice rather than the passive. ("Observers and researchers invariably use comparison" is active; "The comparison is invariably used by observers and researchers" is passive.) But often textbook prose tends to have elaborate syntax that makes reading it difficult. One of my favorite textbook sentences is this: "That Henry VIII would be the cause of all the trouble was hardly a fact of which people were unaware." Try paraphrasing (writing another and simpler version of) this sentence just to see how simple the point being made here really is and how clearly it could have been written. In his *Philosophy of Composition*, E. D. Hirsch notices that textbook writers are often the worst offenders of what he calls the "readability principle." That principle is that "the sequence for economizing the reader's attention is the sequence that leaves the reader in uncertainty for the shortest period of time" (p. 80). The sentence above certainly fails to do that. Usually, if you want to write an essay that is clear and readable, you would prefer the simple subject/verb ordering of most sentences, and you would prefer active voice to passive. You can write long, Byzantine sentences in your essays if you wish. You should remember, however, that such sentences make your reader work harder and may even make your reader down-

right impatient with you. A reader who gets impatient just stops reading, and when your reader stops reading, you have lost your audience: lost your chance to be heard.

6. This last point is particularly important. Sadly, I think many beginning writers believe just the opposite: that it is elaborate prose that *earns* them the right to be read. But as a writer, you should want to write as simply as possible, so that the complexity of your ideas can shine through. The harshest judgment on pompous padded prose comes, I think, from Rudolf Flesch in *The Art of Readable Writing*:

> "Great formality seems to be the hallmark of the still-insecure, the not-quite-arrived, the semi-accepted. The social sciences have a more pompous language than the natural sciences, psychology has a more luxuriant lingo than medicine, public administration is more unreadable than law. Among our social groups, the most formalistic style is that of labor. . . . John L. Lewis loved to express himself like this: 'No action has been taken by this writer or the United Mine Workers of America, as such, which would fall within the purview of the oppressive statute under which you seek to function. Without indulging in analysis, it is a logical assumption that the cavilings of the bar and bench in their attempts to explicate this infamous enactment will consume a tedious time.'" Flesch concludes his observations by saying that "those who are secure in their position . . . usually know they don't need such verbal trappings. They know they can forget about false dignity and use language that suits their personality and the purpose in hand" (p. 221).

This seems a fair judgment. The only other reason why a writer would want to sound pompous, obscure, or like a textbook, I think, is that he or she is not quite sure what he or she wants to say and is trying to hide that doubt. We will talk later about what the writer can do when that point comes.

The second writing sample is from Margaret Mead's *Coming of Age in Samoa*, which is a study of adolescence in a primitive culture and an analysis of the differences between young people in Samoa and in Western countries. I would call this a true essay. What are its characteristics?

1. It is addressed to its readers in a matter-of-fact, straightforward voice, tone, and style. Sentences such as the one that begins "We have been comparing point for point . . . " make it very clear that this writer is much more interested in being clear and being understood than in being thought to be writing something "weighty."

2. This style and tone, however, do not signal a casual or haphazard attitude toward the material discussed. Instead, if you look closely, you will see that Mead is carefully building an analysis—point by point, sentence by sentence. In contrast to textbook sentences, each of her sentences leads into the following one, as well as supports, refutes, elaborates, or makes a connection with the preceding one. The unmistakable signs of a building analysis are there in the words: "If . . . then. . . . But . . . however, because . . . therefore. . . ." Much of this book will lead you through the steps necessary to produce analysis, but for now you might simply notice that her analysis is made up of *propositions* ("If adolescents are only plunged into difficulties and distress because of conditions in their social environment, then by all means let us so modify that environment so as to reduce this stress and eliminate this strain and anguish of adjustment"). Her analysis is made up of *qualifiers* made upon those propositions ("But unfortunately the conditions which vex our adolescents are the flesh and bone of our society, no more subject to straightforward manipulation upon our part than is the language which we speak"). It is also made up of statements *asserting a relationship* between separate propositions ("The principal causes of our adolescents' difficulty are the presence of conflicting standards and the belief that every individual should make his or her own choices, coupled with a feeling that choice is an important matter"). The essay is also full of statements *demonstrating the truth of* those propositions Mead makes. All of these kinds of statements—propositions, qualifications, exemplifications, and demonstrations—make up the essay form.

3. Because the material Mead is discussing is inherently complex, the writing is characterized by a fierce attempt to be simple and clear. Unlike "creative" writing, which strives to be richly ambiguous, her writing strives to be as unambiguous as possible. This is not to say that the prose is not colorful and full of images and analogies or comparisons: "At first blush," "Conditions . . . vex our adolescents," "are the flesh and bone of society," "conditions . . . are no more subject to straightforward manipulation . . . than is the language which we speak." But those images and comparisons are used to clarify her points, not to make the prose rich in ambiguities.

4. What this last point suggests is that the writing of an essay takes as much imagination as the writing of a poem: the essay writer needs imagination to choose exactly the right metaphor, the absolutely best word, the best order in which to convey ideas and findings most clearly. The essay writer uses his or her imagination to be as flexible as possible in order to see how best to arrange the parts of the discourse. The "imaginative" or "creative" writer simply uses his or her imagination for different purposes.

5. You will notice that Mead does not assume her audience "knows what she means" about anything. She takes great pains to lead the reader through her essay. In this instance, she begins by summarizing what she has been doing. She explains why she has done it. She announces that she is going to take up a new subject ("If we now turn from the Samoan picture . . ."). That kind of careful leading of the reader by the hand is absolutely essential in good essay writing, in which you might take as a rule of thumb the principle that your reader is a stranger, who is intelligent but does not know much about your subject. In this respect, college classes, I fear, often mislead us. The atmosphere in the class is that we are "all friends," who share a classroom, a set of beliefs, certain sets of assumptions, and a certain body of knowledge. This assumption leads to the writing of essays that are far too elliptical, too brief, too sketchy. When a reader responds to your essays by saying, "You haven't told me enough," your response

is often, "But *you* know what I mean." In theoretical terms, there is confusion here about whether the writer is in a "restricted code situation" (in which writers and readers all know each other and agree on everything and therefore do not have to explain and defend everything), or an "elaborated code situation" (in which we as writers need to be more explicit, more public, and assume our readers are strangers to our ideas). These are Basil Bernstein's conclusions about different "codes" that operate for writers (pp. 165–66).

6. One of the most dramatic and interesting features of a true essay, however, is not its tone or grammatical features or the sentences one finds in it, but its status in quite a different sense. You will notice that Mead's essay is completely composed of a challenge to the old, accepted truism "Adolescence is a painful time, caused mostly by physiological changes that are inevitable." This points up one of what I take to be the most exciting and challenging parts of essay writing: essays not only explain, solve, or explore problems; as often as not, *they create a problem or generate and then answer a question where none existed before.* They point out to us how some of those things we thought were obviously and unexceptionably true are not so unexceptionably true at all. Writing essays is engaging in *discourse.* That word is very popular these days. It means writing about topics such as human nature, culture, society, or history: writing about anything in which there is room and need for fresh ways of seeing and thinking. As Hayden White reminds us in *Tropics of Discourse,* the word *discourse* comes from the Latin *discurrere,* which means to move back and forth, or to run to and fro. What is it that we run back and forth between when we write essays; when we compose "discourse"? The answer is twofold: we run back and forth from facts in the world to speculations about what those facts may mean. We run back and forth between what White calls "conceptualization[s] of a given area of experience which have become hardened into a hypostasis that blocks fresh perceptions or denies, in the interest of formalization, what our will or emotions tells us ought not to be the case in a given department of life" (pp. 3–4).

What that means is that we move back and forth between set, long-held notions and ways of looking at something in the world, and some new way of seeing that our hunches, our observations, or our heart tells us is more accurate. This is exactly what Mead does in her essay. Discourse is the way the mind wrestles with what surrounds it. Discourse is a kind of midpoint between the desire to understand some part of experience, and full comprehension of that part of experience (White, p. 22). It is, in other words, what we talked about in the last chapter. It is the way we think beyond what we know.

7. When you write an essay, compose discourse, move back and forth between those old ways of seeing and new ways of seeing, the skill and clarity with which you do those things, according to White, is what *earns* you the right to be heard; *earns* you the right to change other people's way of seeing. The strong and coherent essay, in other words, is your ticket into the world of ideas and into the marketplace where ideas are exchanged. Mead died not so long ago, but her ideas are still alive in the world. The essay makes way for, and finds a place for, our ideas in the world.

The third piece of writing is a newspaper article. It is included here because it shows both what a newspaper article can be and how a newspaper article may transcend that form and become something very much like an essay. It is really, in smaller compass than Mead's essay, an essay itself. It was written by William Henry, who recently and quite deservedly won a Pulitzer Prize for his journalism. The article demonstrates what we have just said about the essay:

1. Most significantly, it points a connection where we had not seen one before. In this case, Henry pinpoints the nature and source of Donald Duck's appeal, as well as the function he serves for his readers and for those who watch him on television. You should note that words like *nature* (what is it?), *source* (where does it come from?), and *function* (what does it do?) are often central in essay writing and, as you surely have noticed, in essay exams as well.

2. Just as does Mead, Henry finds something new to say where

we had thought we knew it all. Adolescence is *not* necessarily a time of pain and turmoil. Donald Duck is *not* just another cartoon character. The essay reevaluates what we all thought was settled forever. It looks at something old in a new way, or reexamines something that is an old problem, but in a new way. In *On Knowing*, Jerome Bruner calls the essay "the literary counterpart of the 'possible world' of the logical or like the 'thought experiment' of the scientist. . . . It begins with a set of connected familiars and seeks by rearranging them to leap to the higher ground of novelty, a novelty rooted in what was previously familiar" (p. vii).

3. One of the features of a good essay, according to Bruner, is that it produces in the reader something he calls "effective surprise" and describes in this way: "Surprise is the unexpected that strikes one with wonder or astonishment. What is curious about effective surprise is that it need not be rare or infrequent or bizarre and is often none of these things. Effective surprises . . . rather seem to have the quality of obviousness about them when they occur, producing a shock of recognition following which there is no longer astonishment" (p. 18).

4. You should notice to do that—to produce surprise in your reader—the essayist chooses a subject about which he or she can say something in depth. Henry did not choose as his subject "Comic Strips in America." That subject would be far too broad for him to say anything but the most superficial things. Instead, he focuses closely on one small area and discovers a new way of seeing that area. It is a wise decision.

5. The *kinds* of surprise a good essay can provide and the kinds of value an essay provides can be specified. An essay can have *predictive* value. It can, that is, devise a formula that will always work. Mead does this: "Wherever choice is a virtue in a society, and young people are forced to make many choices fast, there will be adolescent turmoil." An essay can have formal value. It can order facts in such a way that readers will be able to see a relationship between those facts that was obscured before. (You might read what

Poincaré has to say about this kind of thinking and writing in his study of mathematical invention.) An essay can have *metaphoric* value. It can connect very different experiences by the use of symbol or metaphor or image. We will practice doing this in Chapter 8, but it is possible here to show you what this value can do. Suppose I want to talk about what the self is. Is the self something that may best be described as something like a peach? Does it consist of a soft exterior, with a hard pit or core at the center? Or is the self more like an onion: if you peel away the layers of skins, nothing remains, because the self itself *is* that layering of skins? The metaphor or image in the essay clarifies a way of seeing something.

6. Here in this last point, you can see in a different way how large a part the imagination plays in essay writing. In *The Act of Creation*, Arthur Koestler says that "artists tend to treat facts as stimuli for imagination, whereas scientists use imagination to coordinate facts" (p. 200). I think the essay writer rests somewhere in the middle of those two points. The essayist uses facts, and uses imagination both to coordinate those facts and to venture metaphors that clarify the relationship between those facts. It may seem reasonable to conclude, then, that there is both something of the artist and something of the scientist in the essay writer. If, as Karl Popper contends in *The Logic of Scientific Discovery*, any kind of problem solving or new thinking is "science-making," then Bill Henry is a scientist. And so also are all essay writers; they are part scientist and part artist.

The fourth writing sample is a representative sample of a university writing proficiency exam, and I include it because it is a sample not of a news article, or of an essay, or of textbook writing, but of a specialized creature that seems to exist only in college classes. It is a *theme*, and its features are worth noting, mostly so that they can be avoided by the serious essay writer.

1. The theme resembles textbook writing in that it is built up of a series of assertions, none of which are demonstrated, defended, explained, or proven. To look at its first paragraph is to recognize that it is not a paragraph at all, but

simply two sentences, each of which is a separate proposition that is offered and then dropped.

2. Unlike an essay's paragraphs, those in a theme are short, undeveloped, dropped and left for a new point. The signs that would tell you that an analysis was developing are absent. There are few or no words like "if . . . then", "but . . . however, on the other hand"; "all the same . . . in spite of this . . . because of . . , as a result"—words or phrases that are a part of any analysis.

3. The theme is often characterized by a large number of what S. I. Hayakawa called *buzz words*, or highly charged words calculated to get some emotional response from a reader. These words change from year to year or from decade to decade, but characteristically they are never defined or defended. In this particular piece of theme writing, *depersonalize* and *dehumanize* seem to be the chosen buzz words. This is not to say, of course, that computers may *not* depersonalize or dehumanize. But it is to say that the writer has not thought much about what those things might mean, precisely, or about how a computer will bring those things to pass. In what ways might a computer lead to greater freedom? Exactly how—in what event and by what mechanisms—would computers ensure that "thoughts and feelings and sentiments" have "little or no control over life"? How will computer-assisted diagnoses by doctors "wipe out" the doctor-patient relationship?

4. Although the theme writer is unclear about or fails to explain why or how this depersonalization will take place, he or she is even more unclear about the relationships between the separate concepts in his or her essay. When the theme writer says, for instance, that "technology must work with society," that phrase suggests that "technology" is a volitional, live creature with the capacity to "work with" people. But what relationship does technology have to society? Is not technology itself a creation of society and run by people in society? So society would have to do something with technology, and not the reverse. The theme writer has not clarified relationships; he or she is barely aware that such things exist.

5. We could go on, but the point is clear already. The theme is different from the essay in that it fails to grapple in an honest and serious way with a serious issue. It fails to develop or to analyze. It is an infinitely expandable series of buzz words and stock phrases, such as "one giant step," which no one, least of all the writer, takes seriously. Technically, its paragraphs are modular; that is, they could be shifted around almost at will, with no appreciable effect on the whole piece. Its sentences, for the most part, could also be moved almost anywhere without damaging the piece. It is, in short, more a ritual exercise in not-making-mistakes-in-grammar than a serious attempt to struggle with anything of substance.

Now that we have distinguished the essay from other forms of writing that it resembles in some ways, it may also help to distinguish the different kinds of essays it is possible to write. The ancients classified the essay by the nature of its appeal. *Pathos* was an appeal to the audience's emotions. *Ethos* was an appeal based on the speaker or writer's own moral character. *Logos* was an appeal based in logic. The modern essayist is more likely to decide what and how to write on the basis of some purpose rather than some *appeal*, and the purposes for which you might write are many:

1. An essay may inform.

2. An essay may instruct.

3. An essay may try to persuade.

4. An essay may try to solve a problem.

5. An essay may speculate about a particular issue or a particular phenomenon.

6. An essay may theorize: (a) "what happened"—about historical events or events in your own history or in that of your family, class, group, or sex; (b) "what happens"—it may, that is, generalize about recurring phenomena; (c) about "what will or may happen" in the future if this or that policy, habit, tendency, or belief persists.

7. An essay may be a retrieval of relevant information already known. We would call it, then, a summary.

8. An essay may be an analysis of problematic or puzzling data. What would explain or account for these facts?

9. An essay may be a discovering of some new concepts or ways to order separate facts.

When you are at a loss for a topic and want to write an essay, you might consider going over this list as a means of finding what it is you might want to write. Deciding whether you want to argue or to analyze, to talk about past habits or potential dangers, is a start in the right direction. Deciding whether you want to talk to everyone, or just to a very select audience, is also a start in the right direction.

Below are more exercises, which are designed to get you to think about what an essay is, and about how its language differs from other kinds of writing.

4. If you are taking college courses, gather together whatever you can of the assignments you will have in them. Inventory the skills you will need to do this writing well. What is being asked of you? Analyses? Summaries? Research reports? Notice how often those words we talked about, words like *nature*, *source*, and *function*, appear in essay exams, paper topics, and lecture notes. Remember what those words refer to.

5. Gather together some of your most frustrating-to-read textbooks and try rewriting a paragraph or two of one of them. What are the major differences you see between your paraphrase and the original? What do you learn by rewriting?

6. Be alert to any good writing you see anywhere in the next week and classify it by type. Which of the categories of purpose we talked about does each example fit into? Consider which types appeal to you most, and what kinds of things you would like to write.

7. In his *Philosophy of Composition*, E. D. Hirsch says that it is wrong to equate clear thinking and clear writing. "The word *clear* means something different in the two phrases. Clear thinking means drawing correct inferences from the given premises. Clear writing means an unambiguous and readable expression of one's meaning. . . . Muddy writing can express clear thinking, and clear writing can express muddy thinking" (p. 142). Do you agree with Hirsch? Take an old bit of an essay you may have lying around, preferably one you believe never really came together clearly. See if you can rewrite some portion of it clearly. Did you find that the *thinking* became more clear as the prose became more clear?

The four excerpts discussed in this chapter follow. The first is by Charles Frantz. The second is by Margaret Mead. The third is by William A. Henry 3rd; he wrote this column while he was television critic for the *Boston Globe*. A student wrote the last excerpt for a university writing proficiency exam.

Charles Frantz.
From *The Student Anthropologist's Handbook*

The early Greeks generated the birth of anthropology on a modest scale, since their genius was directed basically toward speculation and the search for ideal social forms. In many ways, better understanding of actual human forms derived from Chinese and Vedic Indian observers and philosophers. These diverse intellectual streams had, however, minimal contact with one another for centuries. It was Alexandrian and Arabic scholars who for almost a millennium principally contributed to the slight advances made toward a mature anthropology, although the extent of their descriptive work has yet to be fully determined. Reformation in Europe stimulated the growth of a kind of individualism, and the Renaissance gave rise to nationalism in the modern sense. An era of great social and economic changes dissolved the hierarchically-based and comparative cultural unity of medieval Europe. The period of Great Discoveries, beginning in the fifteenth century, brought to inquisitive Europeans both correct and fantastically distorted reports about previously unknown races, cultures, languages, plants, and animals. The "glory" of ancient Greece and Rome was discovered about the same time. The invention of the printing press encouraged the wider spread of information from many parts of the globe than history had known before. Compendia and encyclopedia were inaugurated which aimed to delineate human variations very completely. Museums and private cabinets of curios began to appear. The public was increasingly flooded with new explanations of human diversity and commonality. The striking commercial and political success of European nations added support for doctrines about divine guidance working through white men. Christianity provided concepts by which Europeans explained and rationalized their growing economic and political power throughout the world.

By the eighteenth century, rationalism and secularism extensively pervaded intellectual life in Europe. Philosophers and budding social scientists sought "laws of nature" to explain human differences, similarities and regularities. Some invested their explanations with the concept of progress, attributing it either to nature or to divine ordination. Others like Montesquieu wisely noted how little *was* known of the social world, and called for more observation and study, realizing many puzzles could be solved only through more patient study and the accumulation of more reliable data.

In the eighteenth and nineteenth centuries, hundreds of associations and academies dedicated to the pursuit of general knowledge, or the advancement of specialized studies, were established in Europe and North America. Most of these were initiated locally, but national and international associations and congresses were quick to follow. At the same time, an expansion of learned journals and universities occurred.

Many scholars were thoroughly imbued with the ideals of humanism and idealism, believing optimistically that scientific discoveries would help reduce war, halt disease, eradicate poor labor conditions, and end illiteracy and primitivism by "uplifting natives" through Christianity and governance superimposed directly. It was in the midst of these ambitions that a number of questions gained importance for what was taking shape as a distinctive field of anthropology. A resurgence of anatomical and medical studies, the discovery of common roots between the languages of Europe and India, and the opening of prehistoric research by advances in geology all contributed data or posed new problems concerning the nature of *Homo sapiens* and his social and cultural forms, through all time and space. The mid-nineteenth century brought forth such hallmarks of the future as the evolutionary theories of Herbert Spencer, Charles Darwin, Thomas H. Huxley, and

Alfred Wallace. Lewis Henry Morgan sent out the first world-wide questionnaire to procure information about systems of descent and affinity. Others began to make specific inquiries into the beliefs, languages, and practices of non-European peoples. Meanwhile accounts, sometimes exceptionally reliable, increasingly poured in from missionaries, colonial administrators, travellers, and expeditions charged with surveying lands and people with whom economic and political relations might be established.

In Europe, North America, and Australia associations for the advancement of science generally provided the organizational context for anthropological reports and speculations. Later, more specialized societies arose, both in the parts listed and elsewhere. The first specifically anthropological society, founded in Paris in 1839, was soon emulated in many countries. Later in the chapter, more will be said about these societies when the social organization of anthropology is discussed.

For now, suffice it to say that by the beginning of the twentieth century a narrower discipline of anthropology had begun to appear in several universities in the world. From that time, an increasing number of specialized problems about man, although still covering the Earth through all time, came to characterize the work of scholars who labelled themselves anthropologists (pp. 2–4).

Margaret Mead.
"Education for Choice."
From *Coming of Age in Samoa*

We have been comparing point for point, our civilisation and the simpler civilisation of Samoa, in order to illuminate our own methods of education. If now we turn from the Samoan picture and take away only the main lesson which we learned there, that adolescence is not necessarily a time of stress and strain, but that cultural conditions make it so, can we draw any conclusions which might bear fruit in the training of our adolescents?

At first blush the answer seems simple enough. If adolescents are only plunged into difficulties and distress because of conditions in their social environment, then by all means let us so modify that environment as to reduce this stress and eliminate this strain and anguish of adjustment. But, unfortunately, the conditions which vex our adolescents are the flesh and bone of our society, no more subject to straightforward manipulation upon our part than is the language which we speak. We can alter a syllable here, a construction there; but the great and far-reaching changes in linguistic structure (as in all parts of culture) are the work of time, a work in which each individual plays an unconscious and inconsiderable part. The principal causes of our adolescents' difficulty are the presence of conflicting standards and the belief that every individual should make his or her own choices, coupled with a feeling that choice is an important matter. Given these cultural attitudes, adolescence, regarded now not as a period of physiological change, for we know that physiological puberty need not produce conflict, but as the beginning of mental and emotional maturity, is bound to be filled with conflicts and difficulties. A society which is clamouring for choice, which is filled with many articulate groups, each urging its own brand of salvation, its own variety of economic philosophy, will give each new generation no peace until all have chosen or gone under, unable to bear the conditions of choice. The stress is in our civilisation, not in the physical changes through which our children pass, but it is none the less real nor less inevitable in twentieth-century America.

And if we look at the particular forms which this need for choice takes, the difficulty of the adolescent's position is only documented further. Because the discussion is principally concerned with girls, I shall discuss the problem from the girls' point of view, but in many respects the plight of the adolescent boy is very similar. Between fourteen and eighteen, the average American boy and girl finish school. They are now ready to go to work and must choose what type of work they wish to do. It might be argued that they often have remarkably little choice. Their education, the part of the country in which they live, their skill with their hands, will combine to dictate choice perhaps between the job of cash girl in a department store or of telephone operator, or of clerk or miner. But small as is the number of choices open to them in actuality, the significance of this narrow field of opportunity is blurred by our American theory of endless possibilities. Moving picture, magazine, newspaper, all reiterate the Cinderella story in one form or another, and often the interest lies as much in the way cash girl 456 becomes head buyer as in her subsequent nuptials with the owner of the store. Our occupational classes are not fixed. So many children are better educated and hold more skilled positions than their parents that even the ever-present discrepancy between opportunities open to men and opportunities open to women, although present in a girl's competition with her brother, is often absent as between her unskilled father and herself. It is needless to argue that these attitudes are products of conditions which no longer exist, particularly the presence of a frontier and a large amount of free land which provided a perpetual alternative of occupational choice. A set which was given to our thinking in pioneer days is preserved in other terms. As long as we have immigrants from non-English-speaking countries, the gap in opportunities between non-English-speaking parents and English-speaking children will be vivid and dramatic. Until our standard of education becomes far more stable than it is at present, the continual raising of the age and grade until which schooling is compulsory ensures a wide educational gap between many parents and their children. And occupational shifts like the present movements of farmers and farm workers into urban occupations, give the same picture. When the agricultural worker pictures urban work as a step up in the social scale, and the introduction of scientific farming is so radically reducing the numbers needed in agriculture, the movement of young people born on the farm to city jobs is bound to dazzle the imagination of our farming states during the next generation at least. The substitution of machines for unskilled workers and the absorption of many of the workers and their children into positions where they manipulate machines affords another instance of the kind of historical change which keeps our myth of endless opportunity alive. Add to these special features, like the effect upon the prospects of Negro children of the tremendous exodus from the southern corn fields, or upon the children of New England mill-hands who are deprived of an opportunity to follow dully in their parents' footsteps and must at least seek new fields if not better ones.

Careful students of the facts may tell us that class lines are becoming fixed; that while the children of immigrants make advances beyond their parents, they move up in step; that there are fewer spectacular successes among them than there used to be; that it is much more possible to predict the future status of the child from the present status of the parent. But this measured comment of the statistician has not filtered into our literature, nor our moving pictures, nor in any way served to minimize the vividness of the improvement in the children's condition as compared with the condition of their parents. Especially in cities, there is no such obvious demonstration of the fact that improvement is the rule for the children of a given class or district, and not merely a case of John Riley's making twenty dollars a week as a crossing man while Mary, his daughter, who has gone to business school, makes twenty-five dollars a week, working shorter hours. The lure of correspondence school advertising, the efflorescence of a doctrine of short-cuts to fame, all contrive to make an American boy or girl's choice of a job different from that of English children, born into a society where stratification is so old, so institutionalised, that the dullest cannot doubt it. So economic conditions force them to go to work and everything combines to make that choice a difficult one, whether in terms of abandoning a carefree existence for a confining, uncongenial one, or in terms of bitter rebellion against the choice which they must make in contrast to the opportunities which they are told are open to all Americans.

And taking a job introduces other factors of difficulty into the adolescent girl's home situation. Her dependence has always been demonstrated in terms of limits and curbs set upon her spontaneous activity in every field from spending money to standards of dress and behaviour. Because of the essentially pecuniary nature of our society, the relationship of limitation in terms of allowance to limitation of behaviour are more far-reaching than in earlier times. Parental disapproval of extreme styles of clothing would formerly have expressed itself in a mother's making her daughter's dresses high in the neck and long in the sleeve. Now it expresses itself in control through money. If Mary doesn't stop purchasing chiffon stockings, Mary shall have no money to buy stockings. Similarly, a taste for cigarettes and liquor can only be gratified through money; going to the movies, buying books and magazines of which her parents disapprove, are all dependent upon a girl's having the money, as well as upon her eluding more direct forms of control. And the importance of a supply of money in gratifying all of a girl's desires for clothes and for amusement makes money the easiest channel through which to exert parental authority. So easy is it, that the threat of cutting off an allowance, taking away the money for the one movie a week or the coveted hat, has taken the place of the whippings and bread-and-water exiles which were favourite disciplinary methods in the last century. The daughters come to see all censoring of their behaviour, moral, religious or social, the ethical code and the slightest sumptuary provisions in terms of an economic threat. And then at sixteen or seventeen the daughter gets a job. No matter how conscientiously she may contribute her share to the expenses of the household, it is probably only in homes where a European tradition still lingers that the wage-earning daughter gives all of her earning to her parents. (This, of course, excludes the cases where the daughter supports her parents, where the vesting of the economic responsibility in her hands changes the picture of parental control in another fashion.) For the first time in her life, she has an income of her own, with no strings of morals or of manners attached to its use. Her parents' chief instrument of discipline is shattered at one blow, but not their desire to direct their daughters' lives. They have not pictured their exercise of control as the right of those who provide, to control those for whom they provide. They have pictured it in far more traditional terms, the right of parents to control their children, an attitude reinforced by years of practising such control.

But the daughter is in the position of one who has yielded

unwillingly to some one who held a whip in his hand, and now sees the whip broken. Her unwillingness to obey, her chafing under special parental restrictions which children accept as inevitable in simpler cultures, is again a feature of our conglomerate civilisation. When all the children in the community go to bed at curfew, one child is not as likely to rail against her parents for enforcing the rule. But when the little girl next door is allowed to stay up until eleven o'clock, why must Mary go to bed at eight? If all of her companions at school are allowed to smoke, why can't she? And conversely, for it is a question of the absence of a common standard far more than of the nature of the standards, if all the other little girls are given lovely fussy dresses and hats with flowers and ribbons, why must she be dressed in sensible, straight linen dresses and simple round hats? Barring an excessive and passionate devotion of the children to their parents, a devotion of a type which brings other more serious difficulties in its wake, children in a heterogeneous civilisation will not accept unquestioningly their parents' judgment, and the most obedient will temper present compliance with the hope of future emancipation.

In a primitive, homogenous community, disciplinary measures of parents are expended upon securing small concessions from children, in correcting the slight deviations which occur within one pattern of behaviour. But in our society, home discipline is used to establish one set of standards as over against other sets of standards, each family group is fighting some kind of battle, bearing the onus of those who follow a middle course, stoutly defending a cause already lost in the community at large, or valiantly attempting to plant a new standard far in advance of their neighbours. This propagandist aspect greatly increases the importance of home discipline in the development of a girl's personality. So we have the picture of parents, shorn of their economic authority, trying to coerce the girl who still lives beneath their roof into an acceptance of standards against which she is rebelling. In this attempt they often find themselves powerless and as a result the control of the home breaks down suddenly, and breaks down just at the point where the girl, faced with other important choices, needs a steadying home environment.

It is at about this time that sex begins to play a rôle in the girl's life, and here also conflicting choices are presented to her. If she chooses the freer standards of her own generation, she comes in conflict with her parents, and perhaps more importantly with the ideals which her parents have instilled. The present problem of the sex experimentation of young people would be greatly simplified if it were conceived of as experimentation instead of as rebellion, if no Puritan self-accusations vexed their consciences. The introduction of an experimentation so much wider and more dangerous presents sufficient problems in our lack of social canons for such behaviour. For a new departure in the field of personal relations is always accompanied by the failure of those who are not strong enough to face an unpatterned situation. Canons of honour, of personal obligation, of the limits of responsibilities, grow up only slowly. And, of first experimenters, many perish in uncharted seas. But when there is added to the pitfalls of experiment, the suspicion that the experiment is wrong and the need for secrecy, lying, fear, the strain is so great that frequent downfall is inevitable.

And if the girl chooses the other course, decides to remain true to the tradition of the last generation, she wins the sympathy and support of her parents at the expense of the comradeship of her contemporaries. Whichever way the die falls, the choice is attended by mental anguish. Only occasional children escape by various sorts of luck, a large enough group who have the same standards so that they are supported either against their parents or against the majority of their age mates, or by absorption in some other interest. But, with the exception of students for whom the problem of personal relations is sometimes mercifully deferred for a later settlement, those who find some other interest so satisfying that they take no interest in the other sex, often find themselves old maids without any opportunity to recoup their positions. The fear of spinsterhood is a fear which shadows the life of no primitive woman; it is another item of maladjustment which our civilisation has produced.

To the problem of present conduct are added all the perplexities introduced by varying concepts of marriage, the conflict between deferring marriage until a competence is assured, or marrying and sharing the expenses of the home with a struggling young husband. The knowledge of birth control, while greatly dignifying human life by introducing the element of choice at the point where human beings have before been most abjectly subject to nature, introduces further perplexities. It complicates the issue from a straight marriage-home-and-children plan of life versus independent spinsterhood by permitting marriages without children, earlier marriages, marriages and careers, sex relations without marriage and the responsibility of a home. And because the majority of girls still wish to marry and regard their occupations as stop-gaps, these problems not only influence their attitude towards men, but also their attitude towards their work, and prevent them from having a sustained interest in the work which they are forced to do.

Then we must add to the difficulties inherent in a new economic status and the necessity of adopting some standard of sex relations, ethical and religious issues to be solved. Here again the home is a powerful factor; the parents use every ounce of emotional pressure to enlist their children in one of the dozen armies of salvation. The stress of the revival meeting, the pressure of pastor and parent gives them no peace. And the basic difficulties of reconciling the teachings of authority with the practices of society and the findings of science, all trouble and perplex children already harassed beyond endurance.

Granting that society presents too many problems to her adolescents, demands too many momentous decisions on a few months' notice, what is to be done about it? One panacea suggested would be to postpone at least some of the decisions, keep the child economically dependent, or segregate her from all contact with the other sex, present her with only one set of religious ideas until she is older, more poised, better able to deal critically with the problems which will confront her. In a less articulate fashion, such an idea is back of various schemes for the prolongation of youth, through raising the working age, raising the school age, shielding school children from a knowledge of controversies like evolution versus fundamentalism, or any knowledge of sex hygiene or birth control. Even if such measures, specially initiated and legislatively enforced, could accomplish the end which they seek and postpone the period of choice, it is doubtful whether such a development would be desirable. It is unfair that very young children should be the battleground for conflicting standards, that their development should be hampered by propagandist attempts to enlist and condition them too young. It is probably equally unfair to culturally defer the decisions too late. Loss of one's fundamental religious faith is more of a wrench at thirty than at fifteen simply in terms of the number of years of acceptance which have accompanied the belief. A sudden knowledge of hitherto unsuspected aspects of sex, or a shattering of all the old conventions concerning sex behaviour, is more difficult just in terms of the strength of the old attitudes. Furthermore, in practical terms, such schemes would be as they are now, merely local, one state legislating against evolution, another against birth control, or one religious group segregating its unmarried girls. And these special local movements would simply unfit groups of young people for competing happily with children who had been permitted to make their choices earlier. Such an educational scheme, in addition to being almost impossible of execution, would be a step backward and would only beg the question.

Instead, we must turn all of our educational efforts to training our children for the choices which will confront them. Education, in the home even more than at school, instead of being a special pleading for one régime, a desperate attempt to form one particular habit of mind which will withstand all outside influences, must be a preparation for those very influences. Such an education must give far more attention to mental and physical hygiene than it has given hitherto. The child who is to choose wisely must be healthy in mind and body, handicapped in no preventable fashion. And even more importantly, this child of the future must have an open mind. The home must cease to plead an ethical cause or a religious belief with smiles or frowns, caresses or threats. The children must be taught how to think, not what to think. And because old errors die slowly, they must be taught tolerance, just as to-day they are taught intolerance. They must be taught that many ways are open to them, no one sanctioned above its alternative, and that upon them and upon them alone lies the burden of choice. Unhampered by prejudices, unvexed by too early conditioning to any one standard, they must come clear-eyed to the choices which lie before them.

For it must be realised by any student of civilisation that we pay heavily for our heterogeneous, rapidly changing civ-ilisation; we pay in high proportions of crime and delinquency, we pay in the conflicts of youth, we pay in an ever-increasing number of neuroses, we pay in the lack of a coherent tradition without which the development of art is sadly handicapped. In such a list of prices, we must count our gains carefully, not to be discouraged. And chief among our gains must be reck-oned this possibility of choice, the recognition of many pos-sible ways of life, where other civilisations have recognized only one. Where other civilisations give a satisfactory outlet to only one temperamental type, be he mystic or soldier, business man or artist, a civilisation in which there are many standards offers a possibility of satisfactory adjustment to in-dividuals of many different temperamental types, of diverse gifts and varying interests.

At the present time we live in a period of transition. We have many standards but we still believe that only one stand-ard can be the right one. We present to our children the picture of a battle-field where each group is fully armoured in a con-viction of the righteousness of its cause. And each of these groups makes forays among the next generation. But it is unthinkable that a final recognition of the great number of ways in which man, during the course of history and at the present time, is solving the problems of life, should not bring with it in turn the downfall of our belief in a single standard. And when no one group claims ethical sanction for its cus-toms, and each group welcomes to its midst only those who are temperamentally fitted for membership, then we shall have realised the high point of individual choice and universal toleration which a heterogeneous culture and a heterogeneous culture alone can attain. Samoa knows but one way of life and teaches it to her children. Will we, who have the knowl-edge of many ways, leave our children free to choose among them? (pp. 130–38).

William A. Henry 3rd.
"Still Quacking after All These Years"

Life gives him reasons enough to be exasperated—a rich and stingy uncle, three fractious nephews, a comely but finally unattainable girl friend, and distant relatives noteworthy mostly for impractical invention or outright stupidity.

But from his first harsh quack Donald Duck has raged without reason, though not always without rhyme. Just as his ontological cousin Mickey Mouse normally embodies sweet placidity, so Donald Duck embodies excitable resentment. For as long as we have known him he has been mad as hell and he wasn't going to take it anymore. And, of course, like those of us watching, he recognized his anger was impotent and took it time and again.

His outrage, like ours, never entirely extinguished optimism. Those eyes could open wide, that bill could curve in a smile, his sailor suit and cap could seem to bounce as he set off, lighthearted, on some new—and likely doomed—adventure.

Nor did frustration ever entirely efface his grudgingly expressed family duty. If he spanked his nephews they knew it was due. If he gulled his uncle it was to finance a family gathering or at worst to court the fair Daisy.

He was forgiving even with the beasts of the field (although duckly he always saw himself as more than animal). A bird or squirrel might taunt him as he bicycled or strolled through a park or read on a bench. He might, in pursuit, bisect himself or smash his brainpan against a tree. But in the best cartoon tradition he did not long show his wounds and he never wrought lasting violence in his revenge.

These redeeming decencies allowed us to love him without guilt. They scarcely diminished his quick, quick anger, his explosive quack, his headlong retaliatory waddle. As peevish children, then as careworn adults, we have heard him shriek when we would only mutter, and have admired his ardor in his lover's quarrel with the world.

Tonight the National Broadcasting Company repeats its loving tribute, "This is Your Life, Donald Duck," at 8 on Channel 5. Little will be said about what his career has meant, about what weaknesses in our character made us love him. Little will be said even about the species to which he belongs, the humanized animal, created to explain to children (and perhaps adults) the perplexing behavior of beasts who don't act like us: Donald and Mickey and Felix and Rocky and Bullwinkle and all the rest of the penman's peaceable kingdom help us feel we know what to expect from animals. They help us believe animals understand our words when we weepingly apologize for having stepped on their tails.

NBC thinks of Donald the way television thinks of all its stars, beloved for mere familiarity, indistinguishable from every other familiar face, made a star by uniqueness, then stripped of individuality by enduring stardom. For the public, too, Donald has become Dan Rather, Charo, the Fonz, an icon occasioning general adulation rather than particular prayers.

Donald's friends and relatives and victims will talk tonight, even his venerable grandmother (she conceals her age, but Donald is pushing fifty). Their words can evoke memories so intense we see them anew, in caricature and technicolor. Yet they can give us only glimpses, for Donald did not command our attention as an epic hero. He was always a character turn, always a figure of two dimensions and one reel. We saw him in Latin America. We saw him in love. But to remain a figure of childhood fantasy or adult escape, he had to forgo marriage and children and a recognizable, steady job. He was only an emotion and a circumstance, apoplexy looking for a place to happen.

Of all Walt Disney's visions he was the most widely imitated. Any clever child could approximate the squishy squawk of his voice and, more important, comprehend the instant upsurge of his anger. He never became a mere term of derision about inconsequentiality, as "mickey mouse" did. He never symbolized brute incomprehension, as Goofy did. He had a sort of dignity.

Hollywood has told us for four generations that it doesn't want to send us a message, it wants only to make us cry or laugh. That has been its chief technique of sending us a message. Donald told us our anger was out of proportion to trivial annoyances in a bright and lively world. He told us equally that anger needed an outlet, that any personality less calm than Mickey's should let it all wing out.

Some scholar might connect all that to endorsing Freud and rebuking Marx. He might argue that the most cunning message is to tell us what we already believe and want once more to hear.

Perhaps. Whatever he said, Donald spoke to us as one of our own. He never took to the sea or sky. He was earth-bound, frustrated, without the release of flight. He looked like a duck, he walked like a duck, he quacked like a duck. But he ducked life's missiles like a man.

©*Walt Disney Enterprises*

"Will Computers Free Mankind?" not an essay

①The increasing dependence on computer usage will not lead to greater freedom and individuality but will depersonalize and dehumanize life as we know it. ②All thoughts, feelings, and sentiments will have little or no control over life.

The computer-assisted manufacturing techniques are a great step forward for industry but a giant step back for mankind. There will be unlimited gains in productivity but limited jobs! People would lose their sense of security and personal dignity.

The idea of having instant polls in the home deciding on controversial issues is just another way computers deperson-alize life. The public does not always consider all sides of the issue at hand. In our past history it is pointed out that the majority is not always right.

Computers are now taking over the educational program. These new computers will be able to tell whether the student is happy, nervous, sad, or angry. Then the computer will judge your I.Q. and put you into a program which it 'feels' you belong in. Can you imagine a computer telling you what courses are right for you.

Computers are now diagnosing and advising doctors what drugs should be given to patients. The idea of the doctor-patient relationship will be totally wiped out. This is a perfect example of dehumanization.

Technology must not bring about bewilderment, dehumanization, depersonalization. And it does not have to. Technology must work with society if we are to survive.

What Is a Concept, and What
Do Concepts Have to Do with Writing?

We have talked about what writing is, and what it does for us, and about what an essay is. We have looked at a few bits of essays and talked about what makes them essays. We have said that writing essays makes possible, and produces, a certain kind of thinking. But what kind of thinking produces essays? Obviously, it is a rather specialized kind of thinking—we do not usually use words like *nature, function,* or *source* in our everyday conversations with friends, and it is a rare occasion on which we challenge or explore in more than a very casual way the assumptions of our culture, in writing or in talking. But this specialized kind of thinking is certainly not foreign to you, and in this chapter we begin the first of many thinking and writing exercises designed to allow you to watch how it works. Understanding what you read is made much easier if you understand that other writers are thinking in this same way. Writing essays becomes easier once you see that this kind of thinking is largely a natural extension of what you already do. Writing compositions is something people want to do, and can do, in part because people *are* compositions. Below is what I used to call my "Composition Manifesto." It is as concise a statement as I can muster of the way I think thinking works, and of what I see as your own relationship to that thinking process. I have tried to condense the entire world of thinking into a few pages, thus you should expect that you may not understand all that is said in these pages. But you might regard them as a kind of blueprint for the work you will do throughout the book. Whatever puzzles you as you read through this "Manifesto" will become clearer as you continue to do the exercises throughout the book.

1. You *are* a composition. That is, you are made up of (or composed of) concepts that have been defined for you in a particular way. You were told, or you learned from watching the behavior of those around you, that *normal* "means" X and Y, but not Z, that *success* "means" X and Y, but not Z. A concept, then, is a conception: *a way of seeing* something in the world. When we say that normal "means" X and Y, we are defining that concept. Definitions are not absolutes, however, and what you find in the dictionary are only approximations of the way some people in a given culture tend to see a certain concept. Concepts have no "real" definitions; instead they have uses. They are our way of coming to understand the world and deciding how to behave in it. In every instance, what we *call* something and how we define some concept depends entirely upon what our needs, our interests, and our experiences have been. Nearly any word can be defined in very different ways, according to this principle. The folksinger Woodie Guthrie once said, "To a five-year-old boy who doesn't want to go to sleep, a lullaby is propaganda." Defining a lullaby as propaganda makes perfect sense, given the child's point of view. This is what we mean when we say that concepts have no "real" definitions.

2. Not only are you a composition, but you contain a whole set of *copula,* or connectors that connect any one of those concepts you carry around in your head with another or others in very specific ways. These connections determine, quite as much as your separate concepts, your thinking and behavior. Success in business *precludes* sexual happiness for a woman. Maturity *excludes* spontaneity. Money *ensures* happiness (or misery).

3. Obviously, if you want to think in new ways, to be more aware of how you think now, to be more flexible in how

you think, you need to *identify* the constituent parts of your categories. To take a close look at what you call what and decide whether you might not want to consider a new conception: a new way of seeing. I have heard many beginning writers say they have "writer's block." But "writer's block" is not a helpful conception, not a helpful way of seeing the problem. Because a "block" cannot be gotten around. If those people would try reconceptualizing their problem, renaming it, they could have a chance of solving it. What is writer's block? Is it a fear to be heard? A fear to be challenged that prevents writers from saying anything? An inability to know "how I think" that results in an inability to put words on paper? A simple failure of discipline that makes it impossible for them to sit down long enough to compose? A failure to have enough self-esteem and confidence to believe they have anything worth saying? Renaming is not simply a matter of exchanging one word for another. It is a matter of changing the reality.

4. You cannot say anything new until you see something in a new way (Margaret Mead saw adolescence in a new way, and William Henry saw Donald Duck in a new way). You cannot see something in a new way until you let go of your old ways of seeing. But the struggle is well worth the effort; reconceptualizing creates new worlds and new ideas. As Robert Ornstein says in *The Psychology of Consciousness,* we most often say "I'll believe it when I see it." But, he says, it might be more accurate to say "I'll see it when I believe it." Newspaperman Herbert Bayard Swope created the concept "cold war" before World War II. In doing so, he gave the world a way of seeing, and I would venture to say that it is impossible for any of us *not* to see the world as engaging in "cold war." Because of Winston Churchill, all of us "see" that there is an "iron curtain."

5. You cannot understand any writer—philosopher, psychologist, novelist, political historian—until you understand that a book is nothing but a structure that conveys a writer's conceptualizations: the relationships he or she

sees between one concept and another. Stephen Crane's story "The Blue Hotel" can be seen as a piece of writing that explores the assertion "Deception generates violence." One of Bertrand Russell's essays asserts that "Western progress is really only a veiled quest for power." Both are statements of a relationship between concepts. You cannot respond to a writer's work intelligently unless you understand that what happens in reading, writing, and thinking is almost entirely a confrontation between the writer's set of conceptualizations and your own.

6. When I say these things, I am not suggesting that the world is "arbitrary." I am suggesting that the world presents us with infinite opportunities to explain and make sense of what happens in it, and discourse is exploring those different ways of making sense: comparing our ways against other people's ways of making sense. In an interesting book called *Explanations,* Gwynn Nettler gathers together all of the explanations for the assassination of Robert Kennedy that she can find. The murder was "carried out to impede the process of social change now going on in America." It happened because Sirhan Sirhan "grew up in Pasadena, a center of the John Birch Society, a center of radical right reactionaries. . . . Sirhan simply accepted the way people in Pasadena think. He decided that Bobby Kennedy was evil and he killed him." It happened because men like Sirhan "are plainly weak and suggestible men, stamped by our society with a birthright of hatred and a compulsion toward violence." It happened because "the assassin had schizophrenia, [and was] a paranoid type." These and other explanations are quoted by Nettler on pages 51 and 52 of her book. You will notice that some of the conceptions seem to contradict one another, and others seem quite compatible. You will notice that in each case "thinking" involved trying to categorize some phenomenon in the world around us.

7. To the extent that this is true, the writer's job is no different from the scientist's job. Both observe and then make sense out of what they see. The only difference is that scientists are more likely to be able to test their

explanations to see if their conceptualizations are the most fruitful ones. But for both the writer and the scientist, the initial task is simply to try to *see* what is there in front of us. Recently, scientists were inspired to ask why animals lick their wounds, and why when we smash our fingers in a door, we immediately pop the hurt fingers into our mouth. The answer is that saliva contains a substance called nerve growth factor (NGF), which speeds up the healing process. Obviously, that substance can be used to help trauma and surgery patients. But it took us almost 2,000 years of watching animals lick their wounds and of popping fingers into our mouths to really *see* what we were doing. When we compose we first *look* at the world and then make sense of what we see. That is, we make meaning of the world. In *Reflections on Language,* Noam Chomsky calls this process of putting bits of knowledge together "science-making."

8. You should think, then, of both thinking and writing as a kind of "science-making." Think of thinking and writing as composing the world—or at least some small part of it. You can only live in an ordered world (If you did not classify speeding trucks as things-to-stay-out-of-the-way-of, you would have been dead long ago), and it is much better to live in a world that you order than in one that someone else has ordered for you.

9. You compose, however, not only for yourself, but for others. That is, you compose either to make clearer to some audience how someone else composes the world (Marx, Freud, Nixon, Shakespeare, Woody Allen), or to convince others to accept *your* composition of the world. Debate, argument, dialectic, analysis are written and carried on because people disagree about how they see—conceptualize—phenomena, people, facts, events. Joining in that exploration is the only reason any of us have to write. We may write to make ourselves feel better. We may write just for fun. We may write because we "have" to write a paper. But any other kind of writing will concern itself with exactly what I have described.

10. When you write, you define. That is, you set limits on words. You announce that *this* word shall be used to delineate this much or this part of experience, and nothing more and nothing less. You can watch this being done by other writers, and do it yourself, when you read Chapters 5 and 7. Once you define these concepts, you link them together with words that express some kind of connection between one and another. *Is, is like,* and *causes* are kinds of connectors you might use, but there are all kinds of others that you might watch for as you read: *embodies, generates, retards, inspires, supercedes, justifies, requires, precludes, exemplifies,* and hundreds of others. Finding just the right one will clarify—or maybe even create—a thesis statement for you. What relationship exists between a society and its schools? Do the schools *embody,* or *reflect,* or *ameliorate* the frustrations of a society? The right word creates the idea: creates the thesis statement. And, just by the way, when you have discussed one aspect of a concept, you have also written a paragraph.

Below are more writing exercises, designed to get you to feel at ease with concepts and to allow you to see how they work and can work for you.

8. In this chapter we have said that changing the word for something often serves to change the reality as well, or at least serves to change the way people think and behave toward some reality. Therapists who do psychological counseling tend to call the people they work with *clients* rather than *patients* these days. What changes occur as a result of that name-changing? Can you think of another situation or case in which changing the name for something changed your or someone else's reality? Think about and then discuss one of these two questions.

9. Think about conceptions of the world that were conveyed to you by your family when you were a child, choose one of those, and try as much as you can to explore how that conception has affected the way you think or act. One woman student I know was told as a child, "You can do anything you want to do." As a result, she finds herself overwhelmed and afraid to try anything. Another was told, "You are brilliant, but you are not working up to capacity."

When she has trouble in her courses, she seems to make one of two judgments: she must *not* be brilliant after all, but pretty dumb; or, she must be terribly lazy and not know it. What were *you* told, and what have been the effects of those conceptions of yourself that you were given?

10. When there is more than one child in a family, often families have a very specific conception of each child: Susie is the aggressive, self-directed, responsible child. Patty is the sweeter, soft child who craves approval and attention. Jani is the whimsical, funny child. Often those conceptions tend to become, as Hayden White said, "hardened into a hypostasis": we tend, that is, to behave in ways that confirm those conceptions of us. Is this true of you and your family? Describe how this is so. What conception of you is held by your family?

11. In this chapter, we have said that nearly all writing is done to define concepts (determine how a certain word should be regarded and used) and to connect concepts. In the next few days, be alert as you read—textbooks, newspaper articles, or any other things—for such an assertion or statement of a relationship. Summarize (put in your own words) the assertion in one paragraph.

12. We have said that most debate—in politics, in legal cases—hinges on and is caused by different conceptions of an issue. As you read the newspaper, watch for one such issue that involves conceptual disagreement. Clip the article from the paper and write a short discussion in which you do not solve the problem, but discuss what conceptions are at issue. That is, talk about *what conceptual analysis is necessary if we are to solve the problem.* Recently, for instance, a suit was filed by Eastern Airline flight attendants as a result of the airline's automatic grounding of pregnant flight attendants. The flight attendants contended that this was a case of discrimination. The airline contended that the grounding was necessary to ensure that all flight attendants on a given flight were working at optimal efficiency. The flight attendants insisted that those who were pregnant had sufficient ability to perform their duties. What conceptual issues are involved in this case?

13. Below is a short excerpt from Roger Brown's book *Words and Things.* He talks about the process of conceptualizing that we have been talking about here. Read Brown's "The Uses of the Named Category" and then compose a summary and an analysis in response to what he says. That is, you will put in your own words what he says, and then you will consider whether you agree with him, what prompts him to say the things he says, and what the implications of what he says might be.

Roger Brown.
"The Uses of the Named Category."
From *Words and Things*

The usefulness of named categories is not particularly obvious. Why should we group objects and events and, having grouped them, why should we give names to the groups? Suppose it can be shown that categories and names are important for the formation and transmission of trustworthy expectancies. The usefulness of the expectancy will probably be granted. If we can correctly anticipate what is going to happen we are better able to act so as to preserve our lives and satisfy our desires. It seems to be the chief cognitive business of every kind of higher animal to acquire trustworthy expectancies. It is not the chief business of lower animals because their simpler needs and more predictable experiences make useful instincts possible. . . .

Unless we categorize, it is useless to form expectancies for there will be no recurrences. An event, in all its detail or even all of its discriminable detail, does not repeat. There is no use in remembering that event A was followed by event B because event A will never come again. However, types or categories of events do recur. It may be worthwhile knowing that an event of type A led to an event of type B because there may be new instances of both A and B.

The repertoire of categories, which is an important part of the cognitive branch of culture, consists of principles for grouping experience used in one society and its antecedents back through many centuries. When we learn all of these grouping principles we are equipped with many alternative ways of categorizing any experience. Suppose dog A bites me on the ankle. I should like to store that experience in such a way as to avoid further bites. There will be many possible forms in which to store it. I may decide that: a) chow dogs bite; or b) sleeping dogs bite (so let them lie); or c) on a hot day any dog may bite, etc. These alternative categorizations, one or more of which may be useful, are available to me because I have learned the referents of *chow dogs, sleeping dogs,* and *hot dogs* and can recognize new instances of any of these. However, my one experience affords no basis for preferring one categorization over another. I might learn which is the best categorical rule from many encounters with dogs and a number of bites but since the various categories have names there is another way.

I can bring my tentative rule to someone with a large experience of dogs and get his opinion. Do chow dogs bite? He may know that the chow is no more likely to bite than any other dog unless it is startled and then it is almost certain to bite. He suggests, in effect, that I make a new conjunctive category and learn to avoid *startled chow dogs.* This verbal advice can benefit me only because I already know how to recognize the referents of its critical terms. Because I have learned categories and their names this other man's greater experience of dogs can usefully guide my behavior. More generally I can use the accumulated knowledge of my culture only because I have learned to identify the referents for the terms employed.

Everything in the world is susceptible to multiple categorizations. When something important happens, a parent will often name the person or objects involved and, thereby, select for a child the particular categorizations believed to be most relevant to the event. Suppose one man punches another while a child looks on. A parent may label the aggressor as an

Irishman or a *cop* or *an old man* or a *redhead* or something else. All of these can be attributes of the same man. The selection of a name is also the selection of an attribute supposed to be predictive of aggressive behavior. The child who hears the man identified as a *redhead* will have different expectancies from the child who hears the same man identified as an *Irishman*. They will agree on what is to be expected of redheaded Irishmen but disagree on individuals who are one of these but not the other (pp. 224–26).

14. Brown's writing may be a bit difficult for you to follow, if you are not used to reading what is actually a fairly usual kind of "academic discourse." You may also find it a bit difficult to summarize and analyze what he is saying, because doing those things requires that you, too, engage in that same kind of discourse: discuss concepts, abstractions; where they come from and what they do. Becoming able to do this kind of writing with ease simply takes time and practice, and enough discipline to read and reread patiently until you are sure you understand what is being said. As I have said, learning to do this kind of writing also requires a certain kind of attitude: a drive to be absolutely clear and accurate. This clarity and accuracy begins on the sentence level. Read through the following excerpts, all of which were written by students who were asked to analyze Brown's passage. Look at each excerpt with a sharp eye. Decide which ones are accurate, and which are not; which are awkward, and which are not; which ones stay so close to Brown's own wording that they would not really qualify as proper summaries (many beginning writers, when they feel unsure, fall into using almost the exact words of the writer about whom they are talking). As you do this exercise, pay attention to how it is that grammatical awkwardnesses are almost always the result of a fuzziness in thinking. Pay attention also to the ways in which some of the writers try to obscure their lack of understanding about what Brown is saying by retreating into long words that unfortunately do not work. Because I am hoping that what you do here might well teach you something about your own habits in writing, you might record in the "self-study" part of your journal what you are learning about your tactics for responding to this kind of writing. Might you be, for instance, one of those writers who, like some of these, spends more time trying to shape an impressive sentence than trying to understand the ideas they are writing about? The student sentences immediately follow.

1. Roger Brown starts this piece seriously stating that in order to anticipate what is going to happen, a person needs to categorize events, the principles for grouping and categorizing being culture bound. He illustrates this with a dog bite on the ankle.
2. Brown explains that one's whole learning experience is made up of categorization. Therefore, our reaction or behavior in situations will determine how categorization itself is formed.
3. The author seems to be debating the usefulness of categorizing certain experiences, yet seems to hesitate as to how and why.
4. In essence the essay is saying that the phenomenon of formation and transmission of trustworthy expectancies can only come about when

they are put into categories, for without categories expectancies will not recur because they are not recognized as having occurred before.

5. These multiple categories, however, leave many possible interpretations open to the individual, leading to differences of opinion on the same phenomenon.

6. It appears that in this article that the writer is trying to explain the different ways of categorizing groups and objects in different formations.

7. In conclusion categorizing can be beneficial in order to recur, but many terms have analogies and are difficult to differentiate their meanings.

8. The naming process is, in fact, the instrument by which man, over the years, has found cause to make decisions that have dictated the completion of civilization, determining the course of history.

9. Categorizations are important in bringing up children, interaction between people, and to recognize certain recurrences of former experiences.

10. Each daily event must be analyzed in detail and handled as an individual event, with the interpretation being left up to the individual doing the analysis.

11. No matter what happens to a person in life he should be able to categorize an experience whether it is good or bad.

12. The margin of error in this so-called faulty rationale can be infinitesimal depending on the given set of circumstances that make up the topic in question. In short, the essay points out the inherent danger of professed misconceptions when people fail to limit themselves to an objective base when analyzing an incident, object, or person.

How Does Your Mind Work?

In the last chapter we began to talk about concept formation, which I take to be the major process by which minds make sense of the world. If, as Roger Brown suggested, we are bitten by a dog, or watch a red-headed Irish policeman attack another man, the first thing our minds try to do is make sense of our experience. We do that by trying to fit what we see with our eyes into some structure that explains what we have seen. That structure is a structure of categories, and those categories are concepts. What we see, what we encounter in the world around us, we incorporate into our conception of the world. If what we encounter in the world *resists* incorporation into our conception of it, we work harder: we look for further clues to help us understand what we see; we compare what we see with things we have encountered in the past to see if or how the "new thing" may be related to what we know; we imagine a situation or a context in which the "new thing" would begin to make sense to us; we separate the experience into parts to see which part helps us to understand the whole experience. In Brown's example, we try to decide whether it is *hot* dogs, *chow* dogs, *startled* dogs, or some combination of things that causes us to get bit.

Because *analysis*—the kind of thing people do in essays—is simply a matter of going through exactly the procedures I just described, you can learn a great deal about how you now think by watching what you do when you are confronted with something unfamiliar and are asked to analyze it in writing. Below is a series of exercises designed to allow you to try to make sense of—or analyze—a photograph, and then inventory what you do when you are presented with an invitation to "analyze." Later exercises in this series should also allow you to watch how the conceptualization process works and to consider how you might put that process to work for you when you write.

15. At the end of this chapter, you will find a series of photographs. Choose one photograph and write as complete an analysis of it as you can in two or three paragraphs. That is, you will not use the photograph as the inspiration for a flight of fancy, a story, or a poem, but you will try as best you can to explain what you think is happening in it: where you think it was taken; why you think the photographer would have taken it; what the people in it might be doing (if there are people in the photograph you chose); what its context might be. Just as you might want or need to explain an event to yourself (Why did that old red-headed Irish policeman hit that other man? Why does it seem that my tonsils always swell after strenuous exercise? Why did Americans elect Ronald Reagan?), you also might want to explain this photograph. Whether you are explaining an essay you read, an event you have read about or participated in, or a photograph you are looking at, the same procedures are used. Analyze this photograph, then, trying to be as clear, accurate, and thorough as you can be. This means that you will try to construct an analysis that takes into account as much of the photograph as possible and that will convey to people who read your analysis exactly what you think they need to know to understand the photograph.

16. After you have written two or three paragraphs analyzing the photograph and are satisfied that they are as complete as they can be, answer the questions that follow. Many of these questions ask you to note and count the number of times you have done certain kinds of things in your analysis. Keep track of your answers in your writer's log, because we will use them in the exercises that follow these questions.

1. Draw a circle around, and then count the number of times you used, a concrete, descriptive word.
2. Draw a square around, and then count, every word or place in which you discriminated between one object, face, posture, gesture, and another object, face, posture, or gesture.
3. Draw a line under, and then count, each word you used that could be called an abstraction. Abstractions are words such as *depression, power, maturity, success, fear, poverty, anger*. They are *any* words that describe something you think is represented in the photograph, but that you can not simply point to and say, "*That's* depression, anger,

maturity," and so on. If you said there is a tree, you could point to it; if you said there is poverty, you would have to defend that judgment by pointing to several separate features of the photograph that led you to make that judgment. Such words as the latter are abstractions. How many abstractions have you used?

4. If you have used abstractions, count how many descriptive words you have used to support *each* of those abstractions.

5. Count how many times you used an analogy or a comparison to make yourself clear to your reader. That is, how many times did you say that something in the photograph was *like* something else outside it, but part of your own experience? All kinds of sentences might signal this kind of comparison-making. Did you write some sentences that begin "This X is similar to . . ." or "This X reminds me of . . ." or "This X might be compared to . . ."?

6. Count how many times you contrasted any object, person, expression, physical setting, or anything else in the photograph with something outside it.

7. Count how many times you noted differences between any two things in the photograph, or any two parts of it, using phrases such as "more than . . . less than," "earlier than . . . later than," "in the past . . . now."

8. Count how many times you ventured a speculation about what was happening in the photograph.

9. Count how many times you ventured not only a speculation but also alternate hypotheses about what might be happening in the photograph.

10. Whether you gave one reading of the photograph or several, check to see how much evidence you mustered and listed to support that speculation in each case. Is there one *perhaps* in your analysis? More than one?

11. Did you consider the *context* in which the photograph might have been taken? That is, did you try to imagine why it was taken, by whom, and whether the photographer might have been interested in any particular effects? In making a point? How many of your sentences address these things?

12. Did you discriminate between any two things in the photograph? That is, did you ever say, "This [expression/background/person] is different from this other [expression/background/person]"?

13. Did you foreground any one part or feature of the photograph, emphasizing it over any other part or feature? That is, did you isolate just one part for analysis, and if so, was that a conscious decision, or an accidental one caused perhaps because one feature simply caught your attention?

14. Try to determine, and then record, approximately how much of your analysis you devoted to speculation, description, "creative" writing (writing a story), or the formulation of some moral or message from the photograph.

15. Scanning your paragraphs, determine whether you have composed a coherent analysis that moves in some logical progression from one point to another, or whether you simply devised a kind of grocery list of details. That is, did you simply describe things in the order in which they caught your eye, or did you arrange descriptive details so that they conveyed an organized description of what you thought was happening in the photograph.

17. If you have been alert, you are already aware of what the questions in the previous exercise are about. Whether you are analyzing a photograph, or another writer's theory or account of an event, the procedures you go through to construct an analysis remain the same: you gather evidence, you make a judgment about what that evidence "proves" and then give a name to that judgment, you arrive at that judgment by looking at "what's there" in front of you by comparing "what's there" with something else in your experience, by speculating, by noting that some things are different from some others, and, finally, if you are not sure how best to explain "what's there," you venture two or maybe three possible explanations. You will remember we said in Chapter 2 that discourse is a running back and forth; from what we see to speculations about what the things we see might mean. If you composed your analysis of the photograph as best you could, you did exactly that: you looked, and then you gathered what you saw into some category: call it an abstraction, a generalization, a judgment word, a hypothesis, a concept, a conception. Whatever you call it, what you did was see something, and then you offered to your readers a way to see something: a conception of the photograph. If you did not do this, but simply provided a list of what was "there" in the photograph ("In the left-hand corner I see an X, and just to the right is a Y, and in the back is a Z"), I suggest that for some reason you are not allowing yourself to venture to generalize, hypothesize: form concepts. If when you write about other people's ideas, you seem to produce only summary of their ideas and not analysis, it may well be because you are not going through the procedures outlined in the fifteen questions of Exercise 16. If you rarely or never used analogies or comparisons (*"This* is like *that."*) in your paragraphs, you might consider developing that habit, because comparison is perhaps the world's best way of clarifying things: for yourself, and certainly for your readers. In casual conversation with friends, watch how often you and they say "It's like . . ." in order to communicate some idea. Tap that natural inclination when you write essays. Read over your analysis of the photograph, the fifteen questions of Exercise 16, and your answers to them. Think about what your answers tell you about what you do when you are asked to analyze. Think about what you did when you analyzed the photograph. In your writer's log, write as much as you can about what you have learned about your own writing. What do you want to develop further? What do you want to do more of? Less of?

18. Look at the photograph one more time. Compose a new analysis, again in two or three paragraphs. Compare it to your original analysis. Which one do you like better, and why?

19. So far in these exercises, we have been presuming that you first "see," and then form some hypothesis or explanation of what is "there" in the photograph. However, the relationship between seeing and conceptualizing is much more complex. You may have noticed that the first time you wrote about the photograph, there were some things you did not "see" at all: a shadow, a bit of scenery, a poster on a wall, a facial expression, a gesture of the hands, a slant of light. Several philosophers and psychologists have written about this phenomenon, among them Rudolf Arnheim in *Visual Thinking*, Erving Goffman in *Frame Analysis*, and the Russian linguist, philosopher, and psychologist Lev Vygotsky. Vygotsky determined that labeling things—putting a name on things— is the primary function of language in the very young child. But, he says, after the child has labels for things, he or she begins to combine those labels in ways not available before. "The child begins to perceive the world not through his or her eyes," Vygotsky says, "but through his or her speech." Vygotsky calls seeing "integral," whereas "speech requires sequential processing. Each element is separately labeled and then connected in a sentence structure, *making speech essentially analytical*" (*Mind in Society*, pp. 32–33). Go back to your two analyses of the photograph and consider these questions: Did you first see, and then label, and then construct a hypothesis, or did all three activities happen to some extent simultaneously? Did your second analysis improve over your first one as a result of your becoming aware that you could *rearrange* what the eye sees by means of language? In your second analysis, did you write differently because you *saw* differently? Can you notice now how you may have failed to see some things in the photograph because those things simply did not fit into your original conception of it? Can you see now how what we said in Chapter 3 ("You cannot say something new until you see something in a new way.") may be true?

20. Thinking back through your own life, write an account of an episode or an issue about which there was argument because two or more people saw that episode or issue in different ways. What things was one side seeing that the other side could not or would not see, and vice versa?

All photographs courtesy of Thomas D. Reed

5

Writing about Readings

In the last chapter we wrote and talked about a photograph. But, of course, little of the analysis you write and few of the essays you write will be about photographs. What does what we did in the last chapter have to do with the kind of writing you will be doing, which will be mostly responses to other people's ideas and not responses to photographs?

The answer is simple. Whether you are analyzing a photograph, another writer's argument, or some part of the world around you, you are still doing the same things: creating a way of seeing and, when you are analyzing what someone else has written, comparing his or her way of seeing with your own. If we wanted, we could translate each of the fifteen questions we asked in Exercise 16 into questions that should be asked no matter what we are writing about. For instance, we said you should count how many descriptive words you had used in your analysis of the photograph, and then how many times you gathered those descriptive words into a category, a hypothesis, a conception. If you were writing about another writer's essay, you would be concerned with the same thing: making a judgment (this writer is a conservative, a Marxist, a Freudian) and giving evidence (a description of things the writer says) that lead you to your hypothesis. We said that you should note how many times you discriminated between any two things in the photograph. Writing about another writer's ideas, you often do the same kind of discriminating. If, when you described the photograph, you said something like, "The person in the photograph is surrounded by great wealth, and yet seems to be dressed poorly," you have made a discrimination. In the same way, you might say of a writer, "This writer seems to be in favor of self-determination for smaller nations, and yet he also wants a strong government to lead the people in what he thinks is the 'right' direction." Whether you are talking about a photograph or an idea, the process of analysis remains the same. When we talked about taking into account the context of the photograph, we were really talking about something you would want to do when you analyzed another writer's book or essay. You would, that is, ask yourself questions like "What might have prompted this writer to say the things he says?" Many of the questions we asked of your analysis of the photograph had to do with finding relationships: between one part of it and another; between something in it and something outside it; between something in it and something you remember from the past. Finding relationships is also one of the central features of all writing and thinking.

Becoming aware of the extent to which this is true tends to make all of us sharper readers as well as better writers. Once you can see, as we said in our "Composition Manifesto," that most writing you do will be a confrontation between one writer's conceptualizations and your own—an exploration of the relationships that writer sees between concepts and those *you* see—your own reading and writing tend to become sharper. The exercises below are designed to get you to read with as keen an eye as possible, to demonstrate how much both reading and writing essays is a matter of perceiving and communicating relationships, and to begin to point you toward the resources you have at your command when you want to write an essay or analyze someone else's essay.

21. Below is an excerpt from a review by Gore Vidal; it first appeared in the *New York Review of Books* and was reprinted in Vidal's collection called *Matters of Fact and Fiction*. Read through the excerpt once or twice, trying to understand Vidal's ideas as well as you can.

Gore Vidal.
"The Great World and Louis Auchincloss."

"What a dull and dreary trade is that of critic," wrote Diderot. "It is so difficult to create a thing, even a mediocre thing; it is so easy to detect mediocrity." Either the great philosophe was deliberately exaggerating or else Americans have always lived in an entirely different continuum from Europe. For us the making of mediocre things is the rule while the ability to detect mediocrity or anything else is rare. A century ago, E. L. Godkin wrote in *The Nation:* "The great mischief has always been that whenever our reviewers deviate from the usual and popular course of panegyric, they start from and end in personality, so that the public mind is almost sure to connect unfavorable criticism with personal animosity."

Don't knock, boost! was the cry of Warren Harding. To which the corollary was plain: anyone who knocks is a bad person with a grudge. As a result, the American has always reacted to the setting of standards rather the way Count Dracula responds to a clove of garlic or a crucifix. Since we are essentially a nation of hustlers rather than makers, any attempt to set limits or goals, rules or standards, is to attack a system of free enterprise where not only does the sucker not deserve that even break but the honest man is simply the one whose cheating goes undetected. Worse, to say that one English sentence might be better made than another is to be a snob, a subverter of the democracy, a Know-Nothing enemy of the late arrivals to our shores and its difficult language (p. 10).

After you have read the passage through once or twice, answer the following questions.

1. What is this excerpt? Is it a story? A study? A criticism? An evaluation? A polemic? A description? If it is a description, what is it a description of: A person? A place? A thing? A process? A phenomenon?
2. Identify—and maybe even underline or circle with a pen—all the major concepts you find in this excerpt.
3. Determine, very specifically, *what relationship* Vidal sees existing between and among these concepts. To be sure you are as precise as you can be, force yourself to construct a clear one-sentence answer to each of these questions: (a) What does Vidal see as the relationship between critical standards and the work critics do? (b) What does Vidal see as the relationship between free enterprise and mediocrity? (c) What does Vidal see as the relationship between democracy and critical standards?
4. Imagine this piece of writing as what any piece of writing always is: a part in an ongoing dialectic or debate with lots of other people. Try to determine what this piece is a response to. What attitudes does Vidal set himself against? Which sentences could you cite as evidence that he has a particular attitude, or denounces a particular attitude?
5. Define all words you do not know. What is *panegyric,* for instance? *Corollary?*

6. Determine which words recur in the excerpt and try to determine why they recur. Are they always used in the same sense or the same spirit? What, for instance, does Vidal mean by "criticism" and "standards"?

7. Determine as precisely as you can the *tone* of the excerpt. Is it ironic? Straightforward? Bemused? Angry? Sometimes one thing and at other times another?

8. What is the writer's purpose? Are you being asked to do something? Are you being told something? Does this piece seem written to inspire? To aggravate? To warn? To clarify? To question?

9. Remember what we have said about words like *nature, function,* and *source,* and the extent to which they are a part of what people talk about when they analyze. See if any or all of those words could not play a part in your response.

10. Can you list and then *rank* the points Vidal makes? Which seems to you to be his primary assertion; the one he gives the greatest weight and in which he seems the most interested? Then list the subsidiary points, making clear how they relate to Vidal's main assertion.

11. Try to visualize Vidal's argument. Does he lead you over a series of steps to a conclusion? Does he circle back on himself after a long digression? Does the case build up, like a pyramid, to one fine point? Could you even diagram the progression of Vidal's argument? How?

12. Determine the *function* of each sentence. Why, for instance, does Vidal include the sentence, "Don't knock, boost!" Why is Warren Harding in this excerpt? Who *is* Warren Harding? Which sentences are assertions? Which are substantiating evidence for those assertions? Which are qualifiers? Which make distinctions? What do your answers to these questions tell you about Vidal's strategy?

13. Formulate the question to which Vidal's excerpt could be considered an answer.

14. Read the excerpt's last sentence. See if you can explain clearly how the writer arrived at that point.

15. Once you are clear about the concepts being addressed, the definitions Vidal gives them, the assumptions behind his use of them, and the relationships he sees between them, you can begin to make judgments of your own: How do you feel about his assertions? Test them against your own experience, if you have relevant experience. Test them against other things you have read. Against other positions you know about that have been taken on the same issue Vidal addresses. Do Vidal's assertions seem reasonable? Possible? Outrageous? Fair?

16. What you are doing, of course, is joining in the dialectic being carried forward by this writer in this excerpt. To write well in response to something you have read, you will always want to read in a particular way: not as a consumer only, but as a participant. You will read first for understanding, but then you will read saying, "Yes, but . . . but . . . partly, yes, but maybe also. . . . Instead, couldn't it be that . . . perhaps. . . ." Have a dialogue with an essay you read.

17. If, once you have read and understood the essay, you agree with it

or think you do, simply paraphrase the writer's major points, as clearly as you can, in a summary paragraph.

18. Once you have completed your paraphrase, you may be able to see even more clearly not only the structure of the paragraphs but also the structure of the thinking Vidal went through to get to his assertions. In this case, we have a *causal chain*: X causes Y, which in turn causes Z. Fill in the X, Y, and Z if you can.

19. If, once you have completed your paraphrase, you discover holes in Vidal's argument, or discover you do not like his point, formulate your own statement about the true and proper connections to be made between the concepts Vidal is talking about. Or reread the "Composition Manifesto" in Chapter 3, and consider what your other responses might be. You could, for instance, decide to use a *different* connector between Vidal's separate concepts: Does criticism *impede* free enterprise, or *inspire* free enterprise? You could decide that you like Vidal's way of isolating this particular phenomenon, but that you do not like the concept words with which he describes it. *Rename* (which means reconceptualize, as you know by now) the phenomenon he describes. Maybe it is neither "giving a sucker an even break" nor "hustling" that keeps us from criticizing, but *deference, or consideration toward others.* Maybe you think his use of the word *mediocrity* is appropriate, but you do not see that concept as connected causally with *criticism*. What alternative constructions (conceptualizations) can you bring forward? Mediocrity is caused by *what?* Or maybe you do not think American productions are mediocre. In this case, you could challenge the conceptual categorizations Vidal makes in the first place. Maybe you think Vidal himself is not clear in what he means by "standards" or "criticism." Is he talking about the visual arts? All art? Would he include American technology as being "mediocre"? Notice, all the while, how argument, discussion, and analysis consist almost entirely of such conceptual naming and renaming and connecting.

20. Finally, consider how it might be that all of the writing and thinking you do will also be concerned with these same kinds of things.

22. Now that you have written an accurate summary and analysis of the Vidal excerpt, reread what you have written for accuracy, and also to see whether it is, and how it is, that summary inevitably slides off into analysis. What does that tell you about the relationship between summary and analysis, and, by implication, about fact and interpretation?

23. Find a paragraph or two of writing that is as densely packed with assertions as Vidal's paragraphs are. These might come from a newspaper editorial, an essay, a book. Go through the twenty questions above, doing the same kind of summary and analysis you just did with the Vidal excerpt. Notice how much these procedures will work on any writing you read and respond to.

Where and How Does One Get an Idea:
Watching Your Mind Work

So far in these chapters I have assumed that when you write you are responding to other people's ideas and writings. In one sense that will always be true: every new idea is a response to, or a reaction against, someone else's ideas. But what happens when you just plain want to write an essay, or when you *have* to write an essay? In those cases, the first problem you have as a writer is finding ideas you want to write about. The first question you have for yourself as a writer is obviously, How does one get an idea? To some extent this is an artificial question: in a natural state of affairs, you would not be looking for an idea. You would write whenever you were inspired to write, and you would be inspired to write whenever you already had an idea, or something you wanted to say to a particular audience. Nonetheless, there are times when you need to know how to find an idea, and so it is useful to do some exploring, to find out how you may become a more efficient idea-gatherer or idea-generator. Where does an idea come from? What can you do to be sure an idea comes to you? Or do you come to an idea? These are very real questions for any writer, and maybe especially for the student who happens also to be a writer, for the student rightly suspects that not all teachers have a lot of patience with the student who "can't think of anything to write about." In *The Psychology of Invention in the Mathematical Field*, Jacques Hadamard reveals that this impatience teachers sometimes feel is very real: "Students have often consulted me for subjects of research; when asked for such guidance, I have given it willingly, but I must confess that—provisionally, of course—I have been inclined to classify the man as second rate. In a different field, such was the opinion of our great Indianist Sylvain Levi, who told me that, on being asked such a question, he was tempted to reply: Now, my young friend, you have attended our courses for, say, three or four years and you have never perceived that there is something wanting further investigation?" (p. 126).

Of course part of what the poor student being addressed here may need to do is simply learn how to read more carefully and critically, as we did in the previous chapter. Asking questions of what you read, and reading carefully, often yields ideas for further research and writing. Still, for some people, finding the area that needs investigation, or finding the thing to write about, is the hardest part of writing. In this chapter, then, we shall be thinking, reading, and writing about how ideas come. No one, of course, can tell you how your own ideas come. But I can ask what I hope are the right questions so that you can find those answers for yourself, and I can tell and show you how people who are good at analyzing and writing use certain kinds of analytical structures to get and convey ideas. The latter we will do in the next chapter. In this chapter, we will simply watch ourselves think, comparing the way we think with what several philosophers have said people do when they think, solve problems, invent, struggle to explain or make sense of their worlds.

This process is often referred to as the process of *invention,* and philosophers have had different theories about exactly how it works and what triggers it in the first place. For Jacques Hadamard, there are really two kinds of invention. The first becomes necessary when you have a goal you want to reach. The problem, then, and the thing that makes invention necessary, is the need to find a means for reaching that goal. You may want to convince a reluctant friend to lend you his car. Invention is the process by which you struggle to think of ways to persuade him to do that. The United States may want to encourage more people to put more of their money into savings to slow down inflation. Invention is what Congress needs to use to think of ways to get us to do that.

The second type of invention Hadamard describes is different. In this kind, one already has all "the facts," or "an answer," but has a need to decide what question those facts are answering. What we might have, then, is "the fact": the sick child, the serious disagreement, the threat of war. What we would have to do is work backward, trying to figure out the cause of this result. In the Middle Ages, there were great outbreaks of the plague, and thousands of people died. In those times, the "fact" was there: sick and dying people. But invention was necessary as people tried to move backward from the fact to the cause that preceded it. If you are now taking college courses, you might think carefully about an issue central to any one of those courses that requires either kind of invention Hadamard describes. Sociology courses, I think, would be full of the latter kind of problem. The sociologist sees behavior and must work backward to try to decide what caused it.

Curiously enough, Hadamard thinks it is often the "sense of beauty," or the desire for harmony, that makes us start the process of invention. What he means, I think, is that for the creative thinker, it is the sense of something-not-quite-right, something-not-quite-in-harmony, or something missing in our picture of the world that triggers the process of invention and results in our "getting an idea." And it is writing that allows us, as we have said, to wrestle with the emergent idea and give it a shape and, in the process, bring it to full consciousness. Or, as Hayden White says in *Tropics of Discourse,* discourse is "the verbal operation by which the questing consciousness situates its own efforts to bring a problematical domain of experience under cognitive control" (pp. 10–11). That is only a fancy way of saying we think through writing.

For Susanne Langer, especially in *Philosophy in a New Key,* new ideas come primarily in the act of forming new questions and, simultaneously, rejecting old forms of questions. Questions, says Langer, really determine the direction our explorations will take and determine what we can see and know. For as long as scientists in the Middle Ages continued to ask "Which is the original element: Earth, Air, Fire, or Water?" they could never discover atoms, not to mention protons, neutrons, neutrinos, or quarks. Or, more recently, to discover gluons, which hold everything else together. The new idea, then, consists in the generation of a new question. You might think about the new question or questions that might be formulated to replace old questions like: "How can we get more police into high schools to control the growing violence in them?" "How can we produce more domestic oil?" "How can we make sure all college graduates get good jobs after they graduate?"

For Michael Polanyi in *The Tacit Dimension,* invention begins neither with the question nor the answer. The first problem of the thinker is *to see a problem,* for to do so "is to see something that is hidden. It is to have an intimation of the coherence of hitherto not comprehended particulars" (p. 22). To see a problem is to see something "of which the rest of humanity cannot have even an inkling" (p. 22). Quoting Plato in the *Meno,* Polanyi muses that to search for the solution of a problem is an absurdity: "for either you know what you are looking for, and then there is no problem; or you do not know what you are looking for, and then you cannot expect to find anything" (p. 22). How, then, does Polanyi think we ever learn anything new? For him, those who get ideas and solve problems are only those who feel the full "excitement" of problems; those who have "an obsession with hunches and visions that are indispensable spurs and pointers to discovery" (p. 78).

You might want to think for a few minutes about what Polanyi calls the "coherence of hitherto not comprehended particulars." People died of the plague during the Middle Ages because no one connected the disease with the rats breeding in the garbage in the streets, and because no one connected the rats breeding in the streets with the fleas on the rats, or with fleas passing from rats to people, carrying the virus with them. Before someone thought to ask, "Can bacteria and viruses be carried in the air and passed from one person to another?" no one could have answered, "Yes" and begun working on control of disease. But before that, before someone thought to ask, "How do diseases pass from one person to another?" no one could have discovered bacteria or viruses. Even before that, if someone had not asked "What *is* disease?" we would not have had answers containing words like *transmission, bacteria,* or *virus.* And before someone stopped asking the old question, "How have I angered the gods so that they have called down this suffering upon my head?" we could not have talked about *cures* at all.

If we are interested in getting ideas, it may help for us to consider what an "idea" is in the first place, and where it comes from. Listed below are the ideas of six thinkers—philosophers, psychologists, or mathematicians—about what an idea is. Read through the six very carefully and then do the exercises that follow. The exercises will all require that you pay close attention to different people's notions of how an idea comes.

1. The extreme view, probably, is that held by the French psychologist Souriau, who in 1881 maintained that invention occurs by pure chance. We stumble upon an idea, and that is the only way one ever comes to us.

2. For John Locke, "to ask at what time a man first has any ideas is to ask when he begins to perceive; *having ideas* and *perception* being the same thing." For him, then, there is really no difference between seeing and thinking. All mental activity and all consciousness he bundles together under the category of "having ideas." This is exactly what we talked about in Chapter 4, and what we explored in Exercise 19. Even when you look at an object and call it a "tree," you are already thinking; that is, classifying that mass of atoms with that chemical composition and physical configuration in a certain way.

3. Jacques Hadamard thinks that invention or discovery is a matter not of finding "new" ideas, but of combining older, existing ones. He notes that Max Muller remarked that the Latin verb "cogito" ("to think") etymologically means "to shake together." This notion makes invention or the getting of a new idea a matter mostly of "choice"; of deciding which details of each experience we are going to pay attention to, and which ones we are going to ignore. This sounds very much like the process Roger Brown described in "The Uses of the Named Category." This is also probably very much like what happened as you analyzed a photograph in Chapter 4. Some details simply got ignored, because you did not choose to describe them or fit them into your analysis. Like Brown, Hadamard believes that the rules that guide our choice of details are "largely felt rather than formulated" (pp. 30–31).

4. Jerome Brunner, a cognitive psychologist, would probably be in agreement with Hadamard. In his essay "The Act of Discovery," he says that the act of discovery rarely occurs on the frontiers of knowledge, and new facts are rarely "discovered, in the sense of being encountered as Newton suggested in the form of islands of truth in an uncharted sea of ignorance. Or if they appear to be discovered in this way, it is almost always thanks to some happy hypothesis about where to navigate. Discovery, like surprise, favors the well-prepared mind. The history of science is studded with examples of men "finding out" something and not knowing it. . . . Discovery, whether by a schoolboy going it on his own or by a scientist cultivating the growing edge of his field, is in its essence a matter of rearranging or transforming evidence in such a way that one is enabled to go beyond the evidence so reassembled to additional new insights. It may well be that an additional fact or shred of evidence makes this larger transformation of evidence possible. But it is often not even dependent on new information" (pp. 31–32). For both Hadamard and Bruner, then, the new idea comes almost exclusively as a result of our reshuffling existing information.

5. For others, invention is not just a product of reshuffling. For instance, Eliseo Vivas thinks that "creation" is a genuine phenomenon and not, as the majority of psychologists and philosophers seem to think, some sort of complex shuffling of what had already been known: "I believe that in the act of creation the mind adds something to what was there before the act took place," he says in *Creation and Discovery* (p. xi). But in part it may be that Vivas can say what he does because he is most concerned with *artistic* invention, and because he also claims a vast difference exists between what he calls the "creative imagination" and what he calls the "problem-solving" capacity. It is the difference, he says, between "the mind of the genius and the ingenious mind" (p. 236).

6. Henri Poincaré has a different idea about where the new idea comes from. For him, the thinker "seems to watch passively, as if from the outside, the evolution of subcon-

scious idea" (in Hadamard, p. 15). This idea sounds very close to the ideas of Polanyi. Polanyi believes that the thinker in a manner of speaking simply moves toward what he or she in some sense already knows but does not know he or she knows. Polanyi calls this process *emergence*. In this model of getting ideas, the thinker and writer's major problem is simply remembering to stay alert and tuned in so that he or she can catch the ideas that reside in the subconscious and that speak only quietly and in unguarded moments. The thinker, then, thinks best and gets most of his or her ideas exactly at the moment when he or she is not trying to think at all. Ideas reside in the "ante-consciousness," as some philosophers call it, or in the "fringe-consciousness," as American philosopher William James called it. Arthur Koestler's book *The Act of Creation* is full of accounts of how people like Albert Einstein "discovered" their best ideas at exactly the moments when they were not looking for them. It might better be said, then, that the ideas found *them* rather than vice versa.

Now that we have spent some time talking about how other people think that ideas come, it makes sense to check those theories against our own practice. The series of exercises that follows is designed to allow you to test these theories and to see, in the process, whether you can discover how ideas come to you. Knowing how ideas come to you, of course, cannot help but make it easier for you to think of ideas when you want or need to in the future.

24. Follow your own mind around for a week, watching it think. Eavesdrop on it. Whenever an idea comes to you—whether it is about a connection between sports and adulthood; politics and teaching; adolescence and turmoil; television and morality—write up that idea. This write-up can be one paragraph, ten paragraphs, or even ten pages. On his drive to school, one student decided he had discovered at least five reasons why people drive, besides just getting from one place to the other. See if you can think of a fresh idea of your own.

All that is necessary is that you explain your idea completely and explore as much as you can of its implications.

25. After your idea has "cooled," and after your essay about the idea has cooled, write another essay. In this one, describe in detail how that idea you wrote about in the previous exercise came to you: Where were you, what time of day was it, what were the conditions? Did it come full-blown? Half-formed and fuzzy? Did you wrestle it into shape, or did it come complete? What prompted the idea: Something you read, or heard, or nothing apparent at all? When you wrote up the idea, did you find that the *act* of writing clarified the idea? Did writing lead to your discovering further dimensions of the idea that you had not thought of at first?

26. Reread all of the excerpts on invention and discovery at the beginning of this chapter. Discuss in writing which one comes nearest to describing what happened in you as you got the idea; why and how it describes the process as you experienced it. Do you find *all* of the explanations or theories in the chapter partly true? True in *one* instance of discovery, if not in another?

27. Below is a list of very short propositions from several different sources. Choose *one* of them and do *one* of several things: respond to it; provide one or more instances demonstrating how and where it may prove to be true; demonstrate its accuracy (or falsity); or find its "range of convenience." This last is Jerome Bruner's phrase to denote what we do when we try to figure out exactly where this proposition might be true, and how far its implications go.

1. Not all beliefs have *reasons,* but all beliefs probably have causes. (Max Black, *Critical Thinking,* p. 266.)
2. I happen to believe that Freud's fixed quantity of libido (express it here and it must be withdrawn from there) is a kind of first-order nonsense. Passion, like discriminating taste, grows on its own use. You more likely act yourself into feeling than feel yourself into action. (Jerome Bruner, *On Knowing,* p. 24.)
3. From old truths as from old canvases, the grime of time must occasionally be removed. (Eliseo Vivas, *Creation and Discovery,* p. 111.)
4. A fish will be the last to discover water. (Old proverb.)
5. Before sewing one must cut. (Jacques Maritain, *Creative Intuition in Art and Poetry,* p. 44.)
6. A word is not a crystal, transparent and unchanged; it is the skin of a living thought and may vary greatly in color and content according to the circumstances and the time in which it is used. (Justice Oliver Wendell Holmes.)
7. Formerly, the crux of the art of pleasing was 'to shine,' which meant to flatter others' pride by a visible effort of mind, charm, wit—in short, by a gift of something more valuable than plain unvarnished self. Nowadays we coax rather than flatter and we do it by whittling down the self so as to spare vanity the smallest hurt. To shine would be egotistical. One must merely glow. (Jacques Barzun, *The House of Intellect,* p. 70.)

28. Consider the essay you just wrote in response to one of the quotations above. Again, detail the process by which the ideas came to you, just as you did in Exercise 25. Is the process the same for you when you are responding to written material, or does "invention" happen differently when the impetus for it is someone else's ideas?

29. If you have gone through the last five exercises, you have generated some advice to yourself that you can go back to whenever you are stuck for a place to start; for an idea to get you going when you want or need to write. Write up what you have learned about your own idea-gathering process in your writer's log. What state of mind do you need to be in to get ideas? Where do ideas come to you best? Do they disappear if you do not grab a pencil and write them down right away? Do they grow and change as you write about them? Does writing itself become easier when you are concentrating on getting ideas down, and not on "writing"? Can you see how getting ideas may be more a matter of attitude—staying alert, and considering every occasion or encounter as material—than of anything else? What else have you learned that you may want to hang onto for future use?

7

Where and How Does One Get an Idea: Watching Other Minds Work

In the last chapter we tried to get in touch with that mysterious place in our minds where ideas first form. Our emphasis was on the word *ideas*. In this chapter, it is on the word *form*. Of course, in some crucial way this separation into idea and form is completely inappropriate. As I said in the very first chapter, an "idea" really *is* a form: Gore Vidal's idea that American mediocrity is caused by Americans' fear to be criticized, and Americans' fear to be criticized is the result of their misconceptions of democracy and the free enterprise system, is really a wonderfully tight causal chain. His idea, that is, is a structure of causes, one leading to the next. Because "idea" is really "form," writing teachers for centuries have been trying to teach students to think and write by having them imitate rhetorical models or "forms" of writing. In *A Theory of Discourse,* James Kinneavy carefully traces the lines of development from classical rhetoric to modern writing textbook: from Cicero's determining that an argument must have six parts (exordium, narrative, partition, confirmation, repetition, and peroration), to modern textbook writers telling students to write compare/contrast essays, narratives, and cause/effect essays. It is true that looking at other writers' forms of writing can help us become better writers, but not necessarily because we have noticed the form in order to imitate it. We can learn something from other writers' forms of writing because they reveal to us the way the writer's mind moved, and because they suggest that we might make similar kinds of moves when we shape raw data into "ideas." Michel Foucault's *Archaeology of Knowledge and the Discourse on Language* treats all language as if it were—as it is— traces of a culture, able to be "excavated" and studied to see what that culture was like, how it thought, what it believed in. So, too, a writer's essay is really only traces left behind: traces of a mind thinking. Looking at those traces, you may be able to watch how other minds have thought, and, by extension, you might also learn how *you* might think, or might want to think. And here we are not only talking about *what* you might think, but about *how* you might think.

Below are five excerpts of writing, all a version of the same form; that is, all express a causal connection between at least one thing and at least one other thing. Read through the five excerpts one at a time and do the practice exercises that accompany each one.

30. Read the excerpt of writing that immediately follows which is about Italy and Mussolini. It is from a review of *Mussolini: An Intimate Biography by His Widow,* which appeared in the *New York Review of Books.* If you have difficulty reading it, go back to the suggestions for reading in Chapter 5, "Writing about Readings." After you are sure you understand what the writer is saying, compose your own paraphrase of the writer's ideas. That is, simply put in your own words what this writer is saying.

Luigi Barzini.
Review of Rachele Mussolini's *Mussolini*

What ruined Mussolini, above all, was the idea that Garibaldi's career seemed to demonstrate to Italians, the idea that, if only the right superman could be found, there always was an easy way out of the most arduous crisis. Garibaldi's life seemed to prove that Italy could be spared the necessary uphill struggle to improve its lot (and the opinion others had of it) if it trusted its destiny to a demiurge generally resembling him, who would lead the people to glory and prosperity without "blood, sweat, and tears." (The words are Garibaldi's. He used them in an 1849 proclamation.) This belief in the national hero, to be sure, is not an Italian delusion alone. Many nations have been its victims (or beneficiaries), some of them several times—France, for instance, three times in little more than a century and a half. Incidentally, to fire men's imaginations in a sleepy and archaic country such a hero must proclaim outlandish revolutionary ideals, that is, inspire the hope of escaping the present by dreaming of a radiant future, and remind his countrymen of their glorious history, thus giving them the hope of escaping the present by finding refuge in a partly imaginary past (p. 22).

31. After you have written your paraphrase, reread it and decide whether you agree with the writer's assertions. This exercise, of course, presupposes that you have some background in history (European, American, or Far Eastern) and can check what Barzini says against your own knowledge of how people in some other countries have thought in the past. Is there another country in another historical period that resembles what Barzini describes? If so, talk about that in writing.

32. Forget, for the moment, the *content* of this paragraph. Instead, concentrate on its *form*. Write a short piece in which you analyze that. What kind of assertion is being made by Barzini? Where do you find the assertion being made in one sentence? Which sentences carry that assertion and develop it? Which sentences seem to diverge from the main point, and when they do diverge, what are they doing, and why?

33. Once you are familiar with the form of Barzini's paragraph ("What caused X was Y."), carry that form around in your mind for a few days, watching yourself think, and watching to see whether you might want to compose a few paragraphs about some entirely different issue, paragraphs that are in the *same form* as Barzini's. Ask yourself: Did the form generate the ideas, or did the ideas generate the form?

34. The following excerpt is also from the *New York Review of Books*. Read through these three paragraphs carefully and then write a paraphrase that is as accurate as you can make it.

C. Vann Woodward.
Review of Eugene Genovese's *Roll, Jordan Roll*

The slaves embraced the masters' Christianity, but they "conquered the religion of those who had conquered them." They molded it and transformed it to meet their moral and psychic needs. Even St. Paul set limits to "the things which are Caesar's" and left no doubt that there was a Master above the slave's master and moral limits to submission, even of a slave. Slavery might produce a sense of shame but hardly a sense of guilt. Missing from black Christianity were some essentials of the doctrine's Western formulation—original sin, a sense of guilt, a sense of mission, and the terrible inner tensions they produced.

In their place black Christianity "affirmed the joy of life in the face of every trial." Such was not the stuff of revolutionary commitment and holy wars. It accepted the hegemony of the oppressor but denied realization of the master's ideal. It was a theology vital for defensive needs but poor for offensive strategy. It was a source of strength for a people at bay, but also a source of political weakness. It strengthened the individual at the expense of collective assertion. "The accomplishment soared heroically to great heights, but so did the price, which even now has not been fully paid."

Genovese dismisses the theory that blacks merely copied white religion as "unworthy of discussion." Obviously their religion had Western antecedents, but beneath them were divergencies in meaning—of soul, of sin, of hell and heaven, of the very meaning of God. The devil could be a friend and a laughing matter. The survival of African traditions and influences—which the masters never doubted—is sensibly explored [in this book], and so is the compatibility of conjuring, voodoo, Obeah, and witchcraft with fervid commitment to Christianity. Call-and-response, song-style preaching, and the tightrope role of black preachers gain appreciative understanding. Theirs was a gospel of spiritual resistance but rarely of revolutionary defiance (p. 19).

35. After you have written your paraphrase, write a thoughtful response to the assertions in this excerpt, if you know enough about slavery or Christianity.

36. As you did with the first excerpt, concentrate on the *form* of this excerpt rather than its ideas. Do you find, for instance, a form that is repeated often throughout this excerpt, especially in many of its separate sentences? What is that form, and what does it tell you about the kind of analysis in the excerpt?

37. You will notice that this excerpt, short as it is, is neither a simple causal statement (Christianity is what caused these good things and these not-so-good things for black people), or a simple compare and contrast assertion (Black Christianity differs from white Christianity in these ways and for these reasons and with these effects), or a simple distinction-making assertion (Christianity had its effects on black people, but only in certain ways, and not others, and for certain reasons, and not others). Instead, the excerpt is a combination of all those forms. Construct a paragraph, or two or three, in which you use *any part* of this idea structure to convey some idea you have about anything at all. Your writing here may express a causal connection, compare and contrast, or make some crucial distinction between apparently similar things—just as this excerpt makes distinctions between black and white forms of Christianity.

38. The third excerpt follows. It is taken from a review that also appeared in the *New York Review of Books*. Again, paraphrase the excerpt as accurately as you can.

Richard J. Barnet.
Review of Victor Marchetti and John Marks's
The CIA and the Cult of Intelligence

Thus, the same internal suspicions, rivalries, and bribery that keep poor nations from effectively organizing themselves to overcome mass poverty make them attractive targets of the intelligence underworld. Real and ex- aggerated fears of being infiltrated help to keep such societies in a continual state of political disorganization. As Bissell [Richard Bissell, former head of clandestine operations for the CIA] points out, the less totalitarian the society, the easier it is to find out and to influence what goes on there. Salvador Allende's tolerance of forces opposing him made it easy for the CIA and other intelligence agencies to work with them to hasten his down- fall.

[Some theoreticians] argue that espionage in the poorer countries is needed to produce "timely knowledge" of "tactical significance." In fact most clandestine collection of information serves no purpose other than to support covert activities that subvert foreign regimes. Bissell himself con- cedes that sometimes "the task of intelligence collection and political action overlap to the point of being almost indistinguishable." For what legitimate purpose does the United States need to immerse itself in the internal political developments of Third World and other countries which pose no threat to the security of the United States other than the assertion of their own independence? (p. 30).

39. If you are interested in the issue with which Marchetti and Marks are concerned, write your own response to what they are saying.

40. Below is an excerpt from a review that appeared in the New York Review of Books. As you did in the previous exercises, paraphrase this excerpt.

Wilfrid Sheed.
Review of W. C. Fields by Himself
with commentary by Ronald Fields

[W. C. Fields's] persona was the work of genius, and Ronald's book sug- gests that this was more consciously arrived at than we like to think. Fields's native gifts were industry, physical coordination, and mental retentiveness, plus a downright anal stinginess. The two kinds of retention were possibly connected, and together they account for much of his greatness and misery. Their immediate effect was to make him a master of music hall and vau- deville, where shtiks and bits of business had to be hoarded like miser's gold. I am told it was not unknown for comedians to pull knives on each other when they suspected their acts were being stolen. One's act was all one had, and it had to last a lifetime. Fields was superbly equipped for this cutthroat world: or if not he became so. Very few kindly men can have emerged from vaudeville.

Without detracting from W. C.'s uniqueness, I believe it would be rewarding to study the other comedians of the era for technical similarities. For instance, Fields's habit of throwing up his hands and hunching his shoulders when anyone threatens to touch him might be explained as a reflex flinching from his father's blows. But if memory serves, Leon Errol had a similar style; and before either of them, God knows what forgotten comedian working the London halls in the 1900s when Fields was starting out may have inspired them both. In payment, Fields's hands fluttering at the throat may have taught young Oliver Hardy a thing or two. And so on. Just as the genius of comics is customarily overrated, so their craft and attention to detail is proportionately ignored. In an allied field, it is often forgotten that Sydney Greenstreet was a D'Oyly Carte veteran and that he played the Fat Man precisely as any Poo Bah would have, while Peter Lorre was a member of Bertholt Brecht's ensemble. Thus *The Maltese Falcon* was a mating of acting traditions, and not just of individual actors.

Fields once called Chaplin "a goddam ballet dancer," but it is no coincidence that they both came out of this London tradition, where techniques in physical comedy had reached a high polish. All commentators agree that Fields had ferocious dedication, spending up to two years learning one juggling trick. And his first approach to comedy was probably similar: a dogged humorless mastering of each movement, until his body work was so good that he could make side-splitting *silent* movies. To this day, there is no actor I would rather see just enter a room and sit down, with the possible exception of Fred Astaire.

The vocal side of his act was carried at first by the physical and has a consequent freedom and experimentation about it, akin to Will Rogers's offhand patter during his rope-twirling. The people had paid to see a juggler, so the commentary was gravy: and Fields used it partly to cover his mistakes and hold the crowd's attention, but partly one suspects, semiconsciously, as a man mutters to himself when engaged on an intricate task— I suspect Fields would have talked the same with no one around. The result is a dreamlike free-associative quality closer to poetry than to the world of gags (p. 26).

41. In this excerpt, the writer gives an elaborate and plausible list of the causes for W. C. Fields's success and for his peculiar gestures and on-camera patter. Can you think of a contemporary entertainer whose work you are very familiar with and write a similar analysis of the nature, source, and function of those things you take to be central to that entertainer's success?

42. All of the excerpts we have just read and written about—on Italy and Mussolini, on black Christianity, on CIA covert activities in developing countries, and on W. C. Fields's art—reveal something about the mind of the writers as well as something about the issues about which they write. All of these writers were thinking causally; all of the excerpts say, in one way or another, *this* causes *that.* If you reread the excerpt written by Gore Vidal that appears in Chapter 5, you will find that he is doing the same thing. There are differences, however, between the five pieces. Below are some simple diagrams depicting different kinds of causal forms. Think about and reread the five excerpts— including Vidal's—and determine which of the excerpts is an example of which of the five kinds of causal forms.

1. Simple cause and effect

A———▶B

2. Multiple causes for one effect

3. One cause; two or more effects

A $\longleftarrow$ B
C
D

4. Two causes; two effects (one good, one bad)

A $\times$ C
B   D

5. The causal chain (A causes B, which in turn causes C)

A
D
B
C

43. Even though you can find these causal forms in each of the excerpts, and even though it is the causal form that holds the argument together, notice also how much elbow room each writer gives himself in which to do other things: refer to a similar case in some other time and place; anticipate some of his readers' objections to one of his points and address those objections; muse about the implications of what he is considering. What does this flexibility tell you about the essay as a form? What does it tell you about what *you* might do as you write essays?

Other People's Concepts

If you have read all of the writing excerpts we have encountered so far, you may have been struck by the extent to which
each writer's major job seems to be to argue that we have not
been regarding one or another concept as accurately as we should.
It is a faulty definition of democracy, Vidal says, that makes us
think that criticism is an attack on democratic principles. The
writer discussing Christianity and slavery tells us that there is
simply no one conception of Christianity, and that it was the black
slaves' own conception of Christianity that gave them their strength
and their ability to survive—even if it was also their conception
of Christianity that kept them from rebelling against their white
masters more and sooner than they did. For another writer, it
was the Italians' conception of "the hero" that kept them from
improving their lot and their country. Deciding how we should
and should not see concepts is at the heart of all analytical writing.

Because this is so, it makes sense, now that we are in the
heart of the book, to address this directly. In this chapter, we will
do lots of conceptual play: we will watch what happens if we look
at an issue first one way and then another; we will think about
what it means to say that looking at something one way (*perceiving*) is the same as *looking* at something one way (*conceiving*).
When we say "I see what you mean," we really do mean I *see*
what you mean. The exercises that follow are designed to allow
you to see what happens when we define concepts one way and
then another; to encourage conceptual flexibility; to discover how
and why it is that the definitions we give our concepts really do
make a difference in how we live our lives, how we see ourselves,

and how others see us; to make us yet more aware of how central a part conceptual thinking plays in all writing.

44. The Russian philosopher and psychologist Lev Vygotsky, whom we talked about earlier, says that *every* word is a concept; that *"each word* is already a generalization" (p. 5). Even the word *I*, says Vygotsky, is a concept. Think about Vygotsky's assertion for awhile and then write a short essay in which you explore how it is, why it is—or, if you wish, if it is—that *I* is a concept. If you need help to get started, reread the "Composition Manifesto" in Chapter 3.

45. Vygotsky also suggests that the meanings of words evolve for each of us during childhood and that, even more crucially, abstract words (like *love, duty,* and *success*) undergo a similar evolution as we mature mentally. Think about a concept that has changed its meaning for you over the years and discuss what it meant for you as a child, how it changed for you as you matured, and as a result of what experiences, and what it means to you now.

46. Below is a cartoon. It could be said that the process of conceptualization is itself the subject of the joke. (Jokes often depend on a sudden shift in context for their success. We are tricked into *seeing* in one context, and then that context is suddenly shifted. The result is laughter.) Consider the following:
Q: "What would you do with an elephant with three balls?"
A: "Walk him and pitch to the giraffe."
There are object lessons—for writing and for life—in this cartoon. One is that the *name* we put on something is crucial because it determines how we will respond to that thing, how we will act, and how we will be acted upon. Write a short analysis of the cartoon that tells your reader something about how a concept works. The object will not be, of course, to "explain" the joke, but to discuss what it tells you about the joys, dangers, necessities, and process of forming concepts.

47. A short excerpt by Thomas S. Kuhn follows. Read it carefully and then compose a short essay in which you give special attention to his sentence, " 'Oxygen was discovered' misleads by suggesting that discovering something is a simple act assimilable to our usual (and also questionable) concept of seeing." Try to include an exploration of the following questions: What is implied by Kuhn about the relationship between *seeing* and *conceptualizing*? What can you learn and say about the nature of some philosophical disagreements and how they might be solved, simply by reading what Kuhn is saying?

Thomas S. Kuhn.
"Anomaly and the Emergence of Scientific Discoveries."
From *The Structure of Scientific Revolutions*

Normal science, the puzzle-solving activity we have just examined, is a highly cumulative enterprise, eminently successful in its aim, the steady extension of the scope and precision of scientific knowledge. In all these respects it fits with great precision the most usual image of scientific work. Yet one standard product of the scientific enterprise is missing. Normal science does not aim at novelties of fact or theory and, when successful, finds none. New and unsuspected phenomena are, however, repeatedly uncovered by scientific research, and radical new theories have again and again been invented by scientists. History even suggests that the scientific enterprise has developed a uniquely powerful technique for producing surprises of this sort. If this characteristic of science is to be reconciled with what has already been said, then research under a paradigm must be a particularly effective way of inducing paradigm change. That is what fundamental novelties of fact and theory do. Produced inadvertently by a game played under one set of rules, their assimilation requires the elaboration of another set. After they have become parts of science, the enterprise, at least of those specialists in whose particular field the novelties lie, is never quite the same again.

We must now ask how changes of this sort can come about, considering first discoveries, or novelties of fact, and then inventions, or novelties of theory. That distinction between discovery and invention or between fact and theory will, however, immediately prove to be exceedingly artificial. Its artificiality is an important clue to several of this essay's main theses. Examining selected discoveries in the rest of this section, we shall quickly find that they are not isolated events but extended episodes with a regularly recurrent structure. Discovery commences with the awareness of anomaly, i.e., with the recognition that nature has somehow violated the paradigm-induced expectations that govern normal science. It then continues with a more or less extended exploration of the area of anomaly. And it closes only when the paradigm theory has been adjusted so that the anomalous has become the expected. Assimilating a new sort of fact demands a more than additive adjustment of theory, and until that adjustment is completed—

until the scientist has learned to see nature in a different way—the new fact is not quite a scientific fact at all.

To see how closely factual and theoretical novelty are intertwined in scientific discovery examine a particularly famous example, the discovery of oxygen. At least three different men have a legitimate claim to it, and several other chemists must, in the early 1770's, have had enriched air in a laboratory vessel without knowing it. The progress of normal science, in this case of pneumatic chemistry, prepared the way to a breakthrough quite thoroughly. The earliest of the claimants to prepare a relatively pure sample of the gas was the Swedish apothecary, C. W. Scheele. We may, however, ignore his work since it was not published until oxygen's discovery had repeatedly been announced elsewhere and thus had no effect upon the historical pattern that most concerns us here. The second in time to establish a claim was the British scientist and divine, Joseph Priestley, who collected the gas released by heated red oxide of mercury as one item in a prolonged normal investigation of the "airs" evolved by a large number of solid substances. In 1774 he identified the gas thus produced as nitrous oxide and in 1775, led by further tests, as common air with less than its usual quantity of phlogiston. The third claimant, Lavoisier, started the work that led him to oxygen after Priestley's experiments of 1774 and possibly as the result of a hint from Priestley. Early in 1775 Lavoisier reported that the gas obtained by heating the red oxide of mercury was "air itself entire without alteration [except that] . . . it comes out more pure, more respirable." By 1777, probably with the assistance of a second hint from Priestley, Lavoisier had concluded that the gas was a distinct species, one of the two main constituents of the atmosphere, a conclusion that Priestley was never able to accept.

This pattern of discovery raises a question that can be asked about every novel phenomenon that has ever entered the consciousness of scientists. Was it Priestley or Lavoisier, if either, who first discovered oxygen? In any case, when was oxygen discovered? In that form the question could be asked even if only one claimant had existed. As a ruling about priority and date, an answer does not at all concern us. Nevertheless, an attempt to produce one will illuminate the nature of discovery, because there is no answer of the kind that is sought. Discovery is not the sort of process about which the question is appropriately asked. The fact that it is asked—the priority for oxygen has repeatedly been contested since the 1780's—is a symptom of something askew in the image of science that gives discovery so fundamental a role. Look once more at our example. Priestley's claim to the discovery of oxygen is based upon his priority in isolating a gas that was later recognized as a distinct species. But Priestley's sample was not pure, and, if holding impure oxygen in one's hands is to discover it, that had been done by everyone who ever bottled atmospheric air. Besides, if Priestley was the discoverer, when was the discovery made? In 1774 he thought he had obtained nitrous oxide, a species he already knew; in 1775 he saw the gas as dephlogisticated air, which is still not oxygen or even, for phlogistic chemists, a quite unexpected sort of gas. Lavoisier's claim may be stronger, but it presents the same problems. If we refuse the palm to Priestley, we cannot award it to Lavoisier for the work of 1775 which led him to identify the gas as "the air itself entire." Presumably we wait for the work of 1776 and 1777 which led Lavoisier to see not merely the gas but what the gas was. Yet even this award could be questioned, for in 1777 and to the end of his life Lavoisier insisted that oxygen was an atomic "principle of acidity" and that oxygen gas was formed only when that "principle" united with caloric, the matter of heat. Shall we therefore say that oxygen had not yet been discovered in 1777? Some may be tempted to do so. But the principle of acidity was not banished from chemistry until 1810, and caloric lingered until the 1860's. Oxygen had become a standard chemical substance before either of those dates.

Clearly we need a new vocabulary and concepts for analyzing events like the discovery of oxygen. Though undoubtedly correct, the sentence, "Oxygen was discovered," misleads by suggesting that discovering something is a single simple act assimilable to our usual (and also questionable) concept of seeing. That is why we so readily assume that discovering, like seeing or touching, should be unequivocally attributable to an individual and to a moment in time. But the latter attribution is always impossible, and the former often is as well. Ignoring Scheele, we can safely say that oxygen had not been discovered before 1774, and we would probably also say that it had been discovered by 1777, or shortly thereafter. But within those limits or others like them, any attempt to date the discovery must inevitably be arbitrary because discovering a new sort of phenomenon is necessarily a complex event, one which involves recognizing both *that* something is and *what* it is. Note, for example, that if oxygen were de-phlogisticated air for us, we should insist without hesitation that Priestley discovered it, though we would still not know quite when. But if both observation and conceptualization, fact and assimilation to theory, are inseparably linked in discovery, then discovery is a process and must take time (pp. 52–55).

48. We have said that how we see ourselves and how the world sees us is largely determined by our own conceptualizations of ourselves, and by others' conceptualizations of us. When psychologists decided to call the people they worked with and for *clients* rather than *patients*, a major change was made in the relationship between the two people involved. Think about this suggestion for a few moments and then read the short interview with MIT neuropsychologist Stephan Chorover that follows. Then write an essay in which you talk about the part conceptions (certain ways of seeing the self, the doctor, the mind) played in the treatment and mistreatment of Leonard Kille. In your essay, you should talk about the doctors' concepts, Kille's concepts, and Chorover's concepts as well.

49. Write a short essay if you can think of another instance—one that you have encountered in your own life or in your reading—in which an existing conceptualization of a person, place, or thing has brought about what you think is a faulty or dangerous attitude or behavior toward that person, place, or thing.

"The Battle of the Brain."
From the *Real Paper*

ROCHELLE SEMMEL ALBIN TALKS WITH MIT
NEUROPSYCHOLOGIST DR. STEPHAN
CHOROVER, WHO DEFENDS THE HUMAN
BRAIN AGAINST CONTROVERSIAL MEDICAL
TECHNOLOGY

MIT neuropsychologist Stephan Chorover is known for his outspoken crit-
icism of the hard tools of American psychiatry and psychology—behavior
modification, electroshock therapy, and psychosurgery—which he as-
sailed last year in his book From Genesis to Genocide, *in which he links*
use of these "psychotechnologies" to the users' desire to maintain their
own power in modern society.

Chorover's views have become more crucial because of two recent
psychosurgery malpractice cases, the only two to go to trial in this country.
While both cases sprang from operations performed at Massachusetts
General Hospital, psychosurgery is carried out between two and four
hundred times a year around the country. And it is estimated that at least
100,000 Americans a year receive electroshock therapy, a treatment also
received by one of the plaintiffs.

Last year, Leonard Kille lost his suit against neurosurgeon Vernon
Mark and psychiatrist Frank Ervin, who, he argued, misdiagnosed his
personality problems as epilepsy. The psychosurgery, performed in 1967,
rendered Kille, his attorneys insisted, "utterly dependent and unable to
function in a day-to-day world," and "almost a vegetable."

Three years ago, Martha Kapp initiated suit against several physi-
cians, including neurosurgeon Thomas Ballantine, who performed psy-
chosurgery on her when she was twenty years old. Kapp's attorneys have
argued that Ballantine incorrectly diagnosed her condition, that he had
not seriously explored less extreme remedies, and that Kapp is perma-
nently disabled as a result of the surgery. The case has successfully
crossed several legal hurdles, but a trial date has not yet been set. One
of Chorover's critical articles on psychosurgery has served as evidence.

How did you become interested in psychosurgery?
From two directions. First of all, I am a neuropsychologist interested
in the relationship between the brain and human behavior. Justification for
psychosurgery reminds me of the Vietnam soldier's explanation that it was
"necessary to destroy the village in order to save it." Nothing I know about
the brain suggests that its function can be improved by destroying it. I am
also concerned about the use of psychology as a social weapon. The way
in which psychology defines human beings as normal reflects the interests
and objectives of society's more powerful groups. American psychology
has been the psychology of America's upper and middle classes.

But most of the psychotechnology you discuss in your book—psycho-
surgery, drugs, electroshock treatment—is carried out by physicians and
psychiatrists, not by psychologists.

That's true. The modes of intervention available to the physician are more severe. But psychology and psychiatry often have a common goal: to produce patterns of thought, feeling, and action that conform to a particular definition of reality. My book is an attempt to put in one place concepts and technologies that are usually talked about separately so that we can see the underlying similarities.

How have psychologists and psychiatrists taken on the role of defining reality?
This is not a war between good and evil, between thinking and nonthinking people. It is a matter of training and perspective. Physicians and psychologists are trained to see things in terms of pathology. They are trained to localize problems in individuals. The medical model is the chief legitimizer of this. That model dictates that deviance, disturbance, and unrest are the result of sickness in individuals rather than in the social system. The way a problem is defined determines what does and does not get done about it. To localize a problem in a person, and then even further in the brain of a person, is a scientific mistake. Behavior does not arise exclusively or mainly in a single individual, but rather in the larger social system of which he is a part.

You include behavior modification in the group of psychotechnologies that you attack. Yet, psychologists who use this approach claim to eschew the medical model in favor of manipulating the environment.
These psychologists contradict themselves. When they intervene to treat someone, they treat that person in isolation from his social system. No matter how much they may emphasize the environment, it is ultimately the individual they try to change.

Let's talk about the 1978 Leonard Kille psychosurgery malpractice case. It seems that the jury, which exonerated Kille's physicians, was oblivious to the role of psychosurgery as a tool of those in power. Would this have happened had they understood the context of Kille's treatment?
The Kille case was the first trial I attended extensively. One reason that I think it came out as it did has a lot to do with legal procedure in medical malpractice trials. In science, the effort to discover what is going on proceeds openly so as to get as much information as possible. In a court of law, the jury is made up of people preselected for innocence and ignorance on the matter to be investigated. The jury's view of things depends on what the judge and attorneys allow it to know. Because of this, certain information about the context and conditions surrounding the Kille case were not made available to the jury.

Such as?
The project under which Leonard Kille was treated placed him simultaneously in the position of patient and experimental subject. This makes it difficult for physicians concerned about their research to be equally concerned about their patient. Also, Drs. Vernon Mark and Frank Ervin were explicitly seeking to prove a hypothesis about the relation between brain

and violence that they wanted to apply to social violence on a large scale. They labeled Kille as violent when the only person to whom he had acted aggressively was his wife—just once—and they labeled him as a paranoid when he thought his wife was having an affair with a boarder whom, in fact, she later married.

What about Kille? How could he have permitted the surgery?

Very early in his own life, Kille accepted the definition of himself as a sick person. Later, when he faced very severe marital strife, it was defined as the result of a defect in him, a definition that fit with the way he had always seen himself. Also, he was an engineer, which trained him to expect technical solutions.

Many people see themselves this way. You'd expect more to end up with psychosurgery?

There have always been the two nonoverlapping mental health systems in Massachusetts: one based on biological theory and the other on psychodynamic theory. When a person in trouble seeks psychiatric help, he does not know which system he is getting into.

So, people who end up with psychosurgery have gotten referred to the biological track and stay there?

Yes. Kille was never part of the psychodynamic system. Nor was Martha Kapp, the plaintiff in a more recent psychosurgery malpractice case. The two tracks attribute the cause of people's problems to different factors: the biological track to the brain, the psychodynamic tract to the way a person handles feelings and thoughts. But the two tracks do agree that the problem lies in the individual rather than in the social system.

What would be an alternative treatment?

A systems approach such as family therapy. This view refuses to accept definitions of the problem which both psychodynamic and biological theories buy, definitions that blame the individual.

And how did a neuropsychologist become interested in family therapy?

I owe that to my wife, who is a social worker and family therapist. She is responsible for many of my ideas.

In your book, you attack sociobiology as "wholly useless in explaining human existence in modern society" and as merely a new version of "blaming the victim." How is sociobiology related to the use of psycho-technology?

Sociobiology offers justification for the use of psycho-technology. The idea that the way things are in human society merely reflects the working out of an inherent biological form of our species tells us that the powerful are powerful and the weak are weak because that is the way things are supposed to be. Sociobiology justifies helping them stay that way.

Why is it so popular now?

During times of crisis, there is a certain social comfort derived from an authoritatively delivered message that the way things are is the way they are supposed to be. Appeals such as this become more socially acceptable and necessary during these times, especially among those who enjoy power and privilege in society. Sociobiology offers social justifications with the most powerful conceptual device we have: scientific argument.

Why isn't your analysis obvious to other scientists?

Science is neither objective nor value-free, but scientists don't examine or understand the impact of their values and attitudes on their scientific work.

But even sociobiologists such as Edward Wilson agree that science is not value-free.

Yes, they do give lip service to this. But if sociobiologists really understood that the science they do is intimately tied up with their values and their politics, they would not accuse critics of sociobiology of inserting politics into the debate. They would know that politics had always been part of science.

But isn't there another reason behind the popularity of sociobiology— namely, scientists' traditional desire for the simplest explanations?

Yes. But the point-of-view that reduces violence, for example, to something as simple as a brain problem is an inadequate explanation of most things. Even in particle physics, scientists have not been able to locate a fundamental particle that is not a composite of other, even smaller particles. A fundamental building block does not exist. Scientific reductionism does not work.

What are you up to in your own work these days?

I'm working on a theory of the relationship between human biology, psychology, and social life. I am looking at how the different parts of the brain relate to thinking, feeling, and acting, and to the meaning and values people give to life.

That doesn't sound too ambitious. In any case, how likely is your work to help solve some of the dilemmas that confront us?

Not very likely. The probability is high that these small efforts will be overtaken by global events. We are on slippery slopes right now.

50. Obviously, you have a vested interest—as a writer and as a person—in seeing to it that concepts are defined the way you think they ought to be, and a vested interest—as a writer and as a person—in being able to detect how other people are defining concepts, if only so you can decide whether you *like* those conceptualizations. Conceptualization is always a process of setting boundaries around words: saying "I want this word to be used to mean *this* much, and no more and no less." A conceptualization is always a part of a larger picture (and I mean the word quite literally here). It is always a part of a larger structure of argument or explanation. Below are several bits of other people's essays. In each, see if you can tell what *other* conceptions of his or her word the writer is responding to, and why. What has made it necessary for the writer to draw the boundaries he or she has around the word being explored in each case?

51. After you have read through these mini-definitions carefully, choose *one* of them and write a short essay in which you discuss in more detail why it is or is not a satisfying and useful way of looking at the concept.

1. *Creativity.* "The idealization of childbirth obscures the distinction between involuntary and voluntary achievement which we depend upon in describing any achievement as creative." Mary Ellmann, *Thinking about Women*, p. 63.

2. *Common Sense.* "Why level downward to our dullest perception always, and praise that as common sense? The commonest sense is the sense of men asleep, which they express by snoring." Henry David Thoreau, *Walden.*

3. *Normal.* "The word *normal*, in the biological sciences, means that a certain phenomenon is statistically common. That is all it should mean. If what happens to be most common, by benefit of a 51 percent majority is called normal, and by implication the solely desirable, then what is statistically uncommon will be called abnormal, and by implication suspicious, imperfect, even dangerous. If one standard of measurement after another, hundreds of them, of Mean Averages and majority ideals, were taken up, and in each case the minority and deviant massacred as being abnormal and thus interfering with a stable society, there would not be one of us left standing in a fortnight." Ruth Hershberger, *Adam's Rib*, p. 25.

4. *Progress.* "We in the West make a fetish of 'progress,' which is the ethical camouflage of the desire to be the cause of changes. If we are asked, for instance, whether machinery has really improved the world, the question strikes us as foolish: it has brought great changes and therefore great 'progress.' What we believe to be a love of progress is really, in nine cases out of ten, a love of power, an enjoyment of the feeling that by our fiat we can make things different." Bertrand Russell, "The Chinese Character."

5. *Pension.* "It is almost eight years since I retired from the waterfront, but in my dreams I still load and unload ships. I sometimes wake up in the morning aching all over from a night's hard work. One might maintain that a pension is pay for the work we keep on doing in our dreams after we retire." Eric Hoffer, "Works and Days," p. 73.

6. *Relativism.* "Relativism is the bad faith of the conqueror who has become secure enough to become a tourist." Stanley Diamond, *In Search of the Primitive*, p. 110.

7. *Charm.* "What is charm then? The free giving of a grace, the spending of something given by nature in her role of spendthrift. But there is something uncomfortable here, something intolerable, a grittiness, we are in the presence of an injustice. Because some creatures are given so much more than others, they must give it back? Charm is something extra, superfluous, unnecessary, essentially a power thrown away— given. When [my] grey cat rolls, on her back in a patch of warm sunlight, luxurious, voluptuous, delightful, that is charm, and it catches the throat. When grey cat rolls, every movement the same, but with her eyes

narrowed on black cat (of whom she is jealous), it is ugly, and even the movement itself has a hard abrupt quality to it. And black cat watching, or trying to copy something for which she has no natural gift, has an envious furtiveness, as if she were stealing something that does not belong to her. If nature squanders on a creature, as she has done on grey cat, arbitrarily, intelligence and beauty, then grey cat should, in return, squander them as lavishly." Doris Lessing, *Particularly Cats*, pp. 86–87.

8. *Higher education.*   "A system of higher education which results in mere literacy is a social crime, since it allows its recipients to think they understand the forces shaping world history when they are only in possession of a number of unrelated and isolated facts. If mass education at the university level is worth pursuing, its products must be able to read *and understand* such writers as Spengler, Ortega, and Toynbee. It is not enough for a minority to be acquainted with the nature and extent of the crisis confronting contemporary man. If the peasant and the Western-university-educated youth are equally ignorant of the awesome spectre of the possible decline and fall of mankind, then there is little hope for the future." Duncan Williams, *Trousered Apes*, pp. 153–54.

9. *Love.*   "Many Platonists believed that women were not capable of love at all, because they were men's inferiors physically, socially, intellectually. Love is not possible between inferior and superior, because the base cannot free their love from selfish interest, as the desire for either security or for social advantage, and, being lesser, they cannot comprehend the faculties in the superior which are worthy of love. . . . The proper object for love is one's equal, seeing as the essence of love is to be mutual, and the lesser cannot produce anything greater than itself. Seeing the image of himself, a man recognizes it and loves it, out of fitting and justifiable *amour propre*; such a love is based on understanding, trust, and commonality. It is the love that forms communities, from the smallest groups to the highest. It is the only foundation for viable social structures, because it is the manifestation of common good. . . . From the earliest moments of life, human love is a function of narcissism. The infant who perceives his own self and the external world as the same thing loves everything until he learns to fear harm. So if you pitch him into the sea he will swim, as he floated in his mother's womb before it grew too confining. The baby accepts reality, because he has no ego. Even when his ego is forming he must learn to understand himself in terms of his relationships to other people and other people in terms of himself. The more his self-esteem is eroded, the lower the opinion that he has of his fellows; the more inflated his self-esteem the more he expects of his friends. This interaction has always been understood, but not always given its proper importance. When Adam saw Eve in the Garden of Eden he loved her because she was of himself, bone of his bone, and more like him than any of the other animals created for his delectation. His movement of

desire towards her was an act of love for his own kind. This kind of diffuse narcissism has always been accepted as a basis for love, except in the male-female relationship where it has been assumed that man is inflamed by what is different in woman." Germaine Greer, *The Female Eunuch*, pp. 136–37.

10. *Doodle.* "The doodle is the brooding of the hand." Saul Steinberg, in *Time*, 16 October 1978.

52. You may have noticed that as you did the previous writing exercise, it was sometimes difficult to assess the value of the writer's way of conceiving of his or her subject because you could not figure out the context *of* the remarks, or the context *in* the remarks. That is, if you did not know for which audience he or she was writing, you could not always tell if the writer was doing a good job. If you could not tell what the rest of his or her essay looked like, you could not tell if the conceptual statements were appropriate or helpful. If you did not know what ideas of other people's the writer was responding to, you were not sure whether the conceptualizations were good ones.

Below you will find three excerpts of writing. Each one is about *autonomy*. The first is from Bruno Bettelheim's *Informed Heart*, which he wrote in response to the years he spent at Auschwitz and other concentration camps. He considers how the self is to survive in a dehumanizing society. The second excerpt is from Arthur Koestler's *Act of Creation*, subtitled *A Study of the Conscious and Unconscious in Science and Art*. The third excerpt is a chapter from Lewis Thomas's *Lives of a Cell*. In his book, Thomas muses on the place human beings play in the universe as a whole, and our relationship to that universe. Thomas does his thinking and writing from the vantage point of a biologist, and as he calls himself, "a biology watcher." Read through these three excerpts. Determine exactly how all three writers see the concept of *autonomy*. Then write a short essay in which you talk about *what you learn about the process* of concept definition from these three excerpts. Note that this time you are not paraphrasing what they say, but instead are watching the way the writers draw boundaries around the word *autonomy*, considering the contexts out of which they are writing, and the reasons why the word looks so different when it is used by each writer.

Bruno Bettelheim.
From *The Informed Heart*

Obviously modern Western man has not acted without reason in allowing certain areas of his life to be managed by society, nor has he carelessly deputized a selected few to make all-important decisions for him. Modern technology, mass production, and mass society have brought so many tangible benefits to man, that only in self defeat could he turn his back on them simply because they also involve dangers to personal autonomy. On the other hand, because he has gained so much by entrusting large areas of his life to experts, it has grown very seductive to let them take over more and more of what could remain areas of personal freedom.

It is not that modern man is so much quicker to surrender his freedom to society, nor that man was so much more autonomous in the good old days. It is rather that scientific and technological progress has relieved him of having to solve so many problems that he once had to solve by himself if he meant to survive, while the modern horizon presents so many more choices than it used to. So there is both: less need to develop autonomy because he can survive without it, and more need for it if he prefers not to have others making decisions for him. The fewer meaningful decisions he needs for survival, the less he may feel the need, or the tendency to develop his decision making abilities.

It is just as in psychoanalytic theory where the undeveloped ego is helplessly pushed around by the id and superego it ought to be able to control; so man, if he is not using and strengthening his decision making faculties, is apt to be pushed around both by his instinctual desires and by society; by instinctual desires because he cannot organize and control them (and then he feels cheated because society does not cater to his irrational wishes and rush to satisfy them—witness the typical 'beat" attitude to life); and by society which will run his life for him if he does not do it himself.

But if man stops developing his consciousness of freedom it tends to weaken for lack of exercise. And here I do not mean busy activity, but decisions about attitudes. The simplest example might be the decision: "I want to live in this manner," as opposed to "What's the use of trying to be different," though both may result in exactly the same behavior. Therefore too much management of human affairs without personal decisions, even for the best of purposes, is bad because human autonomy is too apt to wither away.

AUTONOMY

I hope by now it is clear that the concept of autonomy used here has little to do with what is sometimes called "rugged individualism," the cult of personality, or noisy self assertion. It has to do with man's inner ability to govern himself, and with a conscientious search for meaning despite the realization that, as far as we know, there is no purpose to one's life. It is a concept that does not imply a revolt against authority *qua* authority, but rather a quiet acting out of inner conviction, not out of convenience or resentment, or because of external persuasion or controls.

Probably the simplest example is obeying speed limits because one likes one's own body and therefore likes orderly traffic, but not because one is afraid of the traffic police. Autonomy does not imply that the individual has or should have free reign. All society depends for its existence and growth on a balance between individual self assertion and the general welfare. If man's instincts were unchecked, society could not exist. The continuous balancing and resolving of opposing tendencies within oneself, and between self and society—the ability to do this in keeping with personal values, an enlightened self interest, and the interests of the society one lives in—all these lead to an increasing consciousness of freedom and form the basis for man's deepening sense of identity, self respect and inner freedom, in short his autonomy.

One's sense of identity, the conviction of being a unique individual, with lasting and deeply meaningful relations to a few others; with a particular life history that one has shaped and been shaped by; a respect for one's work and a pleasure in one's competence at it; with memories peculiar to one's personal experience, preferred tasks, tastes and pleasures—all these are at the heart of man's autonomous existence. Instead of merely allowing him to conform to the reasonable demands of society without losing his identity, they make it a rewarding experience, quite often a creative one.

The man who can afford rich food and drink, who enjoys it and hence consumes it, may need a much better stomach than the fellow who has to get along on simpler fare. By the same token the citizen enjoying an economy of plenty and great freedom in arranging his life, needs a much better integrated personality in order to choose well and restrict himself wisely, than the citizen who needs no inner strength to restrain himself because there is very little around to enjoy or abstain from. True, in any society there will be some who simply do not enjoy rich food or drink and hence need no strong personality or even a strong stomach for their continued well being. But such men are no problem to society in this sense, nor does a society of plenty tempt them beyond what they can handle. Obviously, in this simpleminded example, a society of plenty is a problem only to the person who has neither a strong stomach nor the inner strength to control his desires, but who also loves rich food and too much drink.

Perhaps my everyday practice may further illustrate why today, because of scientific progress, man needs a much better integrated personality. At all times there are a minority of parents who reject one of their children, and quite a few more who sometimes feel ambivalent about one of them. So far so good. If neither situation is too drastic, most children manage to survive fairly well, though they experience a loss.

A better understanding of psychology has taught us that such parental attitudes are, or can be, quite damaging to the child. So the educated parent of today who has negative or ambivalent feelings about his child feels quite guilty and wants to do something about it. As likely as not, having to feel guilty about his attitude toward one of his children aggravates the negative feelings, and the child now suffers doubly. In addition to the parent's ambivalence he also suffers now from the parent's annoyance with him for causing pangs of guilt.

Thus having learned that it is bad for one's child to have negative feelings about him, the parent needs a much stronger personality and greater inner security to integrate his guilt. This was not true for yesterday's parent who did not know that his negative feelings could be damaging. He may have been convinced that he did enough by feeding and otherwise providing for the child; about the rest he felt easy in his mind. Now, in order to rid himself of guilt feelings, a parent may even convince himself that the child is defective; that his own negative reactions are based on defects that no one is to blame for. So I face many parents who at other times would have rejected their child and simply left him alone but who now, in order to shake off their sense of guilt, are insisting he is brain damaged, or otherwise defective.

The lesson to be learned from such experience is again not that we should condemn our new knowledge, but that each step toward greater consciousness—in this case recognition of the potentially damaging nature of some human emotions—requires that much stronger and better integrated a personality before it can represent true progress.

Both a rejecting parent and his child are better off if the parent does not feel guilty about his rejection, but the situation is still not desirable. Nevertheless, where before such a parent had no choice, now various possibilities are open to him, all of them for the better. He can integrate his guilt and not burden the child or anyone else with it. He can find out about the origins of his rejection and remove them, so that he will neither have to reject or feel guilty. Either solution would help everyone concerned. But when the parent simply responds to the more advanced knowledge (that rejection is damaging) and does not move on to achieve inner changes (integrating his guilt; removing the cause for rejection) then scientific advances lead to a deficit instead of the great benefits we can derive from them.

This one example must stand for many to indicate that social, scientific or technological progress, in order to better, not worsen man's lot, requires a more elaborate consciousness and an integration of personality that reaches into deeper levels than heretofore. Personal autonomy and a consciousness of freedom are only other aspects of these higher stages of personal integration.

It is this need for inner growth that leads some students of social and technological progress to take a dim view of the future. They despair of man's ability to achieve, with each step of external advance, a like progress in personal integration; thus their fear for man's future in our age of technology is really nothing but a consequence of their original low opinion of man.

We have, in fact, taken many such steps toward external progress, each one becoming viable only as we achieve the higher integration that our changed environment called for. But this is usually overlooked by those who hold a pessimistic outlook on the future. Their a priori low estimate of man and his potentials keeps them from realizing that from the time he became a social being, man has been meeting this problem and meeting it successfully.

In the preceding chapter I mentioned the attitude of the modern nomad toward dwellings and dwellers of the city. And it is true, the former nomad will not make a successful citizen unless he learns to control his tendency to take up and move away at whim or the slightest frustration; until he masters the wish to take bloody revenge at any offense. Nor will he achieve this control over himself until such time as close and permanent relations to a group larger than his family or tribe becomes meaningful to him, until the economic and cultural advantages of the city become very attractive. For the sake of these desired benefits he may be willing to restrain himself and to develop new social abilities; in short, to achieve a higher personal integration.

Most formerly nomadic tribes have been willing and able to do this, and to do it in a few generations. So there seems little doubt that today too, man can achieve the higher integration he needs if his new living conditions are to become freeing, not oppressive; provided, of course, that they offer him as many worthwhile advantages as city life offers the nomad. That technology offers great advantages we do not doubt. What may be in doubt is whether and how much these advantages add to the successful living together of man with his fellow men; because that alone will make further integration seem so worthwhile that he will readily achieve it.

This book was written mainly to suggest the direction I believe this higher integration will have to take, and to sensitize the reader to some aspects of modern mass society that hinder the process (pp. 71–76).

Arthur Koestler.
From *The Act of Creation*

It must be admitted . . . that the social climate of the nineteenth century did not favor the contemplative life, nor the arousal of genuine self-transcending emotions. The Victorian versions of religion, patriotism, and love were so thoroughly impregnated with prudery and hypocrisy that the experimental psychologist, devoted to measuring sensory thresholds and muscle twitches could hardly be expected to take such attitudes seriously, and to put them on a par with the sex and hunger drives. Around the turn of the century, the so-called James-Lange theory of emotions emphasized the importance of visceral processes, but it was nevertheless taken for granted that the "true" or "major" emotions were characterized by impulses to muscular action—mainly to hit, run, or rape. When Cannon showed that hunger, pain, rage, and fear were, so to speak, variations on a single theme, it was tacitly taken for granted that *all* emotions worthy of that name were of the active, adreno-toxic, hit-run-mate-devour kind. Laughter and tears, awe and wonder, religious and aesthetic feelings, the whole "violet" side of the rainbow of emotions was left to the poets to worry about; the so-called behavioural sciences had no room for them. Hence the paucity of the literature on weeping for instance—although it is certainly an observable behavioural phenomenon.

The emotions of the neglected half of the spectrum are as real as rage and fear; that much we know for certain from everyday experience. The theory which I have proposed assumes that they form a class, characterized by certain shared basic features. These are partly negative: the absence of adreno-sympathetic excitation alone puts them in a category apart from the emergency responses. On the positive side, emotional states as different as mourning and aesthetic enchantment share the logic of the moist eye: they are passive, cathartic, dominated by parasympathetic reactions. From the psychological point of view, the self-asserting emotions, derived from emergency reactions, involve a *narrowing* of consciousness; the participatory emotions an *expansion* of consciousness by identificatory processes of various kinds.

There exist, however, considerations of a more precise and at the same time, more general nature on which this theory of the emotions is based. These are discussed in Book Two, but I must briefly allude to them. In that wider context, the polarity between the self-asserting and participatory tendencies turns out to be merely a particular instance of a general phenomenon: namely, that evey member of a living organism or social body has the dual attributes of "wholeness" and "partness." It acts as an autonomous, self-governing whole on its own subordinate parts on lower levels of the organic or social hierarchy; but it is subservient to the co-ordinating centre on the next higher level. In other words it displays both self-assertive and participatory tendencies.

THE CONCEPT OF HIERARCHY

The word "hierarchy" is used here in a special sense. It does not mean simply "order of rank" (as in the "pecking hierarchy" of the farmyard); it means a special type of organization (such as a military hierarchy) in which the overall control is centralized at the apex of a kind of genealogical tree, which branches out downward. At the first branching-out, the commanders of the land-, sea-, and air-forces would correspond to the co-ordinating centres of, say, the digestive, respiratory, and reproductive organ-systems; each of these is subdivided into units or organs on lower levels of the hierarchy with their own co-ordinating centres, C.O.s and N.C.O.s; the organs in turn are subdivided into organ-parts; and so the branching-process goes on down to the cellular level and beyond.

But each sub-organization, regardless on what level, retains a certain amount of *autonomy* or self-government. Without this delegation of powers the organization could not function effectively: the supreme commander cannot deal with individual privates; he must transmit strategical orders through "regulation channels," which at each level are translated into tactical and sub-tactical moves. In the same way, information on what is happening in the various fields of operation (the sensory input) is selectively filtered on each level before being transmitted to the higher echelons. A living organism or social body is not an aggregation of elementary parts or elementary processes; it is an integrated hierarchy of semi-autonomous sub-wholes, consisting of sub-sub-wholes, and so on. Thus the functional units on every level of the hierarchy are double-faced as it were: they act as wholes when facing downwards, as parts when facing upwards.

On the upper limit of the organic hierarchy, we find the same double-aspect: the individual animal or man is a whole relative to the parts of his body, but a part relative to the social organization to which he belongs. All advanced forms of social organization are again hierarchic: the individual is a part of the family, which is part of the clan, which is part of the tribe, etc.; but instead of "part" we ought in each case to say "sub-whole' to convey the semi-autonomous character and self-assertive tendency of each functional unit.

In the living organism, too, each part must assert its individuality, for otherwise the organism would lose its articulation and efficiency—but at the same time the part must remain subordinate to the demands of the whole. Let me give a few examples. The heart as an organ enjoys, of course, an advanced form of self-government: it has its own "pacemakers" which regulate its rhythm; if one is knocked out a second automatically takes over. But the kidneys, intestines, and stomach also have their autonomous, self-regulating devices. Muscles, even single muscle cells, isolated from the body, will contract in response to appropriate stimulation. Any strip of tissue from an animal's heart will go on beating *in vitro* in its own, intrinsic rhythm. Each of these organs and organ-parts has a degree of self-sufficiency, a specific rhythm or pattern of activity, governed by a built-in, organic "code." Even a single cell has its "organelles" which independently look after its growth, motion, reproduction, communication, energy-supply, etc.; each according to its own sub-code of more or less fixed "rules of the game." On the other hand, of course, these autonomous action-patterns of the part are activated, inhibited or modified by controls on higher levels of the hierarchy. The pacemaker-system of the heart, for instance, is controlled by the autonomous nervous system and by hormones; these in turn depend on orders from centres in the brain. Generally speaking, each organ-matrix (e.g. a cell-organelle) has its intrinsic code which determines the fixed, invariant pattern of its functioning; but it is at the same time a member of a matrix on a higher level (e.g. the cell), which in turn is a member of an organ or tissue, and so forth. Thus the two complementary pairs: matrix and code, self-asserting and participatory tendencies, are both derived from the hierarchic structure of organic life.

Complex *skills*, too, have a hierarchic structure. However much you try to disguise your handwriting, the expert will find you out by some characteristic way of forming or connecting certain groups of letters—the pattern has become an automatized and autonomous functional sub-whole which asserts itself against attempts of conscious interference. People whose right hand has been injured and who learn to write with the left soon develop a signature which is indistinguishable from the previous right-handed one—"the signature is in the brain," as a neurologist has said. Again, touch-typing is a hierarchically ordered skill, where the "letter habits" (finding the right key without looking) enter as members into "word-habits" (automatized movement-sequences, each with a "feel" of its own, which are triggered off as wholes. . . . Ask a skilled typist to misspell the word "the" as "hte" each time it occurs—and watch how the code of the correct sequence asserts its autonomy. Functional habits must have some kind of structural representation in the neuron-matrices of the brain; and these patterned circuits must be hierarchically organized—as organ-systems are—to account for such complex and flexible skills as, for instance, transposing a tune from one key into another.

Under normal conditions, the various parts of an organism—nerves, viscera, limbs—perform their semi-autonomous functions as sub-wholes, while at the same time submitting to the regulative control of the higher centres. But under conditions of stress the part called on to cope with the disturbance may become over-excited and get "out of control." The same may happen if the organism's powers of control are impaired—by senescence, for instance, or by a physiological blockage. In both cases the self-assertive tendencies of the part, isolated and released from the restraining influence of the whole, will express themselves in deleterious ways; these range from the remorseless proliferation of cancer cells to the obsessions and delusions, beyond rational control, in mental disorder. . . .

The single individual represents the top-level of the organismic hierarchy and at the same time the lowest unit of the social hierarchy. It is on this boundary line between physiological and social organization that the two antagonistic tendencies, which are at work on every level, even in a single cell, manifest themselves in the form of "emotive behaviour." Under normal conditions the self-asserting tendencies of the individual are dynamically balanced by his dependence on and participation in the life of the community to which he belongs. In the body social physiological controls are of course superseded by institutional controls, which restrain, stimulate, or modify the autonomous patterns of activity of its social sub-wholes on all levels, down to the individual. When tensions arise, or control is impaired, a social "organ" (the barons, or the military, or the miners) may get over-excited and out of control; the individual, for the same reasons, may give unrestrained expression to rage, panic, or lust, and cease to obey the rules of the game imposed by the social whole of which he is part.

The participatory tendencies are as firmly anchored in the organic hierarchy as are their opponents. From the genetic point of view, the duality is reflected in the complementary processes of differentiation of structure and integration of function. We may extend the scope of the inquiry even further downward, from animal to vegetable and mineral, and discover analogous pairs of self-asserting and participatory forces in inanimate nature. From the particles in an atom to the planets circling the sun, we find relatively stable dynamic systems, in which the disruptive, centrifugal forces are balanced by binding forces which hold the system together as a whole. The metaphors we commonly use reflect an intuitive awareness that the pairs of opposites on various levels form a continuous series: when in rage, "we fly off at a tangent" as if carried away by a centrifugal force; and contrariwise, we speak of social "cohesion," personal "affinities," and the "attraction" exerted by an idea. These are no more than analogies; the "attraction" between two people of opposite sex does not obey the inverse square law and is by no means proportionate to their mass; yet it remains nevertheless true that on every level of the evolutionary hierarchy stability is maintained by the equilibration of forces pulling in opposite directions: centrifugal and centripetal, the former asserting the part's independence, autonomy, individuality, the second keeping it in its place as a dependent part in the whole. Kepler kept affirming that his comparison between the moving force that emanates from the sun and the Holy Ghost was more than an analogy; the cohesion between the free-floating bodies in the solar system must have a divine cause. Newton himself toyed with similar ideas.

I must apologize for the seemingly sweeping generalizations in the preceding section; the reader will find them substantiated in some detail in the biological chapters of Book Two. For the time being, I only meant to give some indication of the broader theoretical considerations on which the proposed classification of emotions is based—namely, that "part-behaviour" and "whole-behaviour" are opposite tendencies in dynamic equilibrium on evey level of a living organism, and can be extrapolated by way of analogy, both upwards into the hierarchies of the body social, and downward into stable anorganic systems.

Such an approach does not imply any philosophical dualism; it is in fact no more dualistic than Newton's law of action and reaction, or the conventional method of "thinking opposites." The choice of "ultimate" and "irreducible" principles (such as Freud's Eros and Tanatos) is always largely a matter of taste; "partness" and "wholeness" recommend themselves as a serviceable pair of complementary concepts because they are derived from the ubiquitously hierarchic organization of all living matter. They also enable us to discuss the basic features of biological, social, and mental evolution in uniform terms as the emergence of more differentiated and specialized structures, balanced by more complex and delicate integrations of function.

Lastly, increased complexity means increased risks of breakdowns, which can only be repaired by processes of the regenerative, *reculer-pour-mieux-sauter* type that I have mentioned before and which will occupy us again. I shall try to show that seen in the light of the relation of part to whole, these processes assume a new significance as aids to the understanding of the creative mind (pp. 286–91).

Lewis Thomas.
"Autonomy." From *Lives of a Cell*

Working a typewriter by touch, like riding a bicycle or strolling on a path, is best done by not giving it a glancing thought. Once you do, your fingers fumble and hit the wrong keys. To do things involving practiced skills, you need to turn loose the systems of muscles and nerves responsible for each maneuver, place them on their own, and stay out of it. There is no real loss of authority in this, since you get to decide whether to do the thing or not, and you can intervene and embellish the technique any time you like; if you want to ride a bicycle backward, or walk with an eccentric loping gait giving a little skip every fourth step, whistling at the same time, you can do that. But if you concentrate your attention on the details, keeping in touch with each muscle, thrusting yourself into a free fall with each step and catching yourself at the last moment by sticking out the other foot in time to break the fall, you will end up immobilized, vibrating with fatigue.

It is a blessing to have options for choice and change in the learning of such unconsciously coordinated acts. If we were born with all these knacks inbuilt, automated like ants, we would surely miss the variety. It would be a less interesting world if we all walked and skipped alike, and never fell from bicycles. If we were all genetically programmed to play the piano deftly from birth, we might never learn to understand music.

The rules are different for the complicated, coordinated, fantastically skilled manipulations we perform with our insides. We do not have to learn anything. Our smooth-muscle cells are born with complete instructions, in need of no help from us, and they work away on their own schedules, modulating the lumen of blood vessels, moving things through intestines, opening and closing tubules according to the requirements of the entire system. Secretory cells elaborate their products in privacy; the heart contracts and relaxes; hormones are sent off to react silently with cell membranes, switching adenyl cyclase, prostaglandin, and other signals on and off; cells communicate with each other by simply touching; organelles send messages to other organelles; all this goes on continually, without ever a personal word from us. The arrangement is that of an ecosystem, with the operation of each part being governed by the state and function of all the other parts. When things are going well, as they generally are, it is an infallible mechanism.

But now the autonomy of this interior domain, long regarded as inviolate, is open to question. The experimental psychologists have recently found that visceral organs can be taught to do various things, as easily as a boy learns to ride a bicycle, by the instrumental techniques of operant conditioning. If a thing is done in the way the teacher wants, at a signal, and a suitable reward given immediately to reinforce the action, it becomes learned. Rats, rewarded by stimulation of their cerebral "pleasure centers," have been instructed to speed up or slow down their hearts at a signal, or to alter their blood pressures, or switch off certain waves in their electro-encephalograms and switch on others.

The same technology has been applied to human beings, with other kinds of rewards, and the results have been startling. It is claimed that you can teach your kidneys to change the rate of urine formation, raise or lower your blood pressure, change your heart rate, write different brain waves, at will.

There is already talk of a breakthrough in the prevention and treatment of human disease. According to proponents, when the technology is perfected and extended it will surely lead to new possibilities for therapy. If a rat can be trained to dilate the blood vessels of one of his ears more than those of the other, as has been reported, what rich experiences in self-control and self-operation may lie just ahead for man? There are already cryptic advertisements in the Personal columns of literary magazines, urging the purchase of electronic headsets for the training and regulation of one's own brain waves, according to one's taste.

You can have it.

Not to downgrade it. It is extremely important, I know, and one ought to feel elated by the prospect of taking personal charge, calling the shots, running one's cells around like toy trains. Now that we know that viscera can be taught, the thought comes naturally that we've been neglecting them all these years, and by judicious application of human intelligence, these primitive structures can be trained to whatever standards of behavior we wish to set for them.

My trouble, to be quite candid, is a lack of confidence in myself. If I were informed tomorrow that I was in direct communication with my liver, and could now take over, I would become deeply depressed. I'd sooner be told, forty thousand feet over Denver, that the 747 jet in which I had a coach seat was now mine to operate as I pleased; at least I would have the hope of bailing out, if I could find a parachute and discover quickly how to open a door. Nothing would save me and my liver, if I were in charge. For I am, to face the facts squarely, considerably less intelligent than my liver. I am, moreover, constitutionally unable to make hepatic decisions, and I prefer not be obliged to, ever. I would not be able to think of the first thing to do.

I have the same feeling about the rest of my working parts. They are all better off without my intervention, in whatever they do. It might be something of a temptation to take over my brain, on paper, but I cannot imagine doing so in real life. I would lose track, get things mixed up, turn on wrong cells at wrong times, drop things. I doubt if I would ever be able to think up my own thoughts. My cells were born, or differentiated anyway, knowing how to do this kind of thing together. If I moved in to organize them they would resent it, perhaps become frightened, perhaps swarm out into my ventricles like bees.

Although it is, as I say, a temptation. I have never really been satisfied with the operation of my brain, and it might be fun to try running it myself, just once. There are several things I would change, given the opportunity: certain memories that tend to slip away unrecorded, others I've had enough of and would prefer to delete, certain notions I'd just as soon didn't keep popping in, trains of thought that go round and round without getting anywhere, rather like this one. I've always suspected that some of the cells in there are fluffing off much of the time, and I'd like to see a little more attention and real work. Also, while I'm about it, I could do with a bit more respect.

On balance, however, I think it best to stay out of this business. Once you began, there would be no end to the responsibilities. I'd rather leave all my automatic functions with as much autonomy as they please, and hope for the best. Imagine having to worry about running leukocytes, keeping track, herding them here and there, listening for signals. After the first flush of pride in ownership, it would be exhausting and debilitating, and there would be no time for anything else.

What to do, then? It cannot simply be left there. If we have learned anything at all in this century, it is that all new technologies will be put to use, sooner or later, for better or worse, as it is in our nature to do. We cannot expect an exception for the instrumental conditioning of autonomic functions. We will be driven to make use of it, trying to communicate with our internal environment, to meddle, and it will consume so much of our energy that we will end up even more cut off from things outside, missing the main sources of the sensation of living.

I have a suggestion for a way out. Given the capacity to control autonomic functions, modulate brain waves, run cells, why shouldn't it be possible to employ exactly the same technology to go in precisely the opposite direction? Instead of getting in there and taking things over, couldn't we learn to disconnect altogether, uncouple, detach, and float free? You would only need to be careful, if you tried it, that you let go of the right end.

Of course, people have been trying to do this sort of thing for a long time, by other techniques and with varying degrees of luck. This is what Zen archery seems to be about, come to think of it. You learn, after long months of study under a master, to release the arrow without releasing it yourself. Your fingers must do the releasing, on their own, remotely, like the opening of a flower. When you have learned this, no matter where the arrow goes, you have it made. You can step outside for a look around (pp. 75–80).

53. In the exercise you just finished, you noticed how difficult it is to understand someone's writings and respond to them if you do not have some idea of the context of those writings: if you do not know, as some people are fond of saying, "where he's coming from." But *imagining* a context, trying to figure out where somebody or something "is coming from" is what the mind does as naturally and easily as you put one foot in front of the other when you walk. Thinking and writing well is only a matter of putting that natural inclination to use. For instance, below you will find a simple sketch. It is a variation of a sketch used by my colleague Ann E. Berthoff. Look at it and then imagine this structure *in as many different contexts as you can.* Aim for at least fifteen different contexts in which you might run across something that looks like it. What would it be if it were seen in the air? On the ground? Lying flat? Standing up? As part of a body? As part of something mechanical? As part of nature? Can you see that your mind naturally *wants* to classify and categorize? Can you see how much difference *context* makes in what something might be?

54. Try a different version of the same exercise. Imagine that you are standing on a subway platform, or waiting in line to buy a movie ticket. In front of you are a young man and young woman. They do not know each other. The young man obviously wants to get to know the young woman. He is thinking of a way to get her attention. Suddenly, he steps out in front of her and tosses his big furry glove at her feet. She is startled, sees the glove, picks it up, bewildered, turns, looks at him, hands it to him. He smiles impishly. Is he behaving with maturity? How can you answer that question? How does conceptual definition, analysis, and determination of context creep into your answer, and why?

55. So if you're down on your luck,
And you just don't give a damn,
Just find a girl
With Far-Away Eyes.

You might recognize the lyrics. They are from "Far-Away Eyes," by Mick Jagger and Keith Richards. Write a short essay in which you tell your readers exactly what you think is happening in that song. What *is* a girl with far-away eyes? What is the relationship between the-thing-in-the-world, and the word in the song? Does the concept bring the reality into being, or was the reality already there waiting for someone to come along and pin a name on it? Test your conception of a girl with far-away eyes against someone else's. Do you share the same conception?

56. What follows are two different people's conceptions of *culture*. Is there any reconciling the two? Why or why not? Create your own definition of culture, if you are so inclined. Knowing what you now know about how people define and use concepts, explain why these two conceptions are so different.

Duncan Williams.
From *Trousered Apes*

In 1869, Matthew Arnold defined culture as being a "pursuit of our total perfection by means of getting to know, on all the matters which concern us, the best which has been thought and said in the world." Even the most charitable critic would find it difficult to reconcile Anthony Burgess's *A Clockwork Orange* or a play by Harold Pinter, for example, with this definition and one may be pardoned for assuming that the *worst* that has been thought and said has supplanted the Arnoldian ideal and become the temporary cultural norm. Lest I be accused of indulging in unsupported generalizations perhaps I ought to provide specific examples even at the risk of appearing to prove what is only too evident. Three representative and therefore by no means extreme products of the contemporary theatre will perhaps suffice. In Osborne's *A Patriot for Me* two males embrace on the stage; in Picasso's *Le Désir Attrapé par la Queue* a woman, aptly named Tart, squats in a urinating position while a sound track obligingly makes appropriate noises; in Genet's *The Balcony* a man castrates himself. All three dramatists would doubtless claim that men *do* embrace, that women *do* urinate, that perhaps unbalanced men do occasionally castrate themselves. . . . Over the centuries, the cumulative wisdom of society has decreed that if males must embrace they do so in private; urination was also deemed to be a private affair; and presumably if a man must castrate himself then he should do so in the privacy of his own house. . . . In other words, the contemporary literary movement, while ostensibly bent on "liberation," is in effect an attack on one of Western man's last and most cherished liberties—the liberty of privacy (pp. 153–54).

H. L. Mencken.
"The Sahara of the Bozart"

The New England shopkeepers and theologians never really developed a civilization; all they ever developed was a government. They were, at their best, tawdry and tacky fellows, oafish in manner and devoid of imagination. . . . But in the South there were men of delicate fancy, urbane instinct and aristocratic manner—in brief, superior men—in brief, gentry. To politics, their chief diversion, they brought active and original minds. It was there that nearly all the political theories we still cherish and suffer under came to birth. It was there that the crude dogmatism of New England was refined and humanized. It was there, above all, that some attention was given to the art of living—that life beyond and above the state of a mere infliction and became an exhilarating experience. A certain noble spaciousness was in the ancient Southern scheme of things. The Ur-Confederate had leisure. He liked to toy with ideas. He was hospitable and tolerant. He had the vague thing we call culture (p. 185).

Forming Your Own Concepts

So far we have spent a good bit of time reading, thinking, and writing about how other people have defined concepts. But of course you will be and *must* be involved in the defining of concepts yourself—if you want to be a good writer, a happier person, an influential person, a person who changes minds, including your own. In this chapter, then, *you* will become the definer; you will say how words shall and shall not be used. This is not so hard to do, and there are questions you can ask yourself to get started and to help yourself sharpen the concepts you define.

First, it helps to realize that there are more concepts around that could benefit from redefining than any of us may realize. It is not just words like that old chestnut people like to drag out— *freedom*—that need redefinition. Others we have always thought were perfectly clear and unexceptionable can give us trouble too. If *maturity*, for instance, is defined as always being stable, never making an unexpected move, always being predictable, then how many of us are "mature"? If maturity includes behavior that is playful and unpredictable (like throwing gloves in front of women on subway platforms), then lots of people who are excluded under the narrower definition can suddenly be proclaimed to be mature after all. In *The Logic and Rhetoric of Exposition*, a very good writer's book, Harold Martin, Richard Ohmann, and James Wheatley point out that even a verb like "to own" sometimes needs to be reconceptualized. Architect Richard Neutra, they say, claimed that it is absurd to "speak of a man as owning a house that was built, not for his individual needs, but to the specifications of a mass-produceo stereotype, a house with no privacy in a row of identical houses, a house with a thirty-five year mortgage." "Ownership," he says, "should imply more psychological control and more personal involvement than that" (pp. 15–16).

Some words that can successfully be defined or redefined with benefits to the definer and the world at large are those on the list we put together in the previous chapter: love, normal, creativity, progress. But there are lots of others: obscene, old age, selfishness, necessity, sin or evil, virtue, grace, un-American, masculinity and femininity, education, nobility, insanity, efficiency, conservative, art, power, genius, experience, success, poverty, style. All of these seem either impossibly difficult to define, or so simple and "obvious" that they do not need definition. Everyone knows what "conservative" means, doesn't he? But what about a "conservative" diagnosis and treatment in medicine? What would that be? That question sounds easy to answer too, but is it? A young man has a mysterious lump on his neck. The doctor removes it, and the pathologist does tests on it. The cells in the lump are not easy to define. They are not "normal," yet they are not so "abnormal" as to be called "cancerous." But they are not definitely *not* cancerous either. Medicine today dictates a "conservative" response to most medical situations. In this case, what would be the conservative medical response: Should the doctors start surgery and chemotherapy and radiation treatments "just to be safe," so that the cancer, if there *is* one, does not spread? Or should the doctors with a different conception of conservative response just hold back and wait to see what develops? Life and death often do hinge on exactly such conceptual—and definitional—decisions.

In the exercises at the end of this chapter, you are invited to define some concepts in ways you think would be useful. Before you do that, however, it will help if you read the following list of questions and procedures. They are intended to help you sharpen the way you think about any concept and to construct your own definitions. Whenever you have isolated a concept you think ought to be sharpened or defined differently, ask yourself these questions about it:

    1. Should I perhaps think in *plurals*; that is, perhaps I should not ask what is grace, heroism, progress, or success, but what kinds are there. If you define courage, selfishness,

normality, creativity, or anything else, how you do so depends upon your context. Different kinds are appropriate to different contexts. Different occasions demand different ways of seeing. Determine, then, whether you want to talk about *physical* (courage, selfishness, normality, and so on), or *moral* (courage, selfishness, normality, and so on), or *mental*, or *psychological.*

2. Not only might you divide the concept this way, but you might decide which of its ingredients are appropriate and relevant *in all contexts.* If, that is, there might be any common features shared by the word in its uses in all its possible contexts.

3. Are different concepts appropriate in different realms: in public versus private realms; in business versus domestic realms; in business versus religious realms; in any *other* realms of which you might think.

4. What orders are there? That is, do you see a *hierarchy* of sorts at work in your concept? Is there, for instance, heroism appropriate in a child, and is that different from that appropriate in an adult, and is that different from that appropriate in and among world leaders or soldiers? Or doctors, teachers, or priests?

5. In what different contexts might this word be used? Look again at the excerpts on *autonomy.* Think about the contexts in which your word might be used. Decide which context you want and need to talk about.

6. Under what conditions would the having of this characteristic you are categorizing be regarded as good or bad, desirable or undesirable? Selfishness may be good and necessary for some people in some contexts, and bad and unnecessary for some people in some other contexts. Discriminate.

7. What "ingredients" go into this concept? Bravery, for instance, would be made up of a number of different but related habits. Concoct a recipe for your concept. What would one have to have handy to create: success, maturity, normality, grace, wit, intelligence, autonomy, or whatever else you want to talk about?

8. In some cases, it will be appropriate to talk about the source of this concept: concepts like *iron curtain, penis envy, Beat Generation, the Me Generation, id, ego* or *superego, cold war, pacification program,* or *nattering nabobs of negativity* (the last is Spiro Agnew's speechwriter talking) all demand some historical account. Was the word originally created by a specific person? (Freud? Marx?) If not, did it come from a particular field? (Politics? Religion? Psychology?) For what purpose was the concept originally devised?

9. Do you know, or can you find out, or can you guess or imagine, why this concept first was generated? Was there a need for it before there was a word for it? There is a genuine sense in which a phenomenon does not exist until we have created a name for it, and in creating the name, we create the reality. The "iron curtain" became a reality when the phrase was coined. You read part of Margaret Mead's *Coming of Age in Samoa,* so you already can see that in some parts of the world there simply *is* no concept "adolescence." There are simply children (determined by their size, whatever their age) and adults (also determined by their size, whatever their age). There can be in that society, then, no notion of "adolescent rebellion" or "growing pains."

10. How does this concept function? That is, how does it tend to be used by people: *un-American* was a concept that served to make people very cautious of criticizing the government in any way; *normal* is a concept that, as Ruth Hershberger suggests, can make us fear to do or be anything out of the ordinary. It is a pressuring or censuring word. For some people, some concepts create a reality that others do not think exists: *God, the ether, transits* (in astrology) are such concepts. Think of some concepts, used historically or in the present, that you think we might be better off without.

11. What is the history of the concept? How was it defined in the past? Concepts like *grace* or *progress* or *natural* or *fond* or *nice* are all sharpened in our minds once we learn how the word has come to mean what we think it means

today. Look in the *Oxford English Dictionary* to see how certain words have evolved. Not only is doing this useful, it is also fun.

12. Ask yourself if the concept is always regarded in the same way by different classes or groups of people. Is it valued by some, but not by others? By people of one age, but not of another? By young people, but not by old people? By men, but not by women?

13. Sometimes, when a concept is difficult to define (that is, when it is difficult for you to decide how large you want to draw the boundary around your concept), it helps to determine what related concepts you would like to see it include and then list those. It also helps to think of what you would like to be sure is *excluded* from your concept. For instance, you might say, "I don't know for sure yet what X is, but whatever it is, I'm sure it should *not* include Y." In his book *Thinking with Concepts*, John Wilson suggests this approach. "We might wish," he says, "to tie down the word *democracy* in such a way that it excluded Soviet Russia (assuming Soviet Russia to be 'totalitarian' and restrictive in this sense), but included Britain" (p. 37).

14. There will be times when the concept seems clearly enough defined, but your job will be to add something to that category that had never been added before. To call bed-wetting a call for attention would be such a reclassification, or addition to an old concept.

15. Sometimes the good thinker serves a public function by gathering together lots of what had been thought of as micellaneous details, putting them under one conceptual net, and providing a name for that phenomenon that was not even seen as a phenomenon before that thinker generated the name for it. In *The Logic and Rhetoric of Exposition*, Martin, Ohmann, and Wheatley say "No doubt there have always been people who wash their hands every ten minutes, or couldn't stop chewing their nails, or just had to touch every other lamppost, but the psychologist who gathered such quirks and oddities together under the

heading 'compulsive' behavior performed a service for his colleagues and users of the language generally by providing a shorthand term and a definition" (p. 16) for that behavior. You can do the same thing for *your* colleagues and users of the language generally.

16. Sometimes you will decide that the separate bits of behavior or bits of evidence that have been gathered by some other writer is an appropriate gathering, but that you do not like the *name* that has been placed on the category. For instance, Freud observed that young girls seemed to have a certain fascination with the penises of their brothers. From this observation he concluded that young girls felt a loss; felt that they ought to have one, or wished they had one. They felt "incomplete." He called this phenomenon *penis envy*. Perhaps you may feel it is true that girls have a fascination with this bit of anatomy, and yet you might want to put a different name—and thereby a different conceptualization—on the phenomenon. You might call it curiosity. Or desire. Or even *power envy* rather than *penis envy*. What other phenomenon do you think has been misnamed? Are busing foes racists? Fearful parents? Citizens tired of being pushed around? When you put off a paper until the last minute, is that laziness? Or is it subconscious gestation, as one of my teachers called it. Or is it both? And if both, *in what proportions*, do you think? When the teacher tells a class of teen-agers that they will all be forced to sit with a strange partner so they will form new friendships, and the teen-ager responds, "You can't *force* people to get to know one another," is he or she being insubordinate and snotty, or being intelligent about, and sensitive to, the realities of human interaction? When there is debate about most anything, can you see how much that debate is really argument about *how* something ought to be seen? And can you see that *that* is a conceptual issue? A contextual issue?

17. A concept can be relative not only to context, but to other things as well: "Is it cold outside?" demands some attention to the concept of coldness, but the question, simple

In class

as it is, can only be answered once you consider a whole series of other related questions: Relative to last month? Relative to the temperature in Antarctica? Relative to the wearing of shirtsleeves rather than an overcoat? Relative to what I feel when I am running, or relative to what I feel standing and waiting for a ride on the corner? Relative to what my eighty-nine-year-old grandfather feels, or my six-year-old brother? This seems such an obvious point, but such questions as "Is this movie obscene?" seem to demand exactly this kind of attention to the relativity of a concept: relativity of time (historical), person (age), place (small town or city). Is the concept of *nuclear family* one that may have outlived its usefulness—especially because by some accounts as many as 83.7 percent of all American families no longer fit that pattern? Might you not want to devise new conceptual names that reflect more accurately the real living circumstances of Americans?

18. Sometimes it helps, with some concepts especially, to provide yourself and your reader with *images* for your concept. Way back in the first chapter, for instance, I asked whether *the self* might not be thought of best as a peach (with a softer, fleshier outside, but a hard core or pit at the center), or as an onion (with many layers of skin that once peeled away reveal nothing at all except that the self was itself composed of nothing but those layers). There have been centuries of debate about what education— true education—really is. Some writers picture the student as a kind of sponge, soaking up what the teacher provides. For some, education only takes place when the student gradually "opens up" or "blossoms" under the teacher's care, the teacher being a kind of gardener who nurtures these fledgling plants. For some, education is leading people from one point to a higher point. John Dewey once defined education as a process of unsettling minds. For him, then, it is not filling minds or leading minds that constitutes genuine education, but the dismantling of solidly held but faulty visions of things that students hold when they come to the teacher. Charles Dickens, a nineteenth-century British novelist, wrote many

novels in which he portrayed the education of his time and tried to show what was wrong with it. As you can see from the following passage, he viewed bad education as a kind of premature "forcing" of the kind that greenhouse gardeners do. Like the nurseryman's flowers, the student who is "forced" to learn never turns out quite right.

"Whenever a young gentleman was taken in hand by Doctor Blimber, he might consider himself sure of a pretty tight squeeze. The Doctor only undertook the charge of ten young gentlemen, but he had, always ready, a supply of learning for a hundred, on the lowest estimate; and it was at once the business and delight of his life to gorge the unhappy ten with it.

"In fact, Doctor Blimber's establishment was a great hot-house, in which there was a forcing apparatus incessantly at work. All the boys blew before their time. Mental green-peas were produced at Christmas, and intellectual asparagus all the year round. Mathematical gooseberries (very sour ones too) were common at untimely seasons, and from mere sprouts of bushes, under Doctor Blimber's cultivation. Every description of Greek and Latin vegetable was got off the driest twigs of boys, under the frostiest of circumstances. Nature was of no consequence at all. No matter what a young gentleman was intended to bear, Doctor Blimber made him bear to pattern, somehow or other.

"This was all very pleasant and ingenious, but the system of forcing was attended with its usual disadvantages. There was not the right taste about the premature productions, and they didn't keep well. Moreover, one young gentleman, with a swollen nose and an excessively large head (the oldest of the ten who had "gone through" everything), suddenly left off blowing one day, and remained in the establishment a mere stalk. And people did say that the Doctor had rather overdone it with young Toots, and that when he began to have whiskers he left off having brains" (*Dombey and Son*, chapter 11).

Below is a series of exercises designed to get you to form your own concepts and to learn how you and all other writers can turn that process to your advantage. Do as many exercises as you have time for, or as intrigue you.

57. You have just read a bit of a comic description of how Dickens thinks *bad* education is carried on. Below you will find two more conceptions of education. From both excerpts, you will have to extrapolate what the writer thinks constitutes a good approach to education. Read these two excerpts. If you have the time or inclination, you might also read part of John Henry Newman's *Idea of a University*, particularly the section "Knowledge and Skill." (You can find this in most libraries.) After you have read and thought, construct your own essay in which *you* provide a conception of education that is as good and as useful as you can make it.

Jerome Bruner.
From *On Knowing*

Education must begin, as John Dewey concluded his first article of belief, "with a psychological insight into the child's capacities, interests, habits," but a point of departure is not an itinerary. It is just as mistaken to sacrifice the adult to the child as to sacrifice the child to the adult. It is sentimentalism to assume that the teaching of life can be fitted always to the child's interests just as it is empty formalism to force the child to parrot the formulas of adult society. Interests can be created and stimulated. In this sphere it is not far from the truth to say that supply creates demand, that the provocation of what is available creates response. One seeks to equip the child with deeper, more gripping and subtler ways of knowing the world and himself (pp. 117–18).

Jacques Barzun.
From *The House of Intellect*

Vagueness is bound to prevail when the aim of the school is no longer instruction in subjects, but education in attitudes to meet the needs of life. From the premise that life demands other qualities than learning, which is true and important, we have come to the conclusion that in a school scholastic ability and scholastic subjects are indecent and ought to be disguised: I am conscious that in using the word "pupil" here I sound archaic: the child is the real thing. While biology and algebra are made genteel, play-acting goes on with "living predicaments," "panoramas," "junior town meetings," and "research projects" [he is talking about what happens in elementary schools here] all of which can be used in many directions, like a transfer on a busline. . . . Meanwhile, the simple but difficult arts of paying attention, copying accurately, following an argument, detecting an ambiguity or a false inference, testing guesses by summoning up contrary instances, organizing one's time and one's thoughts for study—all these arts, which cannot be taught in the air but only through the difficulties of a defined subject, which cannot be taught in one course or one year, but must be acquired gradually, in dozens of connections—these arts of the mind are believed to be miraculously added unto the child whose creativity has been released by asking his parents to help him with "projects," parents giving haphazard answers to impossible questions [like "What do you think Benjamin Franklin thought when . . ."] and who has received praise for their joint effort in an atmosphere of contact and forebearance (pp. 114–15).

58. Choose a concept that you believe would benefit from your clarifying and defining it more sharply than it has been defined in the past. You might want to go back to words like *love, maturity, charm, normal, discovery, progress,* and all the rest of the words talked about in Chapter 8 and choose one of them to work with. Whichever word you choose, try to make clear why you have chosen it, and what benefits would accrue if people looked at the word the way you would like them to. Write an essay in which you persuasively argue for your conception.

59. Go back once again to the series of photographs in Chapter 4. Using one of the photographs as the basis for your writing, try to regard it as an instance of or evidence of a particular concept. To do this, you might regard the photograph as one of four things:

1. A series of relationships between the people in the photograph, or between the people and the background in which they are placed. Do they demonstrate love? hate? fear? depression? anger? confusion? joy? sociability? poverty?
2. A series of relationships between the natural or urban setting and the people in it. What kind of concept could be said to be being demonstrated?
3. Look at the photograph only as an aesthetic or artistic composition. How would you then conceptualize it? Stark? "A study in contrasts"? An attempt at a balanced composition? Realistic?
4. Consider the photograph as evidence of a particular political or philosophical stance on the part of the photographer. *Then* what concept does the photograph seem to suggest or represent?

60. In the following questions, identify which concepts are at issue in each case, and which concepts would therefore have to be clearly defined and agreed upon before any productive discussion of the question could take place. Decide which of the eighteen questions above on conceptual defining would be most helpful in arriving at such conceptual agreement.

1. Was Jimmy Carter a good president?
2. Are teenagers responsible members of society?
3. Is senility a mental illness?
4. Can plants feel?
5. Is the film *Behind the Green Door* obscene?
6. Is college necessary for success?
7. Are psychology and anthropology sciences?
8. Who discovered America?
9. Is marijuana addictive?
10. Has America improved since 1900?

61. Begin with the concept *confinement.* Write the word at the center of the top of a piece of paper. Draw a line all the way across the top of the paper. Now let the concept start to branch. Divide it into as many kinds, forms, and contexts as you can. See how many refinements you can make in the concept. Your diagram will look like this:

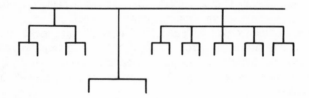

Fill in the blanks.

62. We have said that sometimes simply the existence of a concept word brings into being something that did not exist before. If people believe that certain pestilences and disasters are punishments from God, then the category "punishments-from-God" will fill up very easily, and evidence to "prove" the rightness of the category will be found everywhere. In *Plagues and Peoples,* William H. McNeill tells us that medieval Christians were convinced that Jews were causing the plague and somehow mysteriously making the Christians sick. However, the real explanation was that Jewish dietary and sanitary laws were such that the Jewish sections of cities were kept free of garbage, thus free of rats, thus free of the pests that live on rats and cause the plague by passing viruses from rats to people. But the faulty concept ("Jews cause plague") was readily demonstrated by the "facts." When Senator Joseph McCarthy looked for "subversives," the category's existence made it possible to fill it with a whole host of people. Think of, and discuss in writing, another such category that we have readily and obligingly filled once it existed: "Killer instinct"? "Maternal instinct"? What else?

63. The same "fact" can be seen as evidence of many different things: can be classified as a part of the evidence for the existence of many different concepts. There are 75,000 cars every day on the Los Angeles freeway. That fact can be classified as a bit of evidence to prove the existence of "progress," "pollution," "growth," "the lemming impulse in man," "the bonding impulse in man," and probably a hundred other things as well. Below is a set of facts. Construct as many alternative hypotheses as possible that would explain these facts:

> Jack had lots of friends. He played every high school sport and played them all well. On the soccer field one day, he took a fierce kick, fell, and broke his leg—badly. While he waited for the ambulance to take him to the hospital, he was surprised and hurt to discover how distant his teammates had suddenly become—they were his best friends, after all—and how awkward they were around him, and how eager they were to get away from him. In the hospital, he was visited by a few of them, who were awkward and eager to leave.

64. Some old people seem to carry around on their faces the evidence of their years of work and cares. But others seem almost untouched. Some seem to have gained worlds of experience; others seem to have gone through happenings, but not to have gained experience. (Elizabeth Bowen, the poet, once said "experience is the reaction to what happens, not the happening itself.") How do you explain the differences between the two kinds of elderly people?

As you do these last two writing exercises, you should understand that I am not trying to demonstrate to you that all explanation and conceptualization is "arbitrary," and that therefore all thinking and writing ought to be done cynically. What I am trying to suggest is that the desire to wait until you have absolute certainty or truth in your corner before you begin to write can lead only to paralysis or writer's block. There are different points at which to stand to perceive phenomena; there are different ways to look at situations; there are different "truths" for different people at different times. Writing—or what we have sometimes called "discourse"—is our means of exploring where we might want to stand, and why. It is our way of discovering why other people stand at the point that they do. It is, in short, our means of knowing what we might want to know.

10

Concept-sharpening

Sometimes, as we write an essay, it helps us to sharpen our sense of "how things are" if we simply compare the concept with which we are dealing with others that are closely related to it. In this chapter, then, we will play with closely related concepts: reading excerpts in which other people do the same kind of thing, and then doing that same thing ourselves. You might think of these exercises as a kind of practice in precision.

You should begin by reading carefully the excerpts of writing that immediately follow. In the first two, you will find Richard Hofstadter and Jacques Barzun disginguishing between *intellect* and *intelligence*. Then you will find Jerome Bruner distinguishing between *difficulties* and *puzzles*.

Richard Hofstadter.
From *Anti-Intellectualism in American Life*

Although the difference between the qualities of intelligence and intellect is more often assumed than defined, the context of popular usage makes it possible to extract the nub of the distinction, which seems to be almost universally understood. Intelligence is an excellence of mind that is employed within a fairly narrow, immediate, and predictable range; it is a manipulative, adjustive, unfailingly practical quality; one of the most eminent and endearing of the animal virtues. Intelligence works within the framework of limited but clearly stated goals, and may be quick to shear away questions of thought that do not seem to help in reaching them. Finally, it is of such universal use that it can daily be seen at work and admired alike by simple or complex minds.

Intellect, on the other hand, is the critical, creative and contemplative side of mind. Whereas intelligence seeks to grasp, manipulate, re-order, adjust, intellect examines, ponders, wonders, theorizes, criticizes, imagines. Intelligence will seize the immediate meaning in a situation and evaluate it. Intellect evaluates evaluations, and looks for the meanings of situations as a whole. Intelligence can be praised as a quality in animals; intellect, being a unique manifestation of human dignity, is both praised and assailed as a quality in men.

This distinction may seem excessively abstract, but it is frequently illustrated in American culture. In our education, for example, it has never been doubted that the selection and development of intelligence is a goal of central importance; but the extent to which education should foster intellect has been a matter of the most heated controversy (pp. 24–25).

Jacques Barzun.
From *The House of Intellect*

We ought to remember . . . when the United States is assailed, from within or without, as a nation lacking in Mind and hostile to it [that] we have in fact intelligence in plenty and we use it perhaps more widely than other nations, for we apply it with praiseworthy innocence to parts of life elsewhere ruled by custom or routine. We like ideas, new ideas especially, and we drive a brisk trade in them: the quickest way to get three Americans to travel a thousand miles is to propose an exchange of ideas. And there is reason to believe that this restless searching is becoming a habit the world over.

The modern educated democrat, then, is not anti-intellectual in the sense of shunning novelty or undervaluing intelligence. The truer and more serious charge is that he neglects or resists or shies away from one form of intelligence, which is Intellect. And this we see with peculiar vividness in the United States where, precisely, customs and routines do not mask the defect: it is for lack of Intellect that we have such a hard time judging persons and ideas; it is absence of Intellect that makes us so frightened of criticism and so inept at conversation; it is disregard of intellect that has brought our school system to its present ridiculous paralysis. In any large collective enterprise, such as the production of rockets and satellites, it is dearth of Intellect—not of intelligence—that aggravates the normal causes of friction and slows down accomplishment.

What then is this rare lubricant and propellant that we lack? Intellect is the capitalized and communal form of live intelligence; it is intelligence stored up and made into habits of discipline, signs and symbols of meaning, chains of reasoning and spurs to emotion—a shorthand and a wireless by which the mind can skip connectives, recognize ability, and communicate truth. Intellect is at once a body of common knowledge and the channels through which the right particle of it can be brought to bear quickly, without the effort of redemonstration, on the matter in hand.

Intellect is community property and can be handed down. We all know what we mean by an intellectual tradition, localized here or there; but we do not speak of a "tradition of intelligence," for intelligence sprouts where it will and is spent day by day like income for incessant needs. Intelligence is the native ability of the creature to achieve its ends by varying the use of its powers—living, as we say, by its wits. Accordingly, we can distinguish the intelligent from the stupid throughout the scale of sentient beings: an intelligent, but not intellectual, dog or child; an intellectual, but not intelligent, bluestocking or university professor. Intelligence is by definition the protean faculty. We find it in a political move or in a work of art, in the performance of a football team or in a piece of repartee, none of which are specifically intellectual. And though Intellect neither implies nor precludes intelligence, two of its uses are—to make up for the lack of intelligence and to amplify the force of it by giving it quick recognition and apt embodiment.

For intelligence wherever found is an individual and private possession; it dies with the owner unless he embodies it in more or less lasting form. Intellect on the contrary is a product of social effort and an acquirement. A man cannot help being intelligent, but he can easily help becoming intellectual. Intellect is an institution; it stands up as it were by itself, apart from the possessors of intelligence, even though they alone could rebuild it if it should be destroyed (pp. 4–5).

65. Now that you have read the two writers discriminating between *intellect* and *intelligence*, write a short essay in which you make clear that you understand the distinctions they are making, talk about the ways in which they do or do not see the two concepts as the same or different, and then venture your own definitions of the two words.

66. Reread Gore Vidal's excerpt on page 66. Then think again about Barzun's assertion that "it is absence of Intellect that makes us so frightened of criticism and so inept at conversation." In a short essay, compare Vidal's and Barzun's explanations for Americans' fear of criticism.

67. Read the following excerpt from Jerome Bruner's book *On Knowing*. Then write a summary in which you make it clear that you understand Bruner's distinctions between *difficulties*, *puzzles*, and *problems*. I have included a sizable portion of this chapter "On Learning Mathematics," because a part of it also discusses the importance of the conceptualization process in teaching and learning mathematics.

Jerome Bruner.
"On Learning Mathematics." From *On Knowing*

I take as my starting point a notion of the philosopher Weldon, one I have mentioned before. He said that one can discriminate among difficulties, puzzles, and problems. A difficulty is a trouble with minimum definition. It is a state in which we know that we want to get from here to there, both points defined rather rawly and without much of an idea of how to bridge the gap. A puzzle, on the other hand, is a game in which there is a set of givens and a set of procedural constraints, all precisely stated. A puzzle also requires that we get from here to there, and there is at least one admissible route by which we can do so, but the choice of route is governed by definite rules that must not be violated. A typical puzzle is that of the Three Cannibals and Three Missionaries, in which you must get three missionaries and three cannibals across a river in a boat that carries no more than two passengers. You can never have more cannibals than missionaries on one side at a time. Only one cannibal can row; all three missionaries can. Now Weldon proposes, you recall, that a problem is a difficulty upon which we attempt to impose a puzzle form. A young man, trying to win the favor of a young lady—a difficulty—decides to try out successively, with benefit of correction by experience, a strategy of flattery—an iterative procedure and a classic puzzle—and thus converts his difficulty into a problem. I rather expect that most young men do all this deciding at the unconscious level. The point of mentioning it is to emphasize that the conversion of difficulties into problems by the imposition of puzzle forms is often not always done with cool awareness, and that part of the task of the mathematician is to work toward an increase in such awareness.

The pure mathematician is above all a close student of puzzle forms—puzzles involving the ordering of sets of elements in a manner to fulfill specifications. The puzzles, once grasped, are obvious, so obvious that it is astounding that anybody has difficulty with mathematics at all, as Bertrand Russell once said in exasperation. The answer to our puzzle is simple. The rowing cannibal takes over another cannibal and returns. Then he takes over the other cannibal and returns. Then two missionaries go over, and one of them brings back a nonrowing cannibal. Then a missionary takes the rowing cannibal over and brings back a nonrowing cannibal. Then two missionaries go over and stay, while the rowing cannibal travels back and forth, bringing the remaining cannibals over one at a time. And there are never more cannibals than missionaries on either side of the river. If you say that my statement of the solution is clumsy and lacking in generality, even though it is correct, you are quite right. But now we are talking mathematics.

For the mathematician's job is not pure puzzle mongering. It is to find the deepest properties of puzzles so that he may recognize that a particular puzzle is an examplar—trivial, degenerate, or important, as the case may be—of a family of puzzles. He is also a student of the kinship that exists among families of puzzles. So, for example, he sets forth such structural ideas as the commutative, associative, and distributive laws to show the manner in which a whole set of seemingly diverse problems have a common puzzle form imposed on them.

There probably are two ways in which one goes about both learning mathematics and teaching it. One of them is through a technique that I like to call unmasking, although it is sometimes called empirical generalization. Roughly, it consists in discovering or unmasking certain abstract properties that characterize solutions of more or less practical problems. Thus, the solving of surveying and triangulation problems in the ancient Nile valley, undertaken to reconstruct land boundaries after flooding, provided an empirical starting point for the development of abstract geometry and trigonometry. And so, too, in teaching we use "practical problems" or "concrete embodiments" to equip the learner with the experiences upon which later abstractions can be based. Such devices as the Cuisenaire rods, various of the block sets now on the market, and the "mathematical laboratory" are aids in this approach.

A second approach to mathematics teaching, which by no means excludes the first, is to work directly on the nature of puzzles themselves—on mathematics per se. If the first approach is somewhat semantic, going from things to the symbols used for characterizing them, then the second is principally syntactic in emphasis. For it is concerned not with what mathematical ideas and relations "stand for" or are "derived from" but rather with the grammar of mathematics as such. Empirical reference is put in a secondary position and, if one were to think of an example in teaching, the use of numbers to different bases than the base 10 is a nice one.

Obviously, both the working research mathematician and the person learning mathematics for the first time use both approaches in some optimum sequence.

In what follows, we shall be concerned with four aspects of the teaching or learning of mathematics. The first has to do with the role of *discovery* and if it is important or not that the learner discover things for himself. The second aspect is *intuition*, the class of nonrigorous ways by which mathematicians speed toward solutions or cul-de-sacs. The third is mathematics as an analytic language, and I shall concentrate on the problem of the *translation* of intuitive ideas into mathematics. This assumes that anything that can be said in mathematical form can also be said in ordinary language, though it may take a tediously long time to say it and there will always be the danger of imprecision of expression. The fourth and final problem is the matter of *readiness:* when is a child "ready" for geometry or topology or a discussion of the truth tables?

Discovery. Much has already been said in the preceding essay about the act of discovery. The learning of mathematics provides a test case for some of the notions considered there. Take first the distinction between an active, manipulative approach to learning and the passive approach—the first likened to a speaker's decisions in using language and the second to a listener's. We do a disservice to our subject by calling the stimulation of active thinking, "the method of discovery." For there is certainly more than one method and each teacher has his own tricks for stimulating the quest in his pupils. Indeed, I am impressed by the fact that almost anything that gets away from the usual approach to natural numbers and their mechanical manipulation has the effect of freshening the student's taste for discovering things for himself. It would be better to consider how discovery usually proceeds when it does occur.

My own observation is that discovery in mathematics is a byproduct of making things simpler. Perhaps this is true of growth in pursuing other intellectual disciplines as well, but that is an issue that should not divert us, though a good case can be made for it, I think. In any case, where mathematics is concerned, the issue hinges on *how* simplification occurs. It results most often from a succession of constructing representations of things. We do something that is manipulative at the outset—literally, provide a definition of something in terms of action. A hole is to dig, a yard is to pace off or apply a ruler to, subtraction is to take away. That is the start. But it is a start that provides the material for a second step. For having acted—paced off, taken away, turned upside down, or whatnot—we are then able to turn around on our own actions and represent them. Having considered the ways of "saying-doing" how big or long things are by pacing, putting fingers next to each other, or using a ruler, we may simplify by characterizing all these activities as measuring. In the effort to relate these measuring actions one to the other, it is a very distracted child who will not rediscover the importance of the unit of measure as a means of getting all this welter of activity into a single, simpler framework. Then and only then can there be fruitful discussion of how we construct a unit of measure.

Learning to simplify is to climb on your own shoulders to be able to look down at what you have just done—and then to represent it to yourself. The constructing or doing that precedes the new representation can be well or poorly designed. The good teacher is one who can construct exercises (or, better, provide experiences) that cry for representation in the manner that the one shoe dropped on the floor above cries to have the second one drop. The poor teacher permits so much irrelevant action to occur in such self-obscuring sequences that only a genius could give a coherent account of what he had been up to. Indeed, we can revise a refrain of an earlier chapter to read, "How can I know what I think until I represent what I do?"

Manipulation and representation, then, in continuing cycles are necessary conditions for discovery. They are the antitheses of passive, listenerlike learning. Yet representation is not frenzied activity. Though active, it is still ratiocination, a going back over experience, a listening to oneself. Nor should we think that a teacher cannot play a role. Perhaps, in discussing the functions of teaching we should make a special place for the art of teaching people to listen to what they have been doing so that their actions can be converted into representations of what they have done and what has resulted. If Percy Bridgman's argument in his long effort to persuade scientists to define their concepts in terms of the operations employed in arriving at them could be turned around to read backward, it would fit our case well. Our task as teachers is to lead students to develop concepts in order to make sense of the operations they have performed. Bridgman's dictum should, I think, be converted into a two-way street.

Intuition. It is particularly when I see a child going through the mechanical process of manipulating numbers without any intuitive sense of what it is all about that I recall the lines of Lewis Carroll: "Reeling and Writhing, of course, to begin with . . . and then the different branches of Arithmetic—Ambition, Distraction, Uglification, and Derision." Or as Max Beberman has put it, much more gently, "Somewhat related to the notion of discovery in teaching is our insistence that the student become aware of a concept before a name has been assigned to the concept." I am quite aware that the issue of intuitive understanding is a very live one among teachers of mathematics, and even a casual reading of the twenty-fourth *Yearbook* of the National Council of Teachers of Mathematics makes it clear that they are also very mindful of the gap that exists between proclaiming the importance of such understanding and actually producing it in the classroom.

Intuition implies the act of grasping the meaning or significance or structure of a problem without explicit reliance on the analytic apparatus of one's craft. It is the intuitive mode that yields hypotheses quickly, that produces interesting combinations of ideas before their worth is known. It precedes proof; indeed, it is what the techniques of analysis and proof are designed to test and check. It is founded on a kind of combinatorial playfulness that is only possible when the consequences of error are not overpowering or sinful. Above all, it is a form of activity that depends upon confidence in the worthwhileness of the process of mathematical activity rather than upon the importance of right answers at all times.

I shall examine briefly what intuition might be from a psychological point of view and consider what we can do about stimulating it among our students. Perhaps the first thing that can be said about intuition when applied to mathematics is that it involves the embodiment or concretization of an idea, not yet stated, in the form of some sort of operation or example. I watched a ten-year-old playing with snail shells he had gathered, putting them into rectangular arrays. He discovered that there were certain quantities that could not be put into such a rectangular compass, that however arranged there was always one left out. This of course intrigued him. He also found that two such odd-man-out arrays put together produced an array that was rectangular, that 'the left-out ones could make a new corner." I am not sure it is fair to say that this child was learning much about prime numbers. But he most certainly was gaining the intuitive sense that would make it possible for him to later grasp what a prime number is and, indeed, what the structure of a multiplication table is.

I am inclined to think of mental development as involving the construction of a model of the world in the child's head, an internalized set of structures for representing the world around him. These structures are organized in terms of perfectly definite grammars or rules of their own, and in the course of development the structures change and the grammar that governs them also changes in certain systematic ways. The way in which we gain lead time for anticipating what will happen next and what to do about it is to spin our internal models just a bit faster than the world goes.

68. Finally, here is your chance to practice your own concept-sharpening. Below you will find ten sets or pairs of words that are closely related. In fact, if you go to the dictionary for meanings of these words, you will find that most are synonyms for one another: they "mean" the same thing. But if you think closely and carefully about how the words are used, I think you will find you can discover differences between one and the other. Choose *one* of these pairs or sets of words and discriminate between them, just as Hofstadter and Barzun distinguished between intellect and intelligence, and Bruner between puzzle and problem and difficulty.

1. confident/optimistic
2. vacillate/waver
3. unintentional/inadvertent

 4. correct/proper
 5. suggest/imply
 6. deviation/difference/variation
 7. accident/mistake
 8. intellect/intelligence
 9. mood/emotion/sentiment
10. difficulties/puzzles/problems

You will find a very good discussion of some of these pairs or sets of words in Martin, Ohmann, and Wheatley's *Logic and Rhetoric of Exposition*.

11

Discriminating

In the last few chapters we have seen how central a part
forming, defending, and sharpening our ways of seeing—conceptualizing—plays in writing essays and, of course, in thinking in
general. Sometimes whole books or essays are written to do nothing but create a new concept: one thinks of Charles A. Reich's
Greening of America, or Susan Sontag's *Illness as Metaphor*. But
as I have said before, "writing" is not so easy to separate into
separate "parts" or "kinds." When you define concepts, you are
also automatically involved in making distinctions, because when
you say that X *is* Y, you are also and necessarily saying X is *not*
B, C, or D. When you did Exercise 68 for example, distinguishing
between closely related concepts, you defined *suggest* by setting
it off from and distinguishing it from *imply*. You defined *correct*
by telling your readers how it was something different from *proper*.

In this chapter, then, we shall make distinctions and focus our
attention on exactly how that process works. What does it mean
to make distinctions? This is not so difficult to explain. It means
that we announce that something that appears to be *one* thing is
actually not mostly that, but something else. No one can give you
a list of procedures to follow to discover a distinction, but I can
suggest that what is necessary is that you look closely at something, take it apart and analyze its parts, and in that way you can
discover something about it that does not fit usual ways of thinking
about it. Sometimes, of course, to make distinctions is also the
same thing as to compare and contrast, if you say that what has
been regarded as an A is really a B, because it shares more of
the properties of B than it does of A. But sometimes making

distinctions simply involves pulling something out of a category in which it has been placed—the concept it has been thought to be a part of—and it is not necesary to put it anywhere else.

How will you recognize, as you read and write, that a distinction is being made? Simple. Most times, the language markers will tell you: "Not this, but that." "Not only, but also." "Not merely, but instead." As a reader, you may often find yourself delighted and relieved to discover that a person who has written something saying "Not this, but that" has clarified an issue in a way that you always vaguely realized was necessary; in a way that makes you see why you were always convinced something "wasn't quite right" about the way people were thinking of that issue. For instance, I like Margaret Mead's saying that adolescence is not caused by physiological changes, but by pressures put on a child that are beyond human capacity to handle. And I like William Henry's saying that Donald Duck is not just another cartoon character, but "an emotion and a circumstance, apoplexy looking for a place to happen." For that matter, I like my own distinction making throughout this book: writing well is not a matter of knowing rules and following outlines, but of understanding how thinking and writing work.

The following are some distinction-making sentences or paragraphs, about half from student essays and half from other sources. In each case, notice how the distinction sharpens the way we see, and takes a concept out of one category and puts it into another that the writer finds more accurate, helpful, or relevant.

1. Miss Whetall has also realized that correct testing of deafness in a child depends not only on the loudness of the sound, but on its relevance. A deaf child may not flicker an eyelid at a loud bang behind him, for it is only one more meaningless sound, yet it may turn round to investigate if a teaspoon is tinkled in a cup. (Irene Claremont deCastillejo, *Knowing Woman*, p. 23.)

2. The popularity of Cain, or the outlaw figure, stems not merely from a recognition and affirmation that killing one's brother or breaking the law would bring about social disorder, but from the fact that Cain poses an alternative to the traditional lifestyle of the hero. In spite of the seeming opposition of the two figures, there are many similarities.

Just as the hero, such as Odysseus, breaks away from society to begin a journey where he must rely upon himself to face the perils of the world, so too does Cain leave society to cope with the world alone. However Odysseus returns home to set his household aright, whereas Cain remains outside society and forms his own nomadic tribe. Although we can readily see and understand the appeal of Cain over a static figure like Abel, it is a pessimistic view of society, that we cannot live by our own convictions within society, but can only do so outside, on our own. The popularization of the outlaw or outcast is in keeping with the prevalent feeling in America that we cannot really do anything to change society. But the decision to conform, or to live outside the bounds of society, is sliding back into a much weaker alternative than the hero presents in returning home to correct what has gone awry.

3. For a story to hold the child's attention, it must entertain him and arouse his curiosity. But to enrich his life, it must stimulate his imagination; help him to develop his intellect and to clarify his emotions; be attuned to his anxieties and aspirations; give full recognition to his difficulties while at the same time suggesting solutions to the problems which perturb him. In short, it must at one and the same time relate to all aspects of his personality—and this without ever belittling, but on the contrary, giving full credence to the seriousness of the child's predicaments while simultaneously promoting confidence in himself and in his future. (Bruno Bettelheim, *The Uses of Enchantment,* p. 5.)

4. What has caused South Boston to oppose busing forcibly, primarily, is the chance to have a good fight: the idea that South Bostonians pride themselves on being Number One because they are Irish and from Southie gives them an attitude of superiority and they will go to any lengths to prove this point. The busing issue serves as a way for them to prove to everyone that the people of South Boston are rough, tough, and from a strong neighborhood-oriented group of people. Just as the politicians are making names for themselves in order to further their political careers

over the busing issue, so is Southie making a name for itself by proving to everyone that it is Number One.

5. People often make statements that are half-truths. Through their deceptive rhetoric, they try to hide their true feelings and possible shortcomings. When someone cries in rage, "He deceived me," he's really saying he was outsmarted. Instead of admitting I was embarrassed I might indignantly say, "I was appalled by her questions." If a person tersely states his interests are very concentrated, he might very well be trying to cover for the fact that he knows very little about anything outside his job. When a friend tells me he's getting tired of his girl, I hear "We've been fighting a lot lately." These people don't want to see the truth so they try to paint it to suit their cause. Like the student who tries to downplay his poor math grade by nonchalantly talking about how he hates the subject, or the novice who claims ballet bores him, they are all saying more than they realize.

69. For each of the excerpts above, explain in one sentence what concepts are distinguished from what other ones, if that is what you find being done in each case.

70. From anything you read in the next few days, collect one or two fine, sound distinctions. Copy them or cut them out, put them in your writer's log, and then try to create your own distinction in the same form as the one you found.

71. Write a short essay in which you make some distinction *you* think the world needs. The subject matter will be entirely your own, but you might want to write about an issue in the newspapers, or about something in your own experience. You may have noticed that in several of the distinction-making excerpts above, there are certain sentence forms that carry the distinction. Here are two:

"Just as the _____can be seen as evidence of _____, so also_____suggests _____."

"Although the _____of _____may suggest
_____, one might say that if we see that
_____in combination with _____and
_____, it may rather suggest _____."

See if using these sentence forms helps you formulate your distinction.

12

Comparing

When you make a distinction—that is, when you distinguish one thing from another—obviously you are also comparing one thing with another. In this chapter, we will direct our attention to the act of comparing and contrasting. Comparing and contrasting, as anyone who has ever been a student knows, is one of the most common of writing assignments: Compare pre- and post-war Japan; the U.S.S.R. and China; the ideas of Freud and Jung; middle- and working-class values; conservatives and neo-conservatives. The temptation of the beginning writer is to try to make the job more manageable by talking about one thing, and then about the other, without ever comparing them point by point. But the writer's first task when comparing is always to find some common ground that the two people/attitudes/countries/ideas share, and then to move from there to an even closer look, where one can begin to detect distinctions between the two: in the apparent similarities, we find some subtle differences. That is the essence of comparing and contrasting.

It might help us to begin with a simple comparison and contrast—a description of a meeting between poet W. H. Auden and composer Igor Stravinsky. It appeared in the *New York Review of Books*.

Robert Craft.
"The Poet and the Rake"

The dinner in the restaurant of the Hotel Raleigh that night (March 31, 1948) was memorable mainly as a study in contrasts: in culture, temperament, and mind—as well as appearance, for the shabby, dandruff-speckled, and slightly peculiar-smelling poet (attributes easily offset by his purity of spirit and intellectual punctiliousness) could not have been more unlike the neat, sartorially perfect, and faintly eau-de-cologned composer. At table, too, while the poet demolished his lamb chops, potatoes, and sprouts, as if eating were a chore to be accomplished as quickly as possible, and gulped Stravinsky's carefully chosen Château Margaux, oblivious to its qualities, the composer fussed over his food, and sniffed, sipped, and savored the wine.

These habits illustrate an essential difference between the two men. With Auden the senses seemed to be of negligible importance, whereas with Stravinsky the affective faculties were virtual instruments of thought. Powerful observer though Auden was, he displayed little interest in the visual sense, being purblind to painting for example, and even to "poetic" nature, for he was more concerned with the virtues of gardening than with the beauty of flowers. And whatever the acuteness of his aural sense, the idea of music appealed to him more than music itself, music with words—opera and Anglican hymns—more than Haydn quartets. That the music of Auden's poetry is not its strongest feature, therefore, should hardly surprise us. A conceptualizer in quest of intellectual order, he was a social, moral, and spiritual diagnostician above all.

To return to the contrasts between poet and composer, though both were religious men, equally keen on dogmas, ritual, faith in the redemptive death, the poet had evidently arrived at his beliefs through theology, the composer through "mystical experience" (however diligently he may have applied himself to the *Grammar of Assent*). Theology, at any rate, was a frequent topic in Auden's conversation with Stravinsky, and an exasperating one, except when the poet digressed on Biblical symbolisms (e.g., the moon as the Old Testament, the sun as the New), or on the argument of "*sui generis*" (that "man's image is God-like because the image of every man is unique"). But Auden preferred to theorize about such subjects as angels being "pure intellect," and to postulate that "If two rectangles, with common points between them, can be described on a face, that face is an angel's"—which sounds like a put-on but could have been scholastic exercitation (pp. 30–31).

You might want to notice the following things about how comparing and contrasting proceeds, for it, too, has a form that you can imitate when you construct your own comparison and contrast essays. First, the essay begins with a summary statement: the meeting was "a study in contrasts." From that statement, the writer moves to a specific point-for-point comparison: the dress of one; the dress of the other; the attitude toward the senses in the one; the attitude toward the senses in the other; the attitude toward religion in the one; the attitude toward religion in the other.

From this simple example, you can extrapolate principles to use when you are writing a more complex comparison and contrast. If you are asked, say, to compare the communist state in China with that in the U.S.S.R., you will first have to decide which areas to compare, because obviously you can not do a thorough comparing and contrasting, unless you have five years to write a book. You may want to address the issue of how different states have different attitudes about collective labor; how Chinese and Soviet attitudes toward their party leaders are similar and how they are different. But in any case, your primary decision will be the selection of the *grounds* for comparison. You must never simply begin haphazardly talking about one and the other. Perhaps more than any other kind of essay, this kind must be carefully planned and organized.

Below you will find three student essays that compare and contrast. The first compares the mental state of a person who is alone with the mental state of that same person in the company of friends. The second compares life in the Back Bay of Boston with life in Cambridgeport across the river. The third compares the experience of watching football on television with the experience of playing football. Notice in all three cases the ways in which the writer is careful to choose one aspect of each situation and compare that one aspect with the corresponding aspect in the other situation.

1. When I do anything alone, totally separated from, not so much people in general, but my friends, I seem to deeply

ponder and become depressed. My mind, enhanced by solitude and yearning for someone to talk to, seems to wander aimlessly; about other people around me, about myself, about objects around me. Some of these people are seemingly just like me, alone and sort of depressed looking. But I wonder if they're sitting there thinking the same things about me. Many times, this is really a good time for my mind, sitting alone and contemplating, not about anything in particular, but just thinking. The funny thing about this whole thinking ordeal is that one feels depressed when actually one is not. After a while when friends finally do appear and join you, the whole scene changes. So instead of the little world you were previously in, sharing yourself and your thoughts with yourself alone, you are now sharing them with others, which is the way it's supposed to be. You now become involved in a group and seem to forget about those other people and objects that were so prominent before. But if you happen to look around, you'll notice those same people still there, the same as before, alone and depressed; just waiting for their friends to come and rescue them from their own little world of solitude.

2. In the Back Bay, life is secretive: people are reluctant to acknowledge others on the street, and a constant suspicion lurks in their eyes. They timidly lead docile dogs along uneven sidewalks, and retreat to their households when darkness ensues. Although some suspicion exists in Cambridgeport, life is less inhibited there. Children curse as they play stickball in the streets, and the elderly infrequently take walks at night. Even the dogs are more bold. They man the corners, bark vociferously and defend their territory from invading mongrels.

Yes, life is different in the Back Bay—indeed, death seems to prevail. The Fens, the only vegetation for blocks and blocks, boasts bent trees with grey-green leaves, and a miasmic pond, reeking of sulfur. On a moonlit night, hideous muskrats can be seen skimming the sordid water, as addicts and alcoholics scurry through the park, seeking their pleasure for the evening.

Though Cambridgeport is not exactly dying, it suffers from despair. Poverty and ignorance prevail in the neighborhood: post-adolescent pool sharks relive high school days; teenage girls on welfare mother illegitimate children, and arguments ring from nearly every window. But death has not quite won. People still hope for winning combinations, and occasionally they laugh at their hopeless predicament. And in the back of a few run-down houses, a humble garden may be found.

Certainly both neighborhoods must have experienced a more prosperous era. The austere architecture of the Back Bay suggests it was once inhabited by white collar workers and pseudo-socialites who ventured through the Fens to Symphony Hall. Cambridgeport's worn benches and many archaic churches imply it was once a middle class mecca. Meek white families probably crowded the streets, and Sundays were sober days, not restless, hungover ones. However, only shadows of those periods exist now, and if I must live in shadows, I will live in shadows where there is at least an occasional smile, and where the elderly still walk at night.

3. When I watch a football game I'm restless. I can't sit and watch the game yet I can't leave the room. I'm uncertain of the results and I feel almost cowardly when I realize I'm worrying about losing a little money. But when I play I'm calm and confident. I know what I can do and I know I do it well. My every move is fluid as I comfortably cover my position; there is no place else in the world I would rather be at that moment.

Playing, the sweat feels good on my face; I flick out my tongue and savor its salty taste. I feel clean and purified. As I watch the game I don't sweat, I perspire. I feel foolish for reacting that way in an air-conditioned barroom. It's uncomfortable as my neck chafes against my shirt collar; I feel like an out of shape old man who'd just vainly run to catch a bus. While on the field, no such discomfort haunts me.

When I watch I am uncertain of the results, unsure of the actions of the players. In contrast, as I play, perhaps

I'm a fool but I believe I can control the actions of the game.

Football is an extremely physical game and I like it. I enjoy playing off a blocker twice my size and, head down, making a thunderous tackle. Watching the contact on TV or in the stands leaves me feeling somehow empty. "I should be out there. I'm young and healthy; I should be playing instead of sitting in this barroom, drinking beer, waiting for cash rewards."

As I see a defender intercept a pass, I scream, "Out of bounds! Out of bounds you fool before you fumble!" But when I intercept there is no such chant running through my mind. The ball is rare in the hands of a defender, but I have confidence. I can see the goal line and I know I can score. In the barroom my breathing is unsteady as I'm constantly grasping for air; on the field, with the ball in my hand, it's even and almost melodious. I'm graceful, as I follow my blockers, sidestep a would-be tackler. In the bar nothing is safe: drinks, chairs, and tables all fall prey to my awkward gropings.

When I play I am blinded by loyalty. "My team is the best and we are certain of victory." When I watch no such pride or cause binds me. I am a mercenary, making the percentage bet, the one that will pay the most. When I watch, no sense of loyalty guides me, only my wallet. I am by far, prouder of playing the game than of betting on it.

Perhaps it's foolish to take such pride in playing a game, but I do. If we win I'm ecstatic. We worked hard and were rewarded. The feelings are abstract and different for each player but they're still very real. In constrast, betting to me is like a job. I read the sports pages, study the teams, and sit in the bar waiting for the sucker who's certain his alma mater or hometown team can't lose. I get no pleasure from winning a bet.

When I look within myself I'm not really sure why I bet. It helps make ends meet; it keeps my gas tank on full and I guess I don't hate it as much as I say. But, when I have a choice, the money can go to hell, because you can be sure I'll be out there on some dusty old ballpark turf playing away the biggest prize of all as a reward. The sense of accomplishment is out there for me, the feeling of doing, not watching, of being there sweaty and alive. No amount of money can make me feel so alive.

All three student essays are fine in that the writers struggle with something that is real and give shape to a perception and an experience in ways that they and their readers care about. In each case the writer has a voice that is strong, personable, at ease and at the same time struggling to comprehend and convey what he or she feels. *That* is the voice of the true essayist.

72. Using the student essays as models, consider a subject that you may want to explore in a short essay that compares and contrasts two places, two attitudes, two states of mind. Write that essay.

73. Writing one's own comparison and contrast essay may be quite a bit easier than writing an essay in which you compare and contrast the ideas of two or more writers. This is more difficult because the task is not singular. There are several jobs you need to do. First, you have to read carefully to be sure you understand exactly what each writer is saying. Second, you have to do some translating. That is, you have to determine which word or term in one writer's essay is comparable to which word or term in another writer's essay. Third, you have to construct the comparison itself. And at this point your job is to decide which of those similar terms are precisely equivalent to one another, and which are not. And among those that are not quite equivalent, your job is to decide *at which points* they are the same, and at which they are different. Below you will find several extracts from writers *who are all talking about the same process.* Read through the passages carefully several times, trying to understand them as well as you can. The passages are very difficult; therefore you should not be distressed if you find it takes you some time to do this. After you have read them, I will offer some suggestions to help you construct a comparison and contrast essay in which you compare the ideas in one passage with those in the others.

1. [Biologists] usually proceed in such a way that from certain facts gained by analysis we sketch a picture of the whole organism, which in turn, so long as we encounter discrepancies between this picture and factual experience, stimulates further questions and investigations. Upon the basis of new inquiries the picture of the whole is again modified, and the process of discovering new discrepancies and making new inquiries follows, and so on. By such empirical procedure in a dialectical

manner, a progressively more adequate knowledge of the nature of the organism, of its "essence," is acquired, and an increasingly correct evaluation of the observed facts, and of whether or not they are essential to the organism is obtained. . . . . As skepticism toward a naive copy-theory of knowledge grew, and as it was realized that "empirical" facts are not a simple expression of reality but are also produced through the method of investigation, it became more and more clear that it was the task of natural science to transcend "empirical" facts and create images, "symbols," which are suited for gaining a coherent understanding of the "facts." (Kurt Goldstein, *Human Nature in the Light of Psychopathology,* pp. 26–27.)

2. Every attempt to order the world, to make sense of it, involves a testing of epistemic bonds [linkages between something that we discover and something that is public knowledge]. Mentally, we run back and forth between our postulations and our experiences. Our theories of the world, whether commonsensical or scientific, inevitably contain concepts by postulation so that, with Einstein, we know the public world— the reliable and objective world—"only by speculative means."

The operations we employ in coming to know the world scientifically are operations whose meanings are given by our speculations. Without an embedding in theory, the operations may become as senseless as Benjamin's construction of *hage* [this is a name for a hypothetical concept that could refer to "height plus age" and has no useful purpose.] On the other hand, theories without operations become so flexible as to defy falsification. Operation-free, they can be stretched to explain anything that happens—after the event.

Such unfalsifiable world-views gratify many men. They are called "faiths" to distinguish them, by degree, from those theories that permit a test of the epistemic bond against observable events. The advantage of faiths is that they order and gratify. Their disadvantage is that, devoid of operational meaning, they are immune to disproof and useless for prediction. (Gwynn Nettler, *Explanations,* p. 22.)

3. [Scientists] start with a *problem*, such as the problem of the planets at the time of Plato. This problem (which will be discussed in a somewhat idealized form) is not merely the result of *curiosity,* it is a *theoretical result.* It is due to the fact that certain *expectations* have been disappointed: on the one hand it seems to be clear that the stars must be divine, hence one expects them to behave in an orderly and lawful manner. On the other hand, one cannot find any easily discernible regularity. The planets, to all intents and purposes, move in a quite chaotic fashion. How can this fact be reconciled with the expectation and with the principles that underlie the expectation? Does it show that the expectation is mistaken? Or have we failed in our analysis of the facts? This is the problem.

It is important to see that the elements of the problem are not simply *given.* The "fact" of irregularity, for example, is not accessible without further ado. It cannot be discovered by just anyone who has healthy eyes and a good mind. It is only through a certain expectation that it becomes an object of our attention. Or, to be more accurate, this fact of irregularity *exists* because there is an expectation of regularity. In our case the rule (which is a more specific part of the expectation) asserts a circular motion with constant angular velocity. The fixed stars agree with this rule and so does the sun, if we trace its path relative to the fixed stars. The planets do not obey the rule, neither directly, with respect to earth, nor indirectly, with respect to the fixed stars.

To sum up this part of the [Karl] Popperian doctrine: research starts with a problem. The problem is the result of a conflict between an expectation and an observation which in turn is constituted by the expectation. It is clear that this doctrine differs from the doctrine of inductivism where objective facts enter a passive mind and leave their traces there. (Paul Feyerabend, *Against Method*, pp. 171–72.)

As I promised, the extracts are difficult, but perhaps these questions and procedures will help you make sense of them and start you on the way to an essay in which you compare these writers. These same questions and procedures ought to be of some help whenever you write a comparison and contrast essay.

1. Look for words that recur in the extracts. In this case, the recurrence of words such as *facts, observation, theory*, ought to help you know what the writers are talking about. Look for other such words.
2. I have said that all of these writers are talking about a process. In a sentence or two, explain what that process is.
3. Remember what we have said about words that are always central to analysis; for example, *nature, source*, and *function*. Apply each of those words to *each* of these writers. What, for instance, is the *function* of the process described? What does it yield? Answer these questions for one of the writers, and then for another. What is the *nature* of the process? That is, how does it actually work? Answer that question for each of the writers.
4. Can you do what we did with Gore Vidal's passage in Chapter 5? That is, can you see what the *shape* of each writer's paragraph is? Is there a causal chain in the paragraphs of any of these writers? A gradual progression forward?
5. Are there traces of *an image* that could be visualized and that might help you understand what is being said? We will work on this tactic much more in the next chapter, but for now look closely at phrases like "running back and forth." *Picture* those things in your mind's eye. What do they tell you about how the writers see the process they describe? You might even want to sketch what each writer is describing.
6. Can you detect which term each writer *opposes* to which other terms? See if you can list the oppositions each writer sees.
7. Maybe the best way to force yourself to find similar or equivalent terms is to construct what Ann E. Berthoff calls "grain elevators." These are columns you construct, lining up terms that are equivalent or similar in one writer and another. See an example of this on the next page.

Column A	Goldstein (b)	Nettler (c)	Feyerabend (d)
Need	"adequate knowledge of the essence of the organism"	"coming to know the world scientifically"	"reconciling what we observe, and our expectations of what we observe"
How It Is Served	from available facts, sketching a picture of the whole	running back and forth from our postulations to our experiences	noting irregularity, and trying to come to understand that irregularity
End Product	the creation of "symbols" suitable for explaining the "facts"	the creation of a theory that permits us to test it	not expressed in the excerpt

Berthoff notes that in order for this tactic to work, you must be sure that your separate "elevators" are free standing and, of course, that the items you place across from each other are parallel or equivalent.

8. After you have constructed "elevators," you can force yourself to formulate specific statements that will, in their turn, force you to clarify points of similarity and difference. They might take these forms: "If for [Feyerabend] the _____ is _____, for [Goldstein, Nettler] it is _____."

9. You can also, of course, return to the series of reading questions listed in Chapter 5 and go through the entire list of procedures there. You can, that is, ask such questions as what are the central concepts being discussed (in this case they are *experience, expectation, fact, new ideas,* and so on), and you can then ask yourself how those separate concepts are related to one another by each writer.

10. If we assume that all of these writers are taking somewhat different positions about the same issue, might it not be possible for you to think of these positions as part of a *continuum*? Can you, that is, rank them along a scale of most to least radical? (When I say radical, I do not mean politically radical, of course, but most extreme or most drastic.) Who would you put at the most drastic or extreme end of that continuum, and who on the other end, and where would the other writers fall? Discerning the answer to a question such as this is also deciding how to organize your essay—because you may want to talk about the most extreme position first, the second most extreme position second, and so on. As usual, the organization of your essay will be determined by your thinking, and not by reference to any "rules" of writing.

74. Now that you have composed a comparison and contrast essay based on the writings above, try doing the same thing with the following three short excerpts. In this case also, follow the suggestions given in the last few pages and keep in mind particularly the notion that these three writers may be placed on a continuum. That is, which writer takes the most drastic position, and which the least drastic, and in what ways?

1. The original doctrines of art's "usefulness" were not offered as attacks upon art. Kant, in proposing "purposiveness without purpose" as a formula for the aesthetic, had no intention of providing a "refutation" of art. His formula did, however, mark the emergence of the "use" criterion which was subsequently to place all purely intellectual pursuits upon a defensive basis. His proposition could be readily perverted: if the aesthetic had no purpose outside itself, the corollary seemed to be that the aesthetic had no *result* outside itself. Logically there was no cogency in such an argument, but psychologically there was a great deal. And the damage was perhaps increased through attempts to justify art by the postulating of a special "art instinct" or "aesthetic sense."

   On the face of it, this was a good move. For a time when instincts were gaining considerably in repute, and no complicated human mind could rouse us to admiration so promptly as the routine acts of an insect, what could be more salubrious for the reputation of art than the contention that art satisfies an "instinctive need"? The trouble arose from the fact that the "art instinct" was associated with the "play instinct," thus becoming little more than an adult survival from childhood. The apologists still in the Kantian scheme, associated art with play because both seemed, from the standpoint of utility, purposeless. But in an age when "work" was becoming one of society's catch-words, art could not very well be associated with play without some loss of prestige. (Kenneth Burke, *Permanence and Change*, pp. 72–73.)

2. A work of art can be either "received' or "used." When we "receive" it we exert our senses and imagination and various other powers according to a pattern invented by the artist. When we "use" it we treat it as assistance for our own activities. The one, to use an old-fashioned image, is like being taken for a bicycle ride by a man who knows roads we have never yet explored. The other is like adding one of those little motor attachments to our own bicycle and then going for one of our familiar rides. These rides may in themselves be good, bad, or indifferent. The "uses" which the many make of the arts may or may not be intrinsically vulgar, depraved, or morbid. That's as may be. "Using" is inferior to "reception" because art, if used rather than received, merely facilitates, brightens, or palliates our life, and does not add to it. (C. S. Lewis, *An Experiment in Criticism*, p. 88.)

3. A self-directed enjoyment of nature seems to me to be something forced. More naturally, as well as more properly, we take a self-forgetful pleasure in the sheer alien pointless independent existence of animals, birds, stones, and trees. "Not how the world is, but that it is, is the mystical."

   I take this starting point, not because I think it is the most important place of moral change, but because I think it is the most accessible one. It is so patently a good thing to take delight in flowers and animals that people who bring home potted plants and watch kestrels might even be surprised at the notion that these things have anything to do with virtue. The surprise is a product of the fact that, as Plato pointed out, beauty is the only spiritual thing which we love by instinct. When we move from beauty in nature to beauty in art we are already in a more difficult region. The experience of art is more easily degraded than the experience of nature. A great deal of art, perhaps most art, actually is self-consoling fantasy, and even great art cannot guarantee the quality of its consumer's consciousness. However, what is great can have its effect. Art, and by "art" from now on I mean good art, not fantasy art, affords us a pure delight in the independent existence of what is excellent. Both in its genesis and its enjoyment it is a thing totally opposed to selfish obsession. It invigorates our best faculties and, to use Platonic language, inspires love in the highest parts of the soul. It is able to do this partly by virtue of something which it shares with nature: a perfection of form which invites unpossessive contemplation and resists absorption into the selfish dream of the consciousness. (Iris Murdoch, *The Sovereignty of Good*, pp. 85–86.)

75. We said at the beginning of this book that *all* writing is in a crucial sense a response to what someone else has written or said; all writing picks up where someone else left off. This is particularly true in the above excerpts, in which the reader is almost bound to feel somewhat like an eavesdropper listening in on someone else's argument. But that is the usual condition of the reader and writer. To turn that condition to your own use, try this exercise: imagine what may have prompted each of these writers to say the things he or she says. What attitudes are all three responding to and reacting against? In that more contemporary formulation, "Where are they coming from?" How does knowing where they are coming from help you to understand what they are saying and why they are saying it?

13

Recognizing and Creating Metaphors

Throughout this book we have watched how thinking and writing turn out to be mostly matters of forming concepts, sharpening concepts, and then connecting those concepts. It seems almost too predictable and simple to be true, but it is. Sometimes those connections are causal ones, as they were in Gore Vidal's excerpt about Americans' fear of criticism, or in the excerpts about black Christianity, Italian conceptions of the "hero," CIA operations in Third World countries, and W. C. Fields's appeal as a comedian. Sometimes those connections are simply equations. Such equation happens whenever we define concepts: "Normal *is* what we call something that is statistically common"; "Love *is* an attraction of like for like"; "Charm *is* the giving generously of what we were given generously." That *is* announces the equation of one concept with another. And you certainly have noticed that conceptual defining, equating and connecting happens in the same way whether the subject is science, politics, religion, history, or the arts and entertainment. Thinking is thinking, whatever the field.

There is, however, one last kind of relationship between concepts that we have yet to talk about, that which can only be expressed in an image: in a picture. To my mind, the idea-in-image is both the most difficult to create and to recognize as you read, and the most fun to play with. The idea-in-image never announces its presence loudly and conveniently with a single word like *is* or *causes*. Instead, ideas-in-image announce themselves in much more subtle ways, and to see how they work and what they do for our thinking and writing, it makes sense for us to play with a few. Mircea Eliade writes well about the place of religion in society. In the following passage, he talks about the work of another writer, Jacques Ellul:

> Just how devoid of religion is contemporary society? Could it be that the more secular a culture becomes, the more it secretes new forms of the sacred? Jacques Ellul argues that, despite his apparent lack of interest, modern man is as religious as were his forebears. New forms of religion, especially technology and politics, have filled the spiritual void left by the "death of God."

Where are the concepts here, and how are they related? By now you should be able to say easily enough that Eliade is talking about *religion* and *society* or *culture*, but where is the connector connecting those separate concepts? It lurks in the word *secretes*. What this means is that the person who wants to read well and write with clarity must be alert for conceptions—ways of seeing— that are really *ways of seeing*; are picture-able. Beyond that, the good reader and writer knows that language itself began with pictures, and that words refer to a real, physical world. Several things follow from this recognition. First, as a writer, you will never want to write about "facilitating mutual interaction between parents and siblings," because such language is a crust that gets between your reader and the reality you want to talk about; in this case, the reality of things like holding hands with your children. Second, as a writer, you will want to remember that the more abstract and complex the ideas you talk about, the more you should search for concrete, down-to-earth images to convey them. Philosophers, maybe more than any other writers, use simple images to clarify. Ludwig Wittgenstein called philosophy itself a way of getting the fly in—or out—of the bottle. I might note that this book is full of images; for example, the image of writing practice as jump-starting your car on cold mornings. The writer who wants to be understood has a natural inclination to provide pictures. Remnants of this inclination exist in the speech of teenagers, who frequently say, "You know, it's like . . . it's like." The only problem is that teenagers do not always say *what* "it's like."

As a reader, your job is to notice those images when they occur and to take time to picture what the writer is asking you to picture. In the passage above, Eliade is saying "Society *secretes* religion." As a sharp reader, you will want to ask yourself: What is implied by his choosing that word? What kinds of things secrete? What is the function of a secretion? And how does what I learn by answering these questions help me understand Eliade's way of seeing (conceiving of) religion and society? A skunk secretes to protect itself from intruders. Skin secretes sweat to protect the body and to help it maintain a balance so that it will be neither too hot nor too cold, and so that it will have neither too much nor too little moisture. An oyster secretes a substance around a grain of sand that has gotten inside it and is irritating it. Furthermore, that secretion, which begins as a protection against pain, hardens into something quite valuable: a pearl. What relationship does Eliade see between a society and its religions? Do religions protect society? Do religions help society maintain its balance? Do religions grow in response to human pain and become something of great value, just as the pearl? Obviously, part or all of this is what Eliade must have had in mind when he chose the word *secretes*, and your job as a reader is first to *recognize* that idea-in-image and then try to decide insofar as you can what it—and its creator—are trying to tell you. The idea-in-image is more complex and perhaps more fun than any other kind of idea because one never knows exactly how far the implications of the image can be pushed. For instance, maybe Eliade intended us to see religion as functioning as protection or balance, but had not thought of its being "the pearl of great price." It is in the nature of image or metaphor not only to convey ideas, but to *generate* them as well. Using metaphor—seeing one thing as a kind of another thing—is a way of discovering something new, and a way of communicating a relationship that cannot be communicated in any other way except by and through that image. Below are excerpts from, as usual, lots of different sources. In each excerpt, the writer is conveying his or her idea in an image. See if you can discover what the image is, picture it, and determine what its "range of convenience" might be. That is, you will see how many of the implications called up by the image seem to apply to the idea.

1. But an idea or a notion, when unencumbered and undisguised, is no easier to get hold of than one of those oiled and naked thieves who infest the railway carriages of India.

Indeed an idea, or a notion, like the physicist's ultimate particles and rays, is only known by what it does. (I. A. Richards, *Philosophy of Rhetoric*, p. 5.)

2. The future is like the layout of Boston's streets, which we inherited and are stuck with unless we want to tear it all up. (Harvard sociologist Daniel Bell, quoted in "The Future of Business," Marguret Del Giudice, the *Boston Globe*, 8 June 1980.)

3. David C. McClelland, a Harvard psychologist, has frequently criticized use of the S.A.T. as an admissions criterion for college on the grounds that it ignores motivation. "To use a crude example," he wrote, "a psychologist might assess individual differences in the *capacity* to drink beer, but if he used this measure to predict actual beer consumption over time, the chances are that the relationship would be very low." The testing movement, he continued, "is in grave danger of perpetuating a mythological meritocracy in which none of the measures of merit bear significant demonstrable validity with respect to any measures outside of the charmed circle." (Edward B. Fiske, "Finding Fault with the Testers," p. 162.)

4. "Marrying is barred to me," he tells his father, "because it is your domain. Sometimes I imagine the map of the world spread out and you stretched diagonally across it. And I feel as if I could consider living in only those regions that either are not covered by you or are not within your reach." (Philip Roth, "I Always Wanted You to Admire My Fasting: or, Looking at Kafka," p. 106.)

5. A poem compresses much in a small space and adds music, thus heightening its meaning. The city is like poetry: it compresses all life, all races and breeds, into a small island and adds music and the accompaniment of internal engines. The island of Manhattan is without any doubt the greatest human concentrate on earth, the poem whose magic is comprehensible to millions of permanent residents but whose full meaning will always remain illusive. (E. B. White, "Here Is New York," p. 426.)

76. For the next several days, be as alert as you can be to images and metaphors in what you read. Collect a few of the best, save them in your writer's log, and if you have time, consider teasing out all of the implications of each image or metaphor.

77. Generate your own image or metaphor to clarify some idea, situation, person, or attitude. This can be difficult to do "cold," especially if you are unaccustomed to thinking in this way, but try doing it anyway. If you need a form to use as inspiration, try this: "This [case, person, object, situation, phenomenon] serves the same function, or is, or acts like this [earlier, other, apparently different] [case, person, object]." If you need even more help, consider this: what you will be doing is using a phenomenon from the natural world or the world of machines, as a kind of heuristic; as a way of discovering something you did not know you knew. If you need more help, see the following list of "fertile" objects that can be used to describe some person, place, phenomenon, situation. See if you can, just for fun and practice, identify what the feature or features of these things are that might make them good analogy or metaphor material. Ask yourself, that is, questions like:

1. What are the properties, features, characteristics, habits, functions, or behavior of this object or phenomenon?
2. What other object or situation can be compared to this object or situation because it shares some of the same properties, features, functions, or habits?
3. In each case, of course, it will help if you first find out exactly what this object is and does.

The list immediately follows.

1. a drive shaft
2. fire
3. an oyster
4. a wedge
5. the sail of a boat
6. a clam's propulsion system
7. the snail's escape route
8. akido
9. a kaleidoscope
10. the pupil and iris of the eye
11. a sphygmomanometer
12. particle board
13. a ratchet
14. an artichoke (or a planed board)

78. After you have written your short paper comparing one thing to something unlike it, but similar in unexpected ways, check to make sure you have created an image that is picture-able. Even professional writers sometimes fall into very garbled images. Here are a few howlers. See if you can tell exactly where and how they go off the rails.

1. From the *Boston Globe*, in an article about prisons: "Mr. Johnson said, 'Our objective is to break the cycle of self-destruction called recidivism that engulfs the ex-offender and his or her family in an endless tangle of police, courts, and prison.'"
2. From (sigh) a paragraph from a textbook for writers: "Arranging details, facts, examples, reasons, and evidence provide the muscle that gives shape to your overall strategy."
3. From a review of a book on education: "The writer shows that the roots of this frightening situation are deeply embedded in the structure of American education as it has been developed over the last two hundred years."
4. From a student essay, talking about physical handicaps. The point the writer wanted to make is that the problem a handicapped student has is not so much the physical handicap as it is the other people's attitudes toward the student: "The roots of the problem are not embedded in the physical handicap."

In each of these cases, the idea was wonderful, the execution terrible. See if you can get in the habit of not only creating images as you write to clarify what you are saying but also of *picturing* those images to be sure they work.

79. The kind of thinking and writing you are being asked to do in this chapter is of a special kind, one that may come easier to some people than to others. It requires a mind that is used to seeing some things as metaphors for other things. It requires a mind that is sharpened to see, as Ralph Waldo Emerson said, "sermons in stones." It requires a mind that is inclined to explain itself to others by saying "It's like this; like this; like this." I was taught in grade school by a nun who was very good at this. She would tell us, for instance, "Saying the rosary during Mass is like taking a radio to the movies." She knew that saying "It's like *this*" clarifies ideas. If you need more practice seeing how images can provide clarifications, and more time to see how teasing out all of the implications of an image allows us to think beyond what we now think, choose one of the proverbs out of the following list and then write a short essay in which you tease out the proverb's implications and then try providing several examples of situations in which it might apply. Try to choose your examples from as many different realms or areas of life as you can. Does the proverb apply, for instance, in the world of high finance as well as in that of entertainment? In the world of religion as well as in that of the family? Give yourself plenty of elbow room in which to let the idea grow, and plenty of time in which to muse about the "range of convenience" of the proverb.

1. The sun does not shine on both sides of the hedge at once.
2. The wind in one's face makes one wise.

3. The higher the ape goes, the more he shows his tail.
4. The moon does not heed the barking of dogs.
5. He measures another's corn by his own bushel.
6. Straws show which way the wind blows.
7. When the fish is caught, the net is laid aside.
8. Remove an old tree, and it will wither to death.
9. He that bites on every weed must needs light on poison.
10. Whether the pitcher strikes the stone, or the stone the pitcher, it is bad for the pitcher.
11. Think with the wise, but talk with the vulgar.
12. Eagles catch no flies.
13. When the fox preacheth, then beware your geese.
14. The wine in the bottle does not quench thirst.
15. Fools tie knots and wise men loose them.

14

The Longer Essay from Start to Finish

Throughout this book we have talked about how writing essays is a matter of thinking on paper, and we have said that thinking on paper is a matter of defining concepts, comparing them, distinguishing them, and clarifying relationships between them, partly by using words like *causes* or *is like*, and partly by using images to sharpen the way we see and think. It would be misleading, however, to leave the impression that some essays define, others compare and contrast, and others make distinctions or create metaphors. Few essays are ever "pure" types of one kind or another. The essayist uses combinations of those tactics to explore what he or she might think; to clarify a point; to carry out the analysis; to tease, cajole, intrigue the reader into reading that essay and agreeing with it, or at least entertaining what he or she finds there as possible ways of seeing some part of the world. If you simply flip through the pages of this book and reread some of the writings that we have looked at, you can see that even the shortest bits of writing seem to express connections, create and convey images, and do a dozen other things all at once. It must seem that the good essayist needs to be a good juggler, keeping several balls in the air, with one eye on the distinction he or she is making, and the other eye on the reader, trying to be sure the reader is following the essayist's train of thought. How can the essayist do all those things at once? How can the essayist discover what there is to say, say it, and be sure it is said clearly enough for a reader to follow—all at the same time? Obviously, the essayist cannot do all of those things at the same time. Nobody can. The object of this last chapter, then, is to break the writing process down into steps or stages, all the while recognizing that writing a good essay is not the result of following a neat set of stages like prewriting, outlining, writing, and revising, but of learning how to take advantage of what are really the two most important stages of writing: the mess and the mystery.

By definition, because the writing process is made up of mess and mystery, no one can tell you exactly how your writing process works. But what I can do in this chapter is talk about what has worked for me and what has worked for other writers and, like the bio-feedback doctor, try to set conditions up so that you can discover for yourself what works best for you. One thing I do know is that writing well is more a matter of attitude than of skill, and the attitude most essential is that of welcoming the mess and the mystery that make up the writing process. The neatness of the finished essay, its wonderful coherence, logic, and organization, its orderly progression from one point to the next—all those things obscure the mess and the chaos from which the essay came, and in which it began. Essays never begin with a piece of blank paper, upon which you record an introductory sentence that comes to you whole, from above, almost as if it had been dictated to you by God. Opening sentences tend to come to you *last*, after the essay has been written, and long after your desk has become a blizzard of notes slips and scraps of paper and second and third and fourth drafts. If you are uncomfortable getting your hands dirty and your desk messy, you will cheat yourself out of the chance to discover something new and wonderful to say. Mess is material: material for thinking; for shaping into essays. Somehow Shoe, on the next page, at least *partly* understands this process.

A large part of the writing process is mess; another large part is mystery. We know that "writing" does not begin when we first put pen to paper. Instead, writing is actually only the final stage of a long process. Ideas are born, as we shall see, partly in the act of writing—writing itself generates them—but they are also born out of that rich, primordial slime where we alternatively go after them with our big guns (like definition, compare/contrast, distinction-making) and lie in wait for them to raise their heads out of the smoky swamp like some Nessy. The truth is that all of the lists of procedures in the world will not help you write better if you do not acknowledge that the idea, the hypothesis, the new

synthesis, the organization for an essay is likely to appear not so much as a result of applying a rigorous set of procedures, but just when you were not looking for it at all; as you stumbled half asleep to the front door at 4 A.M., to let the dog in, or out.

So in this chapter you will find an account of what I think is the sequence of stages necessary to write an essay, together with some exercises to get you as comfortable as possible passing through those stages. At the same time, however, I want to remind you that in some sense these stages are artificial; that is, they do not necessarily happen one after the other. They overlap. While you are still gathering material, you begin to write sentences or even paragraphs. But that phase tends to run dry, and you go back to reading. From there, you might begin to write longer passages that can be integrated into an essay. But at some point, you may discover that you cannot write more because of a gap in your information, and you need to read more. So you go back to the reading stage. Even in the last stages of writing, when you are polishing sentences, you might discover that finding just the right word changes the way you see your whole subject. At that point, you might backtrack from editing, to reformulate the whole essay. While reading something just for fun, something you think is entirely unrelated to what you are writing, you might stumble on exactly what you need to provide an introduction to your essay.

That messy and mysterious process by which ideas are born and shaped into an essay is described very well by Herbert Spencer, a nineteenth-century thinker whose work is thought to have been influential on Charles Darwin:

Herbert Spencer.
From his *Autobiography*

It has never been my way to set before myself a problem and puzzle out an answer. The conclusions at which I have from time to time arrived, have not been arrived at as solutions of questions raised; but have been arrived at unawares—each as the ultimate outcome of a body of thoughts which slowly grew from a germ. Some direct observation, or some fact met with in reading, would dwell with me: apparently because I had a sense of its significance. It was not that there arose a distinct consciousness of its general meaning; but rather that there was a kind of instinctive interest in those facts which have general meanings. For example, the detailed structure of this or that species of mammal, though I might willingly read about it, would leave little impression; but when I met with the statement that, almost without exception, mammals, even as unlike as the whale and the giraffe, have seven cervical vertebrae, this would strike me and be remembered as suggestive. Apt as I thus was to lay hold of cardinal truths, it would happen occasionally that one, most likely brought to mind by an illustration, and gaining from the illustration fresh distinctiveness, would be contemplated by me for a while, and its bearings observed. A week afterwards, possibly, the matter would be remembered; and with further thought about it, might occur a recognition of some wider application than I had before perceived; new instances being aggregated with those already noted. Again after an interval, perhaps of a month, perhaps of a half a year, something would remind me of that which I had before remarked; and mentally running over the facts might be followed by some further extension of the idea. When accumulation of instances had given body to a generalization, reflexion would reduce the vague conception at first framed to a more definite conception; and perhaps difficulties or anomalies passed over for a while, but eventually forcing themselves on attention, might cause a needful qualification and a truer shaping of the thought. Eventually, the growing generalization, thus far inductive, might take a deductive form: being all at once recognized as a necessary consequence of some physical principle—some established law. And thus, little by little, in unobtrusive ways, without conscious intention or appreciable effort, there would grow up a coherent and organized theory. Habitually the process was one of slow unforced development, often extending over years; and it was, I believe, because the thinking done went on in this gradual, almost spontaneous way, without strain, that there was an absence of those lines of thought which Miss Evans [George Eliot, a novelist and a friend of Spencer's] remarked—an absence almost as complete thirty years later, notwithstanding the amount of thinking done in the interval.

I name her remark, and give this explanation partly to introduce the opinion that a solution reached in the way decribed is more likely to be true than one reached in pursuance of a determined effort to find a solution. The determined effort causes perversion of thought. When endeavouring to recollect some name or thing which has been forgotten, it frequently happens that the name or thing sought will not arise in consciousness; but when attention is relaxed, the missing name or thing often suggests itself. While thought continues to be forced down certain wrong turnings which had originally been taken, the search is vain; but with the cessation of strain the true association of ideas has an opportunity of asserting itself (1:463–65).

So, as we can learn from Spencer's honest account, thinking and writing *are* messy and mysterious processes. His account suggests that a major part of writing is not following steps or stages, so much as it is just continuing to do it until something comes. Writing takes much more time than one might think. As Spencer's description suggests, it takes time to read. Time to think. Time to relax and let your subconscious do its work. Time to let rough drafts cool. Time to wait for the missing link that connects your miscellaneous ideas to come to you. Janet Emig, in *The Com-*

posing Processes of Twelfth Graders, discovered that people tend to choose a subject to write about on the basis of an intelligent guess about how much time they have to devote to the writing project. So if you find yourself writing about the simple thing instead of the more interesting and new and complex thing, you might consider that you are not giving yourself enough time for this musing and subconscious percolating that Spencer describes as essential to thinking and writing. Of course, no one ever has enough time to write the perfect essay, and no essay, by definition, is ever really "finished." Remember that to "essay" means to try, to attempt, to venture, to test out. So *all* essays are ventures that are not quite final. Alfred Kazin even calls the essay "the open form." Essays are always growing. They invite others to join in and respond with a further "essay," or attempt to understand something. Writing essays, then, demands a certain attitude: a willingness to try to shape material into a finished form, and a willingness to share what we called in the beginning of this book a "struggle into consciousness" with other people.

Now that we have said that there are stages or steps in writing the longer essay, and that there are particular attitudes appropriate to each stage, we might now look at each of those stages one at a time.

Stage 1: Beginning before the Beginning

As we have said, writing begins long before the pen touches the paper. For one thing, the good writer is the person who is interested in everything, who is interested and alert at all times, because he or she never knows when a particular bit of material will become useful or necessary—as an analogy, for contrast, for supporting evidence, as a demonstration of an equivalent instance of something he or she is talking about. Even subway riding can provide you with support you might need to make a point in an economics or sociology paper, or an essay you might want to write on television viewing habits of Americans. When Gore Vidal wanted to talk about how critics fail to criticize American art, thus creating the conditions for mediocrity, he referred to Warren

Harding, Dracula, and Diderot in the process. Only having a well-stocked mind, full of information, anecdotes, potential cross-connections, could have allowed him to do that. When Wilfred Sheed wanted to talk about W. C. Fields, he referred, among other things, to the D'Oyly Carte Opera Company and to Fred Astaire. William Henry learned something about the American psyche by watching Donald Duck. I hope that you and I learned something about the writing process by comparing writing essays to becoming an auto mechanic; by comparing the writing teacher to the doctor teaching bio-feedback techniques. I have learned more about how thinking and writing work by reading about science than I have in any other way. So the first "stage" of writing begins long before you even begin to think about writing a particular essay. It begins in a questing consciousness, a desire to know how things work, what things are, who people are, why things happened or happen, what makes things go, what makes *you* go: what catches your fancy, and why. If you have been keeping the writer's log I suggested at the beginning of this book, you should already have a fund of images, ideas, fancy-ticklers, material for analogies. That is the start of your material as a writer. I think you will want to continue writing in this log and collecting things in it for as long as you are interested in being a writer. If you feel uncomfortable using the log, try some alternative. Some writers collect note slips, bundled together by topic. Some write on anything that comes to hand: napkins, scraps of paper, paper bags. Charles Dickens kept a brown paper bag on the corner of his writing desk into which he stuffed all kinds of things that intrigued him and that he thought he might one day turn into material: snips of overheard dialogue, descriptions of the shape of a nose, the sworl of an ear, faces, gestures, costumes. You will want to find some means to hang onto things you can use for material as you write. It makes sense, if you think about it for a second: you can only write about what you have seen, heard, read about, experienced, observed, and the more you see, hear, read, experience, and observe, the more you have to write about; the less time you will spend at a desk staring at a blank piece of paper. Avoid the problem of the poor artist in the cartoon, on the following page, who does not seem to understand the need to go out into the world to gather material.

Stage 2: The Listening Habit

Not only do you need to watch everything and read everything you can, but you also need to *listen*. This seems elementary, and yet those whose business it is to solve problems often talk about how people need training in listening. George M. Prince, in *The Practice of Creativity*, talks a great deal about what he calls "the evaluative tendency" that keeps us from thoroughly understanding what other people propose as solutions to problems, or explanations of events. We are far too ready to judge what other people say and find it wanting, even before we have understood what they say. Prince suggests that we just try to understand: "Hold in abeyance your negative reactions temporarily" (p. 45), he suggests, whenever you read or hear a new idea. Instead he suggests that we think something like, "Well, maybe this is *partly* right. Maybe some of this is useful. If we adjusted this or that, we would have something." Cultivate that listening habit. Even more importantly, *listen to yourself*. Do not be overly critical in the early stages of thinking or writing. Think, again, "Well, parts of that idea are really muddy, but I might be able to play with it a little and make it better." In fifteen years of trying to help people learn to write better, I am still astonished at how tough on themselves beginning writers are. Before an idea is even half out of their mouths, they say "No, that's dumb." The good writer is kind to himself or herself, and that kindness and courtesy includes simply listening to what the mind is trying to say.

Stage 3: Generating Material

If you are an observant, alert, listening, reading, thinking person, when the invitation or obligation to write comes along, you will be at least partially ready for it. In Stage 3, you will sift through your store of information, decide where you need to do research and more reading to fill in the gaps, and begin what some people call *brainstorming*, or *prewriting*. Scientists often call this the *data-gathering* or the *preparation* phase. Whatever we call it, it is characterized by a widespread search for material, and by the generation of as much material about the topic you are going to write about as time and energy allow. You might notice that this suggestion differs quite a bit from what many writing books tell you. One writing book I know of begins with its author telling writers that "the writer's first task is to narrow his topic." But obviously, the writer's first problem is to have enough material and possible things to say that he or she can *afford* to "narrow" the topic. This means you begin by generating so much material— maybe even three times more than you will eventually use— that you can afford to throw out much of it in a later stage. If you begin an essay by trying to squeeze out the ten pages you want to write from a meager store of ideas, you cannot allow youself to be selective; even worse, you will find yourself padding and repeating to get those ten pages.

Of course the kind of writing you are going to do determines the kind of material-gathering you do. If you are writing a research paper or an analysis for a course, common sense tells you that you will spend time in the library, taking notes and reading—with care and precision, as we have already learned to do—the things you are to write about. If the topic is one of your own choosing, and if conceptual analysis plays a part in what you are writing, as no doubt it will, you can do the kind of conceptual play that we have done here in nearly every chapter.

Writers of books about writing are fond of talking about "brainstorming" as a way of generating ideas. Brainstorming is simply jotting down anything and everything you can think of about a particular topic in order to find something to say. It is a tactic I have very mixed feelings about myself and cannot remember ever using, to be honest. It strikes me that there are two different attitudes one might have towards brainstorming. In one spirit, the writer might simply try to get hold of everything it might be possible to say about a topic. Out of that "chaos," the writer bundles together a sufficient amount of "stuff" to fill out the required number of paragraphs or pages. This seems to me a cynical and unsatisfying approach to the business of thinking and writing. But there is a second kind of brainstorming that might be more productive. You might jot down lists of things, freely and unconsciously, in order to discover how it is that you might already be thinking about your subject without having been fully conscious of doing so. In this kind of brainstorming, you do a kind of free association to get in touch with your own half-conscious thoughts. It may prove quite helpful, especially if you follow up the process with an intelligent attempt to gather the miscellaneous items in your list under useful conceptual headings.

80. Below is one student's brainstorming for the concept *maturity*. See if you can provide the potential organization for the essay that would follow from the brainstorming. You might even add seven or eight more terms to the student's list before you do this.

Maturity

age	compromise	ripeness
responsibility	prime of life	patience
commitments	intelligence	love, marriage
goals	psychological	courage
understanding	emotional	sensible
ability to change	biological	tranquillity
confidence	moral	actions
stages	honesty	personality
personal	rational	relationships
national	sophistication	vocabulary
awareness	refined	purpose
eighteen	urbane	sense of humor
the social	change from idealistic	choice
		stability

81. Once you have generated as many terms as possible in your brainstorming, and have bundled those terms together as best you can, write a short essay inspired by *one* of those bundlings of terms.

82. Write another short essay inspired by a *different* gathering of terms. Notice that when you write an essay, you do not automatically consider using everything you can think of about that particular topic.

83. Do the same kind of brainstorming and essay-writing with another concept. You might want to try the word *censorship*. Notice this time too that you need to gather, as well as to generate, terms and that not everything you can think of about a topic "fits" into one essay.

Stage 4: Note-taking

As we have said, if you are doing a research paper or a paper analyzing readings you have read, brainstorming is not quite as helpful a tactic as is standard note-taking. However, most students I have worked with are unaware of how to take notes in the most useful way. Most simply jot down long quotations from sources they read. But this is a misunderstanding of the way note slips can work for you. Note slips can take a wide variety of forms. They can be:

1. Facts you gather

2. Quotations to support an argument or point you plan to make

3. Reminders or notes to yourself ("Don't forget to mention that . . . " or "Remember to defend this point in this way"). Some of these note slips might contain ideas about possible ways to organize your essay ("Do a history of the concept first, and then analyze it" or "Analyze the concept in the course of giving its history").

4. Questions to and for yourself. These questions can be of several kinds. They can be procedural ("Do I want to talk about *all* kinds of bonding I know of, or only about two or three?"). They can be about rhetorical strategies ("Should I mention the opposition to this point, or will doing that obligate me to make a long digression to argue down the opposition?"). They can be substantive ("Do I really believe psychoanalysis ought to address itself to. . . . ").

5. Some note slips will contain thoughts about a potential thesis statement. They will be a place and an occasion for you to do a kind of stock-taking. Where am I now in the writing/thinking process: What have I learned so far, and what do I *think* will be my approach when I write?

6. Some notes you will take simply to get yourself going, to start the adrenalin flowing, to get your mind thinking. Some researchers, Janet Emig for instance, have noticed that "sweat appears within two minutes of the presence of adrenalin in the blood," and that the literal act of writing, with the hand, is "activating, mobilizing. It physically thrusts the writer from a state of inaction into engagement with the process and the task." (Cooper and Odell, *Research on Composing*, p. 61.) This means that not just writing an essay, but *writing* an essay—the physical act of pushing the pen across the page—may in part bring ideas into your mind. The implications of this for you as a writer should be obvious: you do not wait to see what you think before you write, but you *write in order to help yourself think*. Walter Ong calls this "epistemic" writing, and you can begin to do it in the note-taking stage of writing the essay.

Because at this phase of writing the essay you do not yet know, by definition, exactly what your finished essay will look like, or even what it needs to become finished, it makes sense to take a great many more notes than you think you may need. You do not yet know what your main points will be, what kinds of support you will need for them, or what your approach to your topic will be. For that reason, you should be lavish in your note-taking. If necessary, photocopy whole pages, just in case you might find certain parts of those pages useful later. By all means, keep accurate records. Copy notes accurately and be sure the source and page number is marked on each note slip. Nothing is more frustrating than having to retrace your steps later, trying to find out where you found a particular point or quotation.

Remember, too, that you take notes partly to get yourself engaged with a subject, an author, a point of view. If you are taking notes from a book you are reading, do not be afraid to question, challenge, consider alternative hypotheses to those in it. All of those tactics for reading critically, generating questions, imagining alternative explanations that we have talked about throughout this book should help you as you take notes.

84. Throughout this book, you have read short excerpts on a wide variety of topics: education, Christianity and slavery, liberty, cancer and tuberculosis, autonomy in a concentration camp and autonomy in the life of a cell in the body, criticism in the arts, induction and deduction in the sciences, and a whole host of other things. Choose one of those readings or references that would require you to do research if you were to respond to it intelligently, and do some preliminary reading and note-taking on its topic. Keep taking notes—of all the kinds described above—until you have a substantial number with which to work. Do some practice gatherings of those note slips. In a sentence or two, write up the potential thesis statements you could support with your note slips.

85. Choose the one gathering of note slips that appeals to you most and attempt at least the rough draft of the essay that would result from that gathering. Do *not* try to produce a finished, polished essay. The purpose of this exercise is only to allow you to see how the gathering of the notes allows you to create a shape for an essay.

Stage 5: Organizing the Notes

If you have done the exercises above, you can already see how important this next stage of the writing process is. To me, it seems that good essays are born or die during the stage in which notes are organized. As I have already said, there is no possible way in which your mind can keep all you need to know to write and organize an essay together without some help. There is no way in which your mind can master all the material you generate in order to see what organization you might use to convey it. To help your mind handle that unwieldy mass of material, you not only take notes (which are, as we said, your way of thinking-on-paper), but you physically stack, gather, and shuffle them. The shuffling is what allows you to see—to visualize—what all those materials might yield in the way of a new idea, a thesis statement, a relationship, a hypothesis. For this to work, however, you must be absolutely sure to take your notes on note slips (preferably 4 × 6), rather than on full-size sheets of paper. Further, you must not ever take more than one note per note slip. I have seen students with notes of all kinds taken on full sheets of paper try to organize an essay, and they must go through a very frustrating and usually futile exercise in drawing circles and arrows around separate points, scissoring out half-pages and taping them to other half-pages. What they are trying to do is *see*—actually see—what ought to come first, second, and third in their essay. The easiest way to do that, of course, is simply to have one note per note slip, and to spread all of the note slips out in front of you to see what might go where. In my own experience, the sequence goes something like this:

1. You take the notes, of all the kinds named in Stage 4—and perhaps of a few additional kinds you discover yourself.

2. You spread them out on a large desk or table, reading through them and beginning to gather them together into stacks on the basis of a judgement you make about which ones seem to be about roughly the same thing, or to make a similar point.

3. You do a second gathering in which you make a judgement about which of those separate, first gatherings might themselves constitute a subheading under a still larger heading. This process is difficult to talk about or understand in the abstract, but I can give you an example of how it worked for one student. He was writing an essay about Stephen Crane's story "The Blue Hotel" and began by taking notes on the story that revealed that it contained much violence, both submerged and actual. But he discovered that some of the notes he seemed driven to take were not about violence, but about lies or deception in the story. As he bundled and rebundled his note slips, he discovered that both the "violence" bundle and the "deception" bundle could be gathered together under one heading: the story really seemed to say "Deception generates violence." This thesis statement grew out of the bundling and rebundling process, and I doubt that he could have arrived at that

thesis had he not been able to *see*—literally see—the two stacks of note slips in front of him.

4. What this last account suggests is that if, as many researchers (such as Janet Emig) have discovered, the physical act of writing things down helps you to think, it is also true that the physical act of shuffling note slips can help to bring ideas to you. It can certainly, at the very least, help you see how you might organize your ideas and put you in control of what is in my own experience the most frustrating and frightening part of the writing process: that time in which you have lots of material—on your table or desk, written in the margins of books—but absolutely no idea of how to organize all those helter-skelter half-formed ideas and hunches.

5. In this act of grouping and regrouping note slips, you will also practice some selectivity. Some slips simply will refuse to fit into any of the groupings you can imagine, and those will be rejected. However, you can never be sure that they will not eventually work themselves into the essay, so you should never throw them away. Nothing is more frustrating than finding, in the actual writing of your essay, that you *now* can see exactly where a certain idea or quotation can fit, and discovering, too late, that that note has been carried away with the trash. Put the note slips you do not think you will use aside, with a rubber band around them, and save them "just in case."

Stage 6: The Incubation Phase

What happens if you have done all this preliminary research and gathering and shuffling and bundling, and you *still* do not have a thesis forming? This is a tricky problem, for you cannot strangle the Muse and force her to give you an idea. But it helps to know what is happening in you at this phase, if only so that you might be better able to make it work for you.

This phase is called, for better or worse, the "incubation" phase, and it marks the end of what I have called "the mess" end of the writing process and the beginning of "the mystery" end.

It is a distressing phase to live with, and the only consolation the writer has is that eventually it ends, with what scientists call the "Eureka" experience, and mathematician Martin Gardner calls the "Aha!" phase. In my experience, this is the stage during which many students give up and choose a new topic, because they feel they are at a dead end, and just can not see how they can possibly organize the material they have gathered into an essay. But in fact, this is the stage during which there is not much that you can do. What you need to do, having done all the research and thinking and note-taking and brainstorming possible, is simply *lie in wait* for the idea to come to you. And by "idea," here, you understand by now that we mean the order in which you can present your facts in such a way that they constitute a new idea. That idea will come to you from somewhere on the fringes of your consciousness, and undoubtedly when you least expect it. The good writer even has several notions, several hunches incubating at the same time, so that if one thing does not "come together" in time, he or she has others that will.

What is happening during this stage of writing? What *is* this stage of writing? If you tried the exercises at the end of Chapter 6, you watched your own mind shape hunches or "itches" into ideas. You know that you—as do all people—have not only a conscious, thinking mind, but a less accessible part of your mind that is nonetheless thinking—in its own way—all the time. It is this part of the mind that philosopher William James called the "fringe consciousness," and Arthur Koestler and others call the "ante-consciousness." Especially in Koestler's way of describing this part of the mind, we can think of it as a kind of hallway or chamber passing between our conscious and our unconscious. It is there that new ideas form, and because this is so, it helps for the writer to try to foster a special kind of awareness of that special place; it helps for the writer to listen closely to catch those ideas, even though they whisper rather than shout. As far back as Plato, thinkers have said that we must already know something before we can discover it. We have to have some hunch or itch and then let it work itself into our conscious mind. Stories of this process happening among thinkers and writers are easy to find. "One evening," says Henri Poincaré the mathematician, "contrary to my custom, I drank black coffee and could not sleep. Ideas rose in crowds, I felt them collide until pairs interlocked, so to speak, making a stable combination" (Hadamard, p. 14). It was during what Edgar Allen Poe called the "hypnagogic state," the state between waking and sleeping, that the new idea came. This is often the case. If we want to fall asleep, we do not think about falling asleep; we let our mind wander freely. If we want to catch hold of an idea, we do not focus on the idea; we do what some people call "looking aside." We direct our attention else-where and let the idea come to us. If we want to think of a solution to a problem, we partly think about it, and we partly "sleep on it." The "sleeping on it" is as essential to the process as is the active thinking. If you want to dream, go to bed with a half-

"IF IT WANTS TO DREAM, WE COULD GIVE IT SOME VAGUE, UNSTRUCTURED PROBLEM TO MULL OVER DURING THE NIGHT."

shaped idea that needs to be sharpened; if you want to find the thesis that will pull your half-formed ideas together, go to sleep. As Jacques Hadamard describes it:

> It most often happens that such a result [the half-formed idea] needs to be digested, or, to say it differently, to be classed in

our fringe-consciousness, so as to be "ready for use." Then it can easily and rapidly find its place in the synthetic scheme of deduction. That such a process is unconscious and that it corresponds to an incubation stage cannot be denied. Having reached an intermediate result which seems to be useful for further investigation in many cases I deliberately leave the whole work sleeping till the following day, when I find it "ready for use" (p. 63).

Sleeping on it is one tactic for coaxing the preconscious idea into your consciousness; *moving around* is another. Most writing books tell you to find a quiet place in which to sit and write, and this is partially true. Or, rather, it is true for some phases of writing. But when you need to coax the idea into full awareness, it may well be better to move around, to get the blood and the ideas flowing. Here is Nietzsche's account of the way he wrote part of *Thus Spake Zarathustra*:

That decisive section, "Old and New Tables," was composed during the arduous ascent from the station to Eza, that wonderful Moorish Eyrie. When my creative energy flowed most freely, my muscular activity was always greatest. The body is inspired; let us leave the "soul" out of consideration. I might often have been dancing; I used to walk through the hills for seven or eight hours on end without a hint of fatigue. I slept well, laughed a good deal—I was perfectly vigorous and patient (Ghiselin, p. 203).

The moral seems to be if you are stuck for a thesis, go out for a walk. Play ball. Wash the dishes. Let the idea have a chance to sneak in around the edges of your consciousness. Do not, of course, fool yourself into thinking you need to walk around or play or do the dishes if what you really need to do is shape an idea you already have into good, clear paragraphs. But if the idea is still unclear, you might consider moving around while the idea makes its way into your consciousness. Remember the experience you had while you did the exercises in Chapter 6. Remember that you alternated looking for an idea, and waiting for the idea to come to you; remember the alternation of active and passive "thinking."

When an idea comes, it will always be partly as a result of conscious and deliberate thinking, partly as a result of a kind of accidental stumbling upon ideas ("Eureka" thinking), and partly as a result of a simple, unconscious perculating of the ideas found in one of the two other ways. Stephen Jay Gould's account of how Charles Darwin developed his theory of natural selection follows.

86. Read the essay and then summarize it, paying special attention to the *process* by which Darwin reached his theory of natural selection. If possible, give an account of the way some idea came to *you* as a result of some combination of conscious thought, accidental discovery, and subconscious "gestation."

Stephen Jay Gould.
"Darwin's Middle Road." From *Natural History*

"We began to sail up the narrow strait lamenting," narrates Odysseus.

For on the one hand lay Scylla, with twelve feet all dangling down; and six necks exceeding long, and on each a hideous head, and therein three rows of teeth set thick and close, full of black death. And on the other mighty Charybdis sucked down the salt sea water. As often as she belched it forth, like a cauldron on a great fire she would seethe up through all her troubled deeps.

Odysseus managed to swerve around Charybdis, but Scylla grabbed six of his finest men and devoured them in his sight, "the most pitiful thing mine eyes have seen of all my travail in searching out the paths of the sea."

False lures and dangers often come in pairs in our legends and metaphors—consider the frying pan and the fire or the devil and the deep blue sea. Prescriptions for avoidance emphasize either a dogged steadiness—the straight and narrow of Christian evangelists—or an averaging between unpleasant alternatives—the golden mean of Aristotle. The idea of steering a course between undesirable extremes emerges as a central prescription for a sensible life.

The nature of scientific creativity is both a perennial topic of discussion and a prime candidate for seeking a golden mean. The two extreme positions have not been directly competing for allegiance of the unwary. They have, rather, replaced each other sequentially, with one now in the ascendancy, the other eclipsed.

The first, inductivism, held that great scientists are primarily great observers and patient accumulators of information. New and significant theory, the inductivists claimed, can only arise from a firm foundation of facts. In this architectural view, each fact is a brick in a structure built without blueprints. Any talk or thought about theory (the completed building) is fatuous and premature before the bricks are set. Inductivism once commanded great prestige within science and even represented an "official" position of sorts, for it touted, however falsely, the utter honesty, complete objectivity, and almost automatic nature of scientific progress toward final and incontrovertible truth.

Yet, as its critics so rightly claimed, inductivism also depicted science as a heartless, almost inhuman discipline offering no legitimate place to quirkiness, intuition, and all the other subjective attributes adhering to our vernacular concept of genius. Great scientists, the critics argued, are distinguished more by their powers of hunch and synthesis than by their skill in experiment or observation. The criticisms are certainly valid and I welcome the dethroning of inductivism during the past thirty years as a necessary prelude to better understanding. While attacking inductivism so strongly, some critics have tried to substitute an alternative "eureka" view of scientific creativity. (The name refers, of course, to the legendary story of Archimedes running naked through the streets of Syracuse shouting "Eureka" [I have discovered it] when water displaced by his bathing body washed the scales abruptly from his eyes and suggested a method for measuring volumes.) In this eureka view, creativity is an ineffable something, accessible only to persons of genius. It arises like a bolt of lightning, unanticipated, unpredictable, and unanalyzable—and the bolts strike only a few special people. We ordinary mortals must stand in awe and thanks.

I am equally disenchanted by both these opposing extremes. Inductivism reduces genius to dull, rote operations; eurekaism elevates it to an inaccessible status, more in the domain of intrinsic mystery than in a realm where we might understand and learn from it. Might we not marry the good features of each view and abandon both the elitism of eureka and the pedestrian qualities of inductivism.

In the hagiography of science, a few men hold such high positions that all arguments about creativity must apply to them if they are to have any validity. Charles Darwin, as the principal saint of evolutionary biology, has therefore been presented both as an inductivist and as a primary example of eureka. I will attempt to show that these interpretations are equally inadequate and that recent scholarship on Darwin's own odyssey toward the theory of natural selection supports an intermediate position.

So great was the prestige of inductivism in his own day that Darwin himself fell under its sway and, as an old man, falsely depicted his youthful accomplishments in its light. In an autobiography, which was written as a lesson in morality for his children and not intended for publication, he penned some famous lines that misled historians for nearly a hundred years. Describing his path to the theory of natural selection, he claimed:

"I worked on true Baconian principles, and without any theory collected facts on a wholesale scale."

The inductivist interpretation focuses on Darwin's five years aboard the *Beagle* and views his transition from a student for the ministry to the nemesis of preachers as a result of his keen powers of observation applied to the whole world. Thus, the traditional story goes, Darwin's eyes opened wider and wider as he saw, in sequence, the bones of giant South American fossil mammals, the turtles and finches of the Galápagos, and the marsupial fauna of Australia. The truth of evolution and its mechanism of natural selection crept up gradually upon him as he sifted facts in a sieve of utter objectivity.

The inadequacies of this tale are best illustrated by the falsity of its conventional premier example—the so-called Darwin's finches of the Galápagos. We now know that although these birds share a recent and common ancestry on the South American mainland, they have radiated into an impressive array of species on the outlying Galápagos. Few terrestrial species manage to cross the wide oceanic barrier between South America and the Galápagos. The fortunate migrants often find an island devoid of the competitors that limited their opportunities on the crowded mainland. Hence, the finches evolved into roles normally occupied by other birds and developed their famous set of adaptations for feeding—seed crushing, insect eating, even grasping and manipulating a cactus needle to dislodge insects from plants. Isolation, both from the mainland and among the islands themselves, provided an opportunity for separation, independent adaptation, and speciation.

According to the traditional view, Darwin discovered these finches, correctly inferred their history, and wrote the famous lines in his notebook: "If there is the slightest foundation for these remarks the zoology of Archipelagoes will be worth examining; for such facts would undermine the stability of Species." But, as with so many heroic tales, from Washington's cherry tree to the piety of Crusaders, hope rather than truth motivates the common reading. Darwin found the finches to be sure. But at the time he did not recognize them as variants of a common stock. In fact, he didn't even record the island of discovery for many of them; some of his labels just read "Galápagos Islands." So much for his immediate recognition of the role of isolation in the formation of new species. He reconstructed the evolutionary tale only after his return to London, when a British Museum ornithologist correctly identified all the birds as finches.

The famous quotation from his notebook refers to Galápagos tortoises and to the claim of native inhabitants that they can "at once pronounce from which Island any Tortoise may have been brought" from subtle differences in size and shape of body and scales. This is a statement of different, and much reduced, order from the traditional tale of finches. For the finches are true and separate species—a living example of evolution. The subtle differences among tortoises represent minor geographical variation within a single species. It is a jump in reasoning, albeit a valid one as we now know, to argue that such small differences can be amplified to produce a new species. All creationists, after all, acknowledged geographical variation (consider human races), but argued that the differences could not proceed beyond the rigid limits of a created archetype.

I don't wish to downplay the pivotal influence of the *Beagle* voyage on Darwin's career. It gave him space, freedom, and time to think in his favored mode of independent self-stimulation. (His ambivalence toward university life and his middling performance there by conventional standards reflected his unhappiness with a curriculum of received wisdom.) He writes from South America in 1834: "I have not one clear idea about cleavage, stratification, lines of upheaval. I have no books, which tell me much and what they do I cannot apply to what I see. In consequence I draw my own conclusions, and most gloriously ridiculous ones they are."

The rocks and plants and animals that he saw did provoke him to the crucial attitude of doubt—midwife of all creativity. Sydney, Australia, 1836. Darwin wonders why a rational God would create so many marsupials in Australia since nothing about its climate or geography suggests any superiority for pouches: "I had been lying on a sunny bank and was reflecting on the strange character of the animals of this country as compared to the rest of the World. An unbeliever in everything beyond his own reason might exclaim, 'Surely two distinct Creators must have been at work.' "

Nonetheless, Darwin returned to London without an evolutionary theory. He suspected the truth of evolution but had no mechanism to explain it. Natural selection did not arise from any direct reading of facts during the *Beagle's* voyage, but from two subsequent years of thought and struggle as reflected in a series of remarkable notebooks that have been unearthed and published during the past twenty years. In these notebooks we see Darwin testing and abandoning a number of theories, pursuing a multitude of false leads—so much for his later claim about recording facts with an empty mind. He read philosophers, poets, and economists, always searching for meaning and insight—so much for the notion that natural selection arose inductively from the *Beagle's* facts. Later he labeled one notebook as "full of metaphysics on morals."

Yet if this tortuous path belies the Scylla of inductivism, it has engendered an equally simplistic myth, the Charybdis of eureka. In his maddeningly misleading autobiography, Darwin does record a eureka and suggests that natural selection struck him as a sudden, serendipitous flash after more than a year of groping frustration:

> In October 1838, that is, fifteen months after I had begun my systematic inquiry, I happened to read for amusement Malthus on Population, and being well prepared to appreciate the struggle for existence which everywhere goes on from long-continued observation of the habits of animals and plants, it at once struck me that under these circumstances favorable variations would tend to be preserved, and unfavorable ones to be destroyed. The result of this would be the formation of new species. Here, then, I had at last got a theory by which to work.

Yet, again, the notebooks belie Darwin's later recollections—in this case by their utter failure to record, at the time it happened, any special exultation over his Malthusian insight. He inscribes it as a fairly short and sober entry without a single exclamation point, although he habitually used two or three in moments of excitement. He did not drop everything and reinterpret a confusing world in its light. On the very next day, he wrote an even longer passage on the sexual curiosity of primates.

The theory of natural selection arose neither as a workmanlike induction from nature's facts nor as a mysterious bolt from Darwin's subconscious, triggered by an accidental reading of Malthus. It emerged instead as the result of a conscious and productive search, proceeding in a ramifying but ordered manner, and utilizing both the facts of natural history and an astonishingly broad range of insights from disparate disciplines far from his own. Darwin trod the middle path between inductivism and eurekaism. His genius is neither pedestrian nor inaccessible.

Darwinian scholarship has exploded since the centennial of the *Origin* in 1959. The publication of Darwin's notebooks and the attention devoted by several scholars to the two crucial years between the *Beagle's* docking and the demoted Malthusian insight has clinched the argument for a "middle path" theory of Darwin's creativity. Two particularly important works focus on the broadest and narrowest scales.

Howard E. Gruber's masterful intellectual and psychological biography of this phase in Darwin's life (*Darwin on Man*, E.P. Dutton, 1974) traces all the false leads and turning points in Darwin's search. Gruber shows that Darwin was continually proposing, testing, and abandoning hypotheses, and that he never simply collected facts in a blind way. He began with a fanciful theory involving the idea that new species arise with a prefixed life span and worked his way gradually, if fitfully, toward an idea of extinction by competition in a world of struggle. He recorded no exultation upon reading Malthus, because the jigsaw puzzle was only missing a piece or two at the time.

Silvan S. Schweber has reconstructed, in detail as minute as the record will allow, Darwin's activities during the few weeks before Malthus ("The Origin of the *Origin* Revisited," *Journal of the History of Biology*, vol. 10). He argues that the final pieces arose not from new facts in natural history, but from Darwin's intellectual wanderings in distant fields. In particular, Darwin read a long review of social scientist and philosopher Auguste Comte's most famous work, the *Cours de philosophie positive.* He was particularly struck by Comte's insistence that a proper theory be predictive and capable of making quantitative statements.

He then turned to Dugald Stewart's *On the Life and Writing of Adam Smith,* and imbibed the basic belief of the Scottish economists that theories of overall social structure must begin by analyzing the unconstrained actions of individuals. (Natural selection is, above all, a theory about the struggle of individual organisms for success in reproduction.)

Then, searching for quantification, he read a lengthy analysis of work by the most famous statistician of his time—the Belgian Adolphe Quetelet. In the review of Quetelet, he found, among other things, a forceful statement of Malthus's quantitative claim—that population would grow geometrically and food supplies only arithmetically, thus guaranteeing an intense struggle for existence. In fact, Darwin had read the Malthusian statement several times before; but only now was he prepared to appreciate its significance. Thus, he did not turn to Malthus by accident, and he already knew what it contained. His "amusement," we must assume, consisted only in a desire to read in its original formulation the familiar statement that had so impressed him in Quetelet's secondary account.

In reading Schweber's detailed account of the moments preceding Darwin's formulation of the theory of natural selection, I was particularly struck by the absence of deciding influence from his own field of biology. The immediate precipitators were a social scientist, an economist, and a statistician. If genius has any common denominator, I would advocate breadth of interest and the ability to construct fruitful analogies between fields.

In fact, I believe that the theory of natural selection should be viewed as an extended analogy—whether conscious or unconscious on Darwin's part I do not know—to the laissez-faire economics of Adam Smith. The essence of Smith's argument is a paradox of sorts: if you want an ordered economy providing maximal benefits to all, then let individuals compete and struggle for their own advantages. The result, after eliminating the inefficient and appropriate sorting of the rest, will be a stable, harmonious polity. Apparent order arises naturally from the struggle among individuals, not from predestined principles or higher control.

We know that Darwin's uniqueness does not reside in his support for the idea of evolution—scores of scientists had preceded him in this. His special contribution rests upon his documentation and upon the novel character of his theory about how evolution operates. Previous evolutionists had proposed unworkable schemes based on internal perfecting tendencies and inherent directions. Darwin advocated a natural and testable theory based on immediate interaction among individuals (his opponents considered it heartlessly mechanistic). The theory of natural selection is a creative transfer to biology of Adam Smith's basic argument for a rational economy: the balance and order of nature does not arise from a higher, external (divine) control or from the existence of laws operating directly upon the whole, but from struggle among individuals for their own benefits (in modern terms, for the transmission of their genes to future generations through differential success in reproduction).

Many people are distressed to hear such an argument. Does it not compromise the integrity of science if some of its primary conclusions originate by analogy with contemporary politics and culture rather than from data of the discipline itself? In a famous letter to Engels, Karl Marx identified the similarities between natural selection and the English social scene:

> It is remarkable how Darwin recognizes among beasts and plants his English society with its division of labor, competition, opening up of new markets, "invention," and the Malthusian "struggle for existence." It is Hobbes' *bellum omnium contra omnes* (the war of all against all).

Yet Marx was a great admirer of Darwin—and in this apparent paradox lies resolution. For reasons involving all the themes I have emphasized here—that inductivism is inadequate, that creativity demands breadth, and that analogy is a profound source of insight—great thinkers cannot be divorced from their social background.

But the *source* of an idea is one thing; its *truth* or *fruitfulness* is another. The psychology and utility of discovery are very different subjects indeed. Darwin may have cribbed the idea of natural selection from economics, but it may still be right. As the German socialist Karl Kautsky wrote in 1902: "The fact that an idea emanates from a particular class, or accords with their interests, of course proves nothing as to its truth or falsity." In this ironic case, Adam Smith's system of laissez-faire does not work in his own domain of economics, for it leads to oligopoly and revolution, rather than to order and harmony. Struggle among individuals does, however, seem to be the law of nature.

Many people use such arguments about social context to ascribe great insights primarily to the indefinable phenomenon of good luck. Thus, Darwin was lucky to be born rich, lucky to be on the *Beagle,* lucky to live amidst the ideas of his age, lucky to trip over Parson Malthus—essentially little more than a man in the right place at the right time. Yet, when we read of his personal struggle to understand, the breadth of his concerns and study, and the directedness of his search for a mechanism of evolution, we can understand why Pasteur made his famous quip that fortune favors the prepared mind.

Stage 7: Forming or Shaping the Hypothesis: Getting the Thesis Statement

Once the incubation phase ends, you should have the beginnings of some fairly clear notions of what your subject is going to be, of the approach you want to take with it, and its range ("I'm not going to talk about censorship in movies, but about censorship in newspapers"). To find the *specific* form of your thesis statement, however, takes some conscious work, and there are some tactics you can use and some questions you can ask yourself to discover the most precise and satisfying form that thesis statement might take. With all of your note slips in mind and in hand, then, and with all of your research and reading behind you, you can begin answering such questions as those I have listed below.

One of the secrets to success at this stage is not just sitting and thinking about what your thesis is, but actually doing some writing, including writing out answers to the kinds of questions listed below. At this stage, you are not yet "writing the essay," but you are writing preliminary forays, paragraphs, hunches that are on their way to becoming an essay. And you proceed this way for two reasons. First, writing "just for my own eyes, to see what and how I'm thinking or might be thinking" is a tactic for avoiding the horrible paralysis that can come when the writer sits down and realizes "This is it! I'm actually *writing the essay*!" What you need is a kind of transitional stage to ease you into the writing of a rough draft, and writing tentative hypotheses, possible paragraphs, and what scientists call "relay reports" (summaries of what you have now, and where you might go with that material in a next step) are all ways of easing you into a rough draft. It is a much shorter and easier step from this stage to a rough draft and a final essay than it is from a blank page to a finished essay. (And, of course, you never know how many of those more casual sentences you toss off at this stage might work their way into your final essay.)

You also write up tentative hypotheses and answers to questions at this stage for another reason: to be able to *see* what you are thinking. People who have video-taped writers writing are not surprised to discover that good writers pause, scan, and reread what they have written much more frequently than do poor writers. Good writers know that seeing what they have written is a way of seeing what they may want to write next. Jean Paul Sartre gave up writing entirely when his left eye was hemorrhaging (his right eye had been bad from birth), because, he said, "I cannot see what I write." For him, writing was a way of seeing what he was thinking. I think writing works this way for everyone, so at this stage of the writing process, writing up preliminary hunches allows you to *see* what you may be thinking, to test out ways of saying things on paper, and to do that without penalty and without fear of being awkward or "wrong."

To see what you might want to say, try answering the questions below, or following the procedures suggested. Remember these are to be done *on paper*.

1. Never insist, during this stage of writing, that a solution be complete. Never insist that a possible thesis statement or hypothesis be an absolutely precise one. Ask yourself questions like these: "Are there *any parts* of this thesis that I might want to, or be able to, work with?" "Are

there any parts of this thesis that could be expanded? Refined? That might be incorporated into a more comprehensive thesis statement later?"

2. Venture a statement that *might* turn out to be the thesis for the essay: "Conrad's novel is X, X, and X, but not Y." Then, do what Synectics people call the "Itemized Response" tactic. That is, venture the statement and then write down three reasons why you like that idea, or why you might be able to work with it. Your sentences might be something like, "I like this thesis because it will allow me to write a short paper rather than a long one." Or, "I won't have to do any research if I use this thesis." Or, "I already have an interest in X, so this essay will allow me to do some digging I'd like to do anyway."

3. As you generate potential thesis statements or hypotheses, try to articulate to yourself what each such statement will and will not allow you to do and say. For instance: "If I start here, I won't be able to talk about X"; "Connecting A and B will allow me to make a digression and talk about C as well, which I'd really like to do anyway."

4. At the same time, once you have a partial answer or tentative thesis statement, try what the Synectics people call a "wish/goal" process. State to yourself what you want this thesis to do that it is not doing yet: "I wish this thesis would allow me to talk about A, B, and C, as well as about D, E, and F." Expressing the wish, they say, often makes it easier for you to find the way that *will* allow you to say what you want to say.

5. All the while that you are forcing potential thesis statements, also force yourself to come up with tentative titles for this essay. For many beginning writers, a title is an afterthought. But a title is a way of seeing what you are writing, and it may help you shape the materials you have if you imagine a title that pulls them all together. This tentative title will change, of course, maybe as many as five times. But each title encapsulates one way of seeing what you are doing.

6. Each time you think of a potential thesis statement, allow yourself time to explore it *thoroughly* before you abandon it and go on to another. Most people are far too impatient with their own fledgling ideas and do not give them a chance to develop into something sharp and fine. Do not be too critical of new ideas too soon. Give them a chance. By all means, write them down and stand back and look at them before you reject them. As we have said time and again, the physical act of writing them down may well generate refinements in them, and even help them grow.

7. If you are at a loss for a thesis statement to use in writing an essay in response to some material you have read, consider that you may be able to improve upon the ideas you have read that you find to be only partially accurate, partially satisfactory. You need not completely disagree with a writer, but maybe you can see where he or she is partly right, partly wrong. An exploration of the ways in which that writer is partly right and partly wrong can become your essay.

8. If your ideas seem to be going off in two different directions at once, do not arbitrarily decide to throw out one of those sets of ideas. It may be, and often is, that the two apparently different subjects are related quite closely. Remember what we have said about forcing connections between concepts. Try generating a thesis statement that comprehends these apparently disparate ideas by going through the procedures we have used throughout this book, especially in Chapters 3, 9, 10, 11, 12, and 13. All of those exercises we did—including conceptual play in which you tried to discover how X is like Y, and in which you played with definitions, metaphors, analogies, making distinctions and connections—should be useful at this stage of writing. If necessary, go back through the book and look over all those questions on concepts again, checking to see which ones might help you see your way to a thesis statement.

9. When you are looking for connectors between apparently unrelated things, never underestimate the power of common sense. A physician at UCLA has been exploring the

nature and function and effects of Beta Endorphin in the brain. Beta Endorphin is a natural pain killer produced by the body and is much more powerful than morphine. She reasoned that this being so, the levels of Beta Endorphin in the body might be expected to rise during pregnancy and reach a peak at about the onset of labor. She tested the hypothesis. She was right. No amount of reading or research could have yielded that hypothesis; common sense did.

10. If all of your materials seem to be swirling through your head and not settling into anything remotely resembling a thesis statement, try talking out your ideas with a friend. This is not to say that talking and writing are the same skills, but that a person who has some distance from your materials can sometimes provide the magical question that will pull it all together for you. Talk about your fledgling ideas with someone else, and you might find them clarifying and sharpening as you talk. If you are lucky enough to find a listener who will respond with something like "Yes, but what about. . . .," all the better for you. In the act of explaining and defending your ideas to another person, you are also explaining and defending them to yourself.

11. I have said that you do not want to be in too great a hurry to throw out some of your material even though it appears that you are going in two directions at once, because it might turn out that those two separate directions are really two separate parts of a coherent thesis. But if, after a reasonable length of time, you cannot get the two to come together, consider selecting one set and abandoning, at least temporarily, the other set. It becomes, in other words, a time to practice some kind of *selectivity*. As Elisio Vivas says in *Creation and Discovery:* "The artistic process does not consist in lowering a bucket into the muddy current of the actual and emptying all one picks up into a book. The artist must wait till the bucket settles before he can hope to catch the elusive silvery animals that shall make his feast. It is, in plain terms, a process of discrimination and selection" (pp. 24–25).

Of course you will notice that Vivas expresses his idea through an image—just as we did in Chapter 13. But you will also notice that as a writer, selecting will be as important to you as is combining. When you decide, for instance, to write about "censorship," it is not at all true that everything you know or can possibly imagine about censorship immediately becomes a part of your essay. As Daniel Dennett says in his book *Brainstorms*: "It takes two to invent anything: The one makes up combinations; the other one chooses, recognizes what he wishes and what is important to him in the mass of the things which the former has imparted to him" (p. 71). So in a way you have two minds: one that generates material, and another that decides which parts of that material you can and should use, and which you cannot. One mind gathers; the other selects from what you have gathered only the best and most useful. If you decide to write an essay on censorship, the one part of your mind gathers together all you know or can think of on the subject; the other part decides which things are relevant to your thesis, and which things to throw out.

12. What if you have read all the materials you could read, done all of the research, and are still without any notion of what you might use for a thesis statement? In such a case, it may help you to run through all of the practices and procedures we have played with throughout this book. In short, you may want to ask questions like these:

1. What would you like to *call* the phenomenon you have been reading about, and why? (Go back to Chapters 3 and 8 especially for further inspiration, if necessary.) Do you like the writer's namings (or conceptions) for things? Why or why not? A thorough discussion of why you do or do not like the namings can become your essay. Even if you like them, do you think they could benefit from being sharpened?

2. How are A and B related? That is, how is this phenomenon/attitude/habit/person related to that phenomenon/attitude/habit/person? Or how is this idea related to some other idea it does not seem to resem-

ble, but *does* resemble, in origin, function, purpose, or effect?

3. We have talked a good bit about words like *source, nature,* and *function.* Put them to work for you as you look for your thesis. Ask yourself, "What does that X do?" What, that is, is the function of that myth/ phrase/habit/response/behavior/law/point of view? Where does it come from? How did it happen? What caused it?

4. We have also talked about *context.* Put what you know about context to work for you as you look for your thesis. Ask yourself: Why would this writer make the assertions he or she does? What are the suppositions underlying his or her writings? Or, what are the assumptions underlying this essay/theory/behavior/assertion? Do you *like* these assumptions? Why or why not?

5. What is the *range of convenience* of the idea you have just read about? That is, does the thing apply more widely than the writer recognized? More narrowly?

6. Is this phenomenon/attitude/habit/theory part of some larger entity, and if so, what *is* that larger entity? Here, you will be thinking about relationships like part to whole, and saying that, for instance, a certain phenomenon is really not a separate phenomen, but a part of another, larger phenomenon. In such a case, your essay becomes an exploration of that relationship of part to whole. For instance, is the Moral Majority's concern for controlling sex and violence on television a separate, isolated concern, or is it really a part of a larger picture, and if so, what is that larger issue, as you see it?

7. *Whole and part* is only one set of oppositions that a thinker and writer might use to arrive at a new idea. Other useful, generative oppositions are these: alive/ dead; small/great; anterior/posterior; minor/major, in/ out; field/ground; central/peripheral; then/now; present/future; surface/substance; apparent/real. Think

of others. Imagine an essay that is structured in this way: "The apparent cause for X is Y, but the real cause for X is. . . ." Or, "In the past, religion functioned as an X, but now it seems to function as. . . ." Or, "What captures the viewer's attention when he or she looks at this painting is X, but what is also important is. . . ." All of these are essays that are inspired by thinking of such oppositions.

8. We have played a good bit throughout this book, and especially in Chapter 7, with causal connections. You might find your thesis by considering such questions as: "How did this phenomenon/attitude/habit happen? What caused it? How was it created or generated? What circumstances combined to cause it? Whose fault was it? Reread the excerpts of writings in Chapter 7 to see the range of possibilities for the writer who analyzes causes in his or her essay.

9. If you are writing about another person's theory or explanation, you might find your essay topic by considering the *implications* of the writer's theory, hypothesis, or idea, as we did with Roger Brown's excerpt in Chapter 3.

10. One way of discovering a new idea is to turn an existing way of thinking about a phenomenon on its head. Reverse the usual causality. Psychologists have assumed that REM (Rapid Eye Movement) sleep is evidence that the sleeper is dreaming, and that the dreams are causing the rapid eye movements. But in a recent *Science '80* article, some scientists proposed that it is not dreams that cause REM, but the reverse; that is, the eyes move of their own accord, for physiological reasons, and the unconscious feels compelled to provide a narrative that explains the movement of the eyes. These scientists may be correct or incorrect. The point is that the reversal of the usually accepted causality provides a new way of thinking about an old problem or issue and may yield a new idea better than the old one.

11. You might go back to Chapter 11 and review the exercises you did on making distinctions. You might discover that you can find the subject for your essay by making a discrimination between any two things in your data—two facts that have not been distinguished before. It is not X, you will say, that is responsible for Y, but something else. Your essay will be an explanation, justification, and defense of that position.

12. You might focus on the one detail that you encounter that seems to disprove a current theory; the one bit of evidence that does not seem to fit may yield the new idea or new hypothesis, no matter how preposterous that bit of evidence may seem. Here is one of my favorite stories in which that happens:

"In 1795 Lalande failed to discover the planet Neptune, although the logic of events should have led him to it. Lalande was making a map of the heavens. Every night he would observe and record the stars in a small area, and on a following night would repeat the observations. Once, in a second mapping of a particular area, he found that the position of one star relative to others in that part of the map had shifted. Lalande was a good astronomer and knew that such a shift was unreasonable. He crossed out his first observation of the shifting point of light, put a question mark next to his second observation, and let the matter go. And so, not until half a century later did Neptune get added to the list of planets in the solar system. From the aberrant movement, Lalande might have made the inference not that an error had been made but that a new planet of the solar system was present. But he was reasonable. And it was more reasonable to infer that one had made an error in observation than that one had found a new planet" (Bruner, Goodnow, and Austin, *A Study of Thinking*, pp. 104–5).

Consider that an irritatingly inconsistent bit of evidence might also yield a new idea for you—even when that bit of evidence is much simpler: "Why, of all of my brothers and sisters, does only one have drive or ambition?" is a question that might lead you to a new discovery: about yourself, your family; even about people in general.

13. Sometimes, in desperate circumstances in which you simply cannot get your materials to yield a thesis statement, you can find your way out of that difficulty if you simply write a *narrative* of the difficulties you have had with your subject. That narrative can *become* your essay: "When I first began to think about X, I thought that . . . but as time went on, it became clear to me that. . . ."

14. As you think about a possible thesis statement, you will find your job made much easier if you force yourself to predicate. You should force yourself to move from statements like "I'm writing about censorship," to statements with a verb: "Censorship [verb]." "Censorship *inspires* fear. Or trust." Or whatever you want to say.

15. Scan your preliminary scribblings for words that may in any way be construed as vestigial images. (Remember, an *image* is simply a word that can be pictured.) Those images may be trying to tell you something about a form or state of relatedness of which you are not yet fully conscious. We played with relationships expressed in images in Chapter 13, but sometimes such images are hard to tease out, especially when they are in your own sentences, and when they have almost become so common that we cease to be aware that they even are images. Look for words like *links, aspects, masks, involves,* or phrases like *revolves around, flows from, is a key to.* Once you have isolated them, think hard about what *kind* of link or aspect you might be thinking of. Some links are couplings that connect pipes and do not impede the flow between one section of pipe and another. Other links connect two objects, but prohibit free passage between the links. If your image is "links," you might learn something from that image. If your image is

aspects, then think about what aspects (or faces) your phenomenon has. Tease out the implications of those vestigial images, and you will be closer to knowing how you are thinking.

16. Scan your preliminary scratchings for words that seem highly charged in your own mind. A friend of mine is always writing about "the imagination," and yet he has never tried to define what he means by that. Try to see where charged words are in your writings. Get hold of them, wrestle with them, clarify them. They may turn out to be the subject for your essay.

17. In your preliminary writings, there is often one spot at which you touch upon a subject or issue and then pass quickly on to something else because, as students often say, "I don't want to get into that." As often as not, the thing they "don't want to get into" is precisely the thing that would be most interesting and useful and new to write about. When you find such a germ of a new idea, grab it, work with it, clarify it, cultivate it. It might turn out to be the subject for the best essay you ever wrote.

18. Finally, as you write up tentative thesis statements and venture sentences that might become part of your essay, imagine a reader over your shoulder who not only eavesdrops but also interrupts: "But . . . but . . . how about . . . what about . . . what if . . . isn't it possible instead that. . . ." Let your essay become an answer to this critical reader.

87. In the tenth suggestion above, I said that sometimes turning an existing way of looking at something on its head can yield a new idea. Just for fun, see if you can do this with any issue or problem. Does adolescence cause acne, or does acne cause adolescence? Turn something else on its head. See what you can discover.

88. Reread the twelfth suggestion above. See if you can think of or uncover another historical instance in which this failure to take into account the one bit of evidence that disproved the accepted theory cost us lots of lost time, and caused us to lose sight of something we may have wanted or needed to know.

89. Below you will find a short paragraph from Jerome Bruner's *On Knowing*. Carry this paragraph around with you for a week and write a very short essay (two or three paragraphs) in response to this paragraph every day. That is, you will write *seven* short essays, each of which will take a different approach.

> The degree to which a society elaborates a technology determines the amount of division of labor in the society. The rationale of a technology is that its tools are not such that each individual can be equipped with a full set of them. With technological advance more things are possible, but social and technical organization is increasingly necessary to bring them off. In effect, then, the sense of potency—the idea of the possible—increases in scope, but the artificer of the possible is now society rather than the individual (p. 160).

90. Construct a list of approaches that you have discovered are possible for you to use when you are interested in forming a thesis statement. Did you summarize? Provide an example of the process? Talk about how it originated historically? Distinguish between things like necessary and possible adjustments to this state of affairs? Object to Bruner's assertion? Qualify his assertion? What else? What have you learned about the resources you have available to you when you want to write an essay?

Stage 8: Writing the First Draft

In one sense, of course, you have been writing drafts since the beginning: since you first decided you wanted to write an essay. You wrote notes to yourself; you wrote "relay reports" to yourself to see how much information you had and where the holes in your knowledge that might need to be filled were; you wrote questions to yourself; you wrote potential assertions and thesis statements to see how they sounded. If you have been doing all of these things, the pump is primed, and sitting down to do the "real" writing should not be nearly so fearsome as it can be if you are used to sitting down to face a blank piece of paper. As I have said, part of the "secret" to making writing easier is fooling yourself in one of several ways. "I'm not really writing the essay yet; I'm only taking notes," is a good way to *ease into* the first draft.

There is another way of fooling yourself that might work. As I have said, many writing books claim that when you reach the writing stage, you should find a quiet place in which to work. This is partially true, but what you want to do is be careful not to get yourself too comfortable. It is very easy to fool yourself into thinking you are "working" (because you are, after all, sitting at your desk), when your body and mind are just comfortably humming along, producing nothing. The trick then, might be to fool yourself into believing you are in an emergency situation in order to get the adrenalin flowing. Deadlines are great for this. It is amazing how hard you can work on a paper the night before it is due. And it is equally amazing that you cannot persuade yourself to work the night before that. So if you can fool yourself into thinking you are in an emergency situation, before you really are, you will have a much easier time beginning to write a first draft.

How do you know that it is time for the "real" writing? This time may come at a different phase for each writer, and it may be that the signals are different for each writer. I know it is time for me to start writing first drafts when I start sleeping restlessly and keep jumping out of bed to take more note slips, and when the rubber bands around them can no longer hold the stacks together, and when I am afraid that if I do not capture some of the ideas and sentences that are running through my head, I will lose them forever and be sorry to have lost them. But other writers have other ways of working. Here are two accounts from writers whose signals are very different and whose ways of writing are, apparently, very different too.

Paul Horgan. From *Approaches to Writing: Reflections and Notes on the Art of Writing from a Career of Half a Century*

My own habit brings me to my work table at about the same time every day—roughly at half-past nine. But actually, the working day starts earlier. It starts on awakening, with a sort of bated breath in the thought, if I may put it so. Preparation for the morning's task gets under way in an induced and protected absent-mindedness, as if to allow the work in progress to come clear gradually, so that its daily rebirth suffers no jarring collisions with immediate reality, but establishes its own inner reality from which it will draw conviction. Absurd as it may appear to those in other vocations, any contact with a serious distraction or obligation elsewhere may, at this daily moment, disturb a balance already delicate. A phone call is a minor catastrophe and a knock on the door a potential disaster. Until the day's work can actually begin, a frowning selfishness protects all the ingredients of plan, design, idea, and will; and when it begins, it flows forth, if the day is a good one, or it struggles forth, if it is a poor one; but strangely, later it is difficult to tell by the evidence which pages came from fluent work and which from halting. It is again a reflection of a discipline we have mentioned (p. 10).

Horgan talks a great deal in this book about what he calls the "discipline of work," in which the writer simply gets up in the morning and goes about writing, allowing nothing to interfere between him and his writing. Every day, for so many hours, he sits at his desk, no matter what. But in the following extract, another author describes his own habits quite differently.

Philip Lapote. "Helping Children Start to Write."
From *Research on Composing*

With poetry . . . it doesn't hurt for me to feel a little rushed, upset, physically galvanized. I know something is up when I start hearing the echo, which makes even ordinary thoughts like 'I have to pick up the laundry' take on a melancholy bearing, a rhythmic certitude and significance that would be laughable at any other time when I am feeling more skeptical. This sudden conviction that I *know*, that I am walking in the fields of knowledge and everything is very simple, this impression of shadows and depth behind every thought and observation, is partly a function of the echo. . . . I can tell a poem is coming on from my stomach. A churning in the stomach is the infallible sign; it alone assures me that the emotion which precipitated the poem will last at least as long as it takes me to set down the first ten lines. I always worry that the feeling will desert me before I come to the end of the poem. . . . The crucial thing is that these physiological signals do exist, telling the writer when he or she is ready to get down to business. There may be long periods of waiting when nothing is happening: mental states filled with radio static or subvocal complaints whining and quarreling with each other. When I get like that, I don't see any point in writing. The work will only come out fractured and sour. I need to feel whole to write. Which means that I have to be patient with myself when I am feeling dispersed and wait for a better time. *Waiting is half the discipline of writing.*

I am not saying that writers should sit on their hands and do nothing while waiting for those somewhat mystical signals. On the contrary, they can take notes, edit other material— or they can go ahead and fight the mood and hope to bully it around to their way. They can try to stumble on their wholeness in the act of writing; with a bit of luck, they will. . . . But even the stalwarts . . . have to take a day's vacation occasionally before approaching a difficult scene and dally over minor material until they feel their energies have been marshalled for the climax.

I am convinced there is such a thing as *inner ripeness* in writing. One can ignore these signals or follow them, but the ripening process goes on nonetheless. . . . When you have picked the absolutely right moment to write, *then two-thirds of the technical problems which come up in composition are already solved* (pp. 143–44).

I have quoted several sentences of Lapote's, because they sound so right to me. You might consider whether they ring true to your own experience as well.

Once you have reached that stage—whether it comes with a galvanized jumping out of bed to write, a dogged, deliberate forcing of yourself to sit at a desk, a mystical echoic voice that tells you it is time to write, or a sense of simple eagerness and anticipation—there are some procedures you can follow that will make the writing of the first or rough draft much easier. A list of those procedures follows.

1. Never assume that you must—or even ought to—start by writing the first sentence of your essay. By definition, you do not and cannot know what the absolutely perfect open-

ing sentence will be until you have written the whole essay. More likely than not, your conclusion will split in two, and become both introduction and conclusion. *You cannot write an introduction to an essay that does not exist,* and it is a wonder the libraries are not full of the bodies of students who starved to death, sitting and waiting for that perfect introduction to come to them. It is far better simply to start writing a tentative introduction and assume that it will change at least once before the essay reaches its final form. If you read the introductions to essays, you will be able to tell that the confidence and control they exhibit are proof that they were not and could not have been written until the writer knew exactly where the essay was going.

2. Never sit down to write the draft, think of the major idea, and then reject it because you say to yourself, "I'll save that for later, for the grand finale." The natural tendency is to try to hold onto that big idea for last, but holding back is probably the second most common reason that people cannot get going on an essay. (The first reason is that they are waiting for the perfect opening sentence to come to them.)

3. Never try to polish and edit sentences in your draft, or find "just the right word." In the first place, you cannot tell what the perfect form of each sentence is until you see what the whole essay looks like. As I. A. Richards says in his *Philosophy of Rhetoric,* "A word is always a cooperative member of an organization, the utterance, and therefore cannot properly . . . be thought to have a meaning of its own, a fixed correct usage, or even a small limited number of correct usages unless by 'usage' we mean the whole *how* of its successful cooperations with other words" (p. 69). In the second place, as we have said, your mind simply cannot handle thinking, organizing, writing, polishing, and editing all at the same time. No one's can. In your draft, you should be concerned primarily with getting the ideas down in a logical sequence, and with paying attention to being as clear as you can be so that your reader can follow you from one point to the next. That is enough for anyone to concentrate on at one time. Keep your eye and

mind on your exposition and on the clarity of your essay. There is time enough to worry about polishing in later stages.

4. If you have taken notes as you should have and have grouped them, and then arranged the groups into larger groups, you already have a rough notion of what you will talk about first, second, and third. Follow that outline. In an ideal situation, writing the draft will simply be a matter of turning over note slips as you write, providing not much more than the "glue"—the transitions—that hold them together.

5. In a draft, you should not write all the way to the margins of your paper. We have watched how we write much slower than we think. While you are writing sentences down, no doubt other ideas will creep into your consciousness from that "ante-consciousness" or "fringe consciousness" we talked about earlier. Catch them as they fly by and jot them in the margins for development later. Do not go off the track, though. You can decide where these late thoughts fit in later, after you have finished the draft. Given what we have said about the essay, about how it is a way of thinking on paper, it is not surprising that new thoughts will intrude even as you write. If a new idea suddenly intrudes as you write, an idea that is so wonderful it transforms the shape of the entire essay, so much the better. Let it happen. Other ideas that come to you, however, should be "stored" in the margins, where you can pick them up later, consider if and how they might be related to your topic, and integrate them into a later draft if they fit.

6. As you continue through your note slips, shaping the essay as you go, keep one eye on your readers. Be sure you provide enough help so that they can follow your essay, but also be sure you anticipate your readers' objections and puzzlements: "Why?" "How did you get to this point from where you began?" "Haven't you forgotten about. . . ." Answer those curmudgeonly readers.

7. If you have to stop writing in the middle of the draft, try hard not to do so at a "dry spot," a place at which you do

not know what you want to say next. Doing that makes it much more difficult to come back to your desk, not only because you have to get your mind going again, but also because you will know that what confronts you is not just the finishing of a draft, but the struggling to think of what to say next. Ideally, when you leave off, you should jot down a word or two to help you remember exactly where your draft was going next.

8. Once you have written the draft, compare it against your note slips. See where some of those note slips you thought would not fit in might now fit quite well. See if the draft accurately represents what you intended to write.

Stage 9: Revising or Reformulating the First Draft

If *writing* the essay is never a one-stage process, *revising* it is probably never a one-step process either. It is a rare writer, I think, who can write a clear, concise, well-organized essay in a first attempt. It is an equally rare writer who can go from a first draft to a polished final draft with only a bit of tinkering intervening between one stage and the next. Thus several people, including Janet Emig, in *The Composing Processes of Twelfth Graders,* suggest that it may be best to use the word *reformulation* to describe what we do after the first draft, rather than the word *revision,* which has come to mean something more like minor tinkering or correcting of misspelled words. That kind of tinkering happens in the editing stage, which comes later. But in the reformulation phase, you will want to stand far back from your essay to see how the whole thing holds together, rather than standing up close, looking at details. In the reformulation phase, then, you might consider the following procedures:

1. Stand back from your whole essay. See if it all hangs together. Even if there are digressions, does the essay have a structure that you—and your readers—can follow?

2. As you stand back from the whole essay, check also to see if some separate paragraphs can be moved to make a point to better advantage. Are paragraphs five and eight, for instance, related in ways you had not noticed before?

Might it be wise for you to move them closer together to highlight their relationship?

3. Check the proportions in your essay. Is the essay all introduction? If it is about the relationship of one thing to another, is it weighted too heavily toward one thing, and not enough toward the other? If it is a compare and contrast essay, does it only discuss similarities, not dissimilarities? Is it in every possible way balanced? Does it have enough introduction, enough body, enough conclusion? (Keep in mind that very powerful essays often do not need a formal conclusion.)

4. Stand back from the whole essay and ask yourself: Could any sentences be shuffled about with no apparent damage to the essay's meaning? That is, is this essay composed of free-standing sentences, or is it really an essay in which the parts all add up to something in a *cumulative* way? Remember the "essay" about computers taking over the world in Chapter 2, and remember the way we said that it was not an essay, but a collection of miscellaneous observations. Make sure that is not true of your essay.

5. Stand back from your essay and ask yourself if you see any sentences that would be vague to a reader, but that are highly charged for you. If so, circle the phrase that makes the sentence vague and, in a subsequent draft, make sure you specify what you were thinking of when you composed that sentence. For example, the sentence "By having these two jobs, I was able to see the business in an entirely different perspective," may mean a great deal to you, but unless you specify what you mean by "different perspective," it means very little to your readers. After you circle such phrases, *push* on them; push on your own words to make them give up their secrets to you. By now, you should surely know that words not only express what we mean to other people but also teach us what we might be thinking and feeling—without knowing it. Because this is so, you can use the words you have written as a means of pushing you on to ideas beyond those you think you have.

6. Stand back from the draft. Judge what you now take it to be: Is it a reflection of your current place in the composing process? That is, is it full of ideas that are only half-formed? Is it a record of your own confusion or uncertainty about your material? Is it only a recording of the raw material you had on hand, rather than an organized essay? Is it a narrative ("and then, and then, and then"), or an analysis? Are two theses working against one another? Are there two different but possibly compatible theses in it?

7. Standing back from the draft, check to see if you have made an accurate assessment of what your reader can be expected to know and have made sure your reader will be able to follow you. "A shrewd decision about the knowledge that the writer can tacitly assume in his audience may be the most important decision the writer makes," says E. D. Hirsch in his *Philosophy of Composition* (p. 105).

8. As you stand back from the draft, ask yourself: "Do I like the sound and the tone of the voice in this essay? *Am I that person, or do I want to be known as that person?*"

9. With your draft beside you, follow it closely and *write a paraphrase of it,* just as you wrote paraphrases of writing excerpts from other people's essays throughout this book. Compare your paraphrase with your draft. Decide if you meant to say what you have said. Decide whether you might like the paraphrase better than the draft. Is it more clear, more simple, more graceful? If so, you have now finished your revision.

10. Have a friend paraphrase your draft if possible. Compare that paraphrase against your draft. Refine the draft everywhere you feel you were misunderstood.

11. If your tendency is always to say too little, if you fail to explain yourself or defend your assertions, or if you often are told that you make a point and then run from it and do not explain or defend it, try this tactic during the reformulation phase: take your draft and *add two sentences* in between every two in the draft. You may be

surprised at the added clarity and specificity you will find in the expanded version.

12. If your tendency is to repeat yourself, try deleting or combining sentences. See if your condensation makes your draft more powerful. You should be careful, of course, not to take out anything that is necessary to your essay.

13. Standing back from the draft, check to see if you might not be fighting a pull from the essay. Does it really want to take you somewhere other than where you have taken it? Consider whether you might not want to follow that other impulse, and then write the essay that leads you where it wants to go. See if you like that reformulation better than the draft.

Stage 10: Editing the Final Draft

After you have finished your major reformulation, you should have something that is very near a finished essay. At this point, there are several questions you can ask yourself and procedures you can follow to become, in effect, your own editor. This is true even though editing is probably not a skill that can be easily learned. Editing requires that you be able to see your own writing as if it were someone else's: to see it with a cold eye, making sure not only that there are no mistakes—misspellings and awkwardnesses—but that the rhythms of the prose are good; making sure it just, well, sounds "right." To do all this, there are several procedures you can go through:

1. Test *each* of your sentences *in its context*: Is your opening sentence (or your second sentence, perhaps) an announcement of your major premise? If not, is your opening paragraph, at the very least, an introduction to your thesis; does it direct your reader to the subject?

2. Can you judge the role each of your subsequent sentences plays? Can you say to yourself, with confidence: "*This* sentence is a piece of evidence to support that assertion"? "*This* sentence is an exception to the generalization I just made"? "*This* sentence explores the implications of what

I just said"? "*This* sentence contains my hypothesis"? "*This* sentence is a reiteration of my earlier point"?

3. We said earlier that you should not polish your sentences in the draft, because you cannot know what the best form of those sentences will be until the end of the essay. Now is the time to decide what the best form of each of your sentences is, and you should decide on the basis of the *position* of that sentence in your argument and on the basis of its *function* within a paragraph. Do whatever is necessary to lead your reader from one sentence to the next. Provide the transitions, the *since*'s, *because*'s, *therefore*'s, and *however*'s that your essay requires if those are not already in place in the sentences.

4. You should be able to answer the following questions about each sentence: How is this sentence functioning in my essay? What is it doing there, and what is it doing *at this point* in my essay? Does it belong there? Does this particular sentence need a couple of other sentences to support it? Is its relation to the previous sentence unclear? Think about the kinds of relationship between sentences you found in the excerpts we have read throughout this book. Those relationships need not be remorselessly "logical." Remember we said the essay is a place in which you can think on paper: you can muse, examine cases, explore alternatives, provide analogies. But there must be some order to what you write, and sentence must follow sentence by some logic.

5. If you are in doubt about whether your essay holds together and provides its readers with all the help they need to follow it, test it in this way. Read the first sentence, put your hand over the following sentence, and ask yourself, *What kind of sentence must necessarily follow after this one?* Then answer that question honestly. Anything resembling a mysterious, unexpected sentence will *require* subsequent exemplification and explanation. Any apparent jump to a new subject will *require* an explanation of why and how it is not really a jump—or at the very least, a justificaiton for the jump. Any new term introduced will *require* a def-

inition, or at least an explanation of its relationship to other terms in your essay.

6. X-ray each of your sentences; that is, identify the grammatical "bones" of each sentence, especially those that just do not sound quite "right." Identify the principal subject and verb. Then check all the other elements—subordinate clauses, phrases in apposition, modifiers, pronouns. See if your subject and verb are in agreement. See if each pronoun (*it, they, he*) has an easily identifiable noun to modify in the preceding sentence. Grammatical fuzziness is nearly always a symptom of fuzziness in thinking. If you say "It is a matter of . . .," be sure you can identify that *it*.

7. After you have arrived at what you think is the final version of your essay, test it again against your original scribblings and notes. How much of your scribbling has been polished out of your final draft? How much of it do you want to put back in? For years I have read students' roughest rough drafts as well as their finished essays, and I am often astonished at how much exciting material gets left behind on the coffee-stained napkin on which they first got the brainstorm for their essay. Especially things like examples and model cases get left behind. And explanations of why the topic interested them in the first place, and what their personal relationship to the ideas and material is. In this late stage, if this has happened to your essay, consider bringing that necessary material back into the essay. Otherwise, as you revise, the danger is that each of your succeeding drafts tends to get more and more abstract; more and more cut off from both the real material you began with, and from the excitement that prompted you to write about that material in the first place.

8. Once you have your "final" final draft, give it to someone you trust to read. Even the experts—or maybe especially the experts—need someone else to read their writing to see if it is good and makes sense. Look at the acknowledgment pages of books sometime. You will find writer after writer thanking the people who took the time to read and comment on his or her rough drafts. Once we get very

close to our own words, we lose some of our capacity to see them objectively, and when that happens, it helps to have someone else read what we have written. This need not be threatening, and ought to be a chance for you to share, to teach someone else what you have learned. And that, of course, is why we write.

Bibliography

In this kind of book, in which names and theories have been rather cavalierly scattered here and there, one wants to offer a proper bibliography so that the reader may find what those theories look like in the original, in their context, argued and defended by their creators and proponents. But a proper bibliography for such a book as this is impossible to provide, for several reasons.

First, partly what makes the subject of composition so exciting is also what makes putting together a proper bibliography impossible. The field is a lively and fluid one: there is new theory every day, and theories are so widely debated among so many people in so many places that it is sometimes impossible to know where an idea originated any more. The worn-out ballpoint exercise I propose in an early chapter of this book, for instance, was inspired by the research of James Britton. I did not read the account of that research in Britton's own work; instead, I heard reports of it in San Francisco at the 1979 Modern Language Association Convention, in a session on research in composing led by Janet Emig. There it was Walter Ong, I think, who recounted the experiment. But it might only have been that Fr. Ong was standing and responding to a point, and that it was, as I dimly suspect, someone on the other side of the room who made reference to Britton's experiment. However unsure I am of that reference, I am quite certain that it was E. D. Hirsch who commented offhandedly at that same session that "it might be that the process of composing may be inaccessible to teachers at the level at which they would like to know about it." I am also quite certain that it was this comment that set me to the work of creating a composition book that would not try to tell students how the composing process works (because, as Hirsch says, we cannot *know* how it works), but would try instead to set up practice exercises and generate what I hoped were the right questions that would allow students and beginning writers to discover their own inner composing processes for themselves. In this case, one reference that should be central in my bibliography is obviously an oral one. It is curious, and appropriately intriguing, that the field of research in written composition should be proceeding at the moment in what is partly an oral tradition.

Second, a proper bibliography is difficult to provide because much of what I read has served, as Charles Dickens calls it in *Little Dorrit,* as "exercises in How Not to Do It." I have read innumerable composition textbooks but most do not appear in this bibliography because what they tell students to do simply did not ring true to my own experience: neither to my experience as a composition teacher nor to my experience as a writer myself. Most of the mystery and the messiness, as I have said, gets left out of those textbooks, and they are what I was most intent on bringing back into my account of the composing process.

But the reverse is also true. Some things by which I have been most influenced did not find their way into specific references in this book. These things are the warnings, admonishments, and wisdom that lurk behind everything I say and propose. Those who know composition research will find them there readily. William Coles's notion that one learns to write better primarily by learning how writing works has obviously played a central role in what I propose students do. Ann E. Berthoff's notion that complexity must be present in students' writings from the beginning, and that there are no easy bridges to get students from writing about what-I-did-last-summer to more substantive issues is also central to my approach. So is Jerome Bruner's assumption that to learn anything, people must discover it for themselves and must "*know* what it is that they know." I have tried, in every writing exercise, to set up situations so that students will not be *told* what works, but will discover what works for them. It might be said that my exercises—which allow students to check their own prose for its strengths and weaknesses, and which allow them not so much to judge their finished products as to avoid major disasters at the earliest stages of formulating and thinking and writing—are geared to do what Bruner says the good teacher must always do: set things up so that students can "perceive success or failure as information." My interpretation of that advice is that one can only perceive success or failure as "information" if one can experience that success or failure in private. This is why so many of my lists of things to do are procedures writers can carry out themselves—in private. Such things as Janice Lauer's "Toward a Metatheory of Heuristic Procedures," in *College Composition and Communication* (October 1979), will not be found in my text either. But they were things I felt and heard at my back while writing every page.

Third, and consistent with my own assertions about how composing works, much of the thinking that has gone into this book has been percolating in me for years, long before I had any idea of writing a writing book, and references to what inspired it are no longer retrievable, so far in the past did they begin. I know, for instance, that the debate typified in Schopenhauer's assertion, on the one hand, that "Words are the death of thought," and by Coleridge's assertion, on the other hand, that "Words think for us," lurks at the heart of what I have written. I know that Piaget's research into the "ego-centered" language of children lurks here too: Do students fail to provide enough context in what they write because they are still writing childlike or "ego-centered" prose, as Piaget suggests? Or is it more as Lev Vygotsky thought: that such prose is not ego-centered but, quite the contrary, "sociocentric." That is, do students fail to provide enough context because they believe they are already part of a social group that shares so many of their assumptions that they do not *need* to provide elaborate contexts for their writings?

Finally, such is the state of composition research that a good bit of the most helpful tactics and wisest advice will not be found in composition research, books, or articles, but in quite different places: in the sciences, and even in accounts of problem-solving episodes written by Synectics people in "think tanks." (I say this although I do not hold with those in composition research who see the writing of essays being helped by thinking of the act of writing as a kind of "problem solving," narrowly construed.) All of this makes what I provide as bibliography look more than a bit scattered. Nonetheless, if we are in what Thomas Kuhn would call the "pre-paradigm" stage in composition research, one need look where one can and find what works where one will. What "works" for me is listed below. Because the readings I have done often have provided samples of writing that are included in my text as demonstrations or inspirations for writing exercises, I have included full references to these sources in this bibliography as well.

Albin, Rochelle Semmel. "The Battle of the Brain." *Real Paper,* 17 May 1980, pp. 12–13.

Allen, Michael. "Writing Away from Fear: Mina Shaughnessy and the Uses of Authority." *College English* 41 (1980): 857–67.

Anderson, Richard C., and Ausubel, David P., eds. *Readings in the Psychology of Cognition.* New York: Holt, Rinehart & Winston, 1965.

Arnheim, Rudolf. *Visual Thinking.* Berkeley and Los Angeles: University of California Press, 1969.

Barnet, Richard J. Review of *The C.I.A. and the Cult of Intelligence,* by Victor Marchetti and John Marks. *New York Review of Books,* 3 October 1974, pp. 29–31.

Barzini, Luigi. Review of *Mussolini: An Intimate Biography by His Widow,* by Rachele Mussolini. *New York Review of Books,* 17 October 1974, p. 22.

Barzun, Jacques. *The House of Intellect.* 1959. Reprint. Chicago: Midway Reprints, 1975.

Bernstein, Basil. *Class, Codes, and Control.* London: Routledge & Kegan Paul, 1971.

———. "Social Class, Language, and Socialization." In *Language and Social Context,* edited by P. P. Giglioli. London: Harmondsworth, 1972, pp. 165–66.

Berthoff, Ann E. *Forming/Thinking/Writing.* Rochelle Park, N.J.: Hayden, 1978.

———. "Tolstoy, Vygotsky, and the Making of Meaning." *College Composition and Communication* 29 (1978): 249–55.

Bettelheim, Bruno. *The Informed Heart: Autonomy in a Mass Age.* New York: Free Press, 1966.

———. *The Uses of Enchantment: The Meaning and Importance of Fairy Tales.* New York: Random House, 1977.

Black, Max. *Critical Thinking.* Englewood Cliffs, N.J.: Prentice-Hall, 1952.

Blumenthal, Arthur L. *The Process of Cognition.* Englewood Cliffs, N.J.: Prentice-Hall, 1977.

Britton, James. *The Development of Writing Abilities*. London: Schools Council Publications, 1975.

————. *Language and Learning*. Coral Gables: University of Miami Press, 1970.

Britton, W. Earl. "What Is Technical Writing?" *College Composition and Communication* 16 (1965): 113–16.

Bronowski, Jacob. *The Origins of Knowledge and Imagination*. New Haven: Yale University Press, 1978.

Brown, Roger. *Words and Things*. New York: Free Press, 1958.

Bruner, Jerome. "The Act of Discovery." In *Readings in the Psychology of Cognition*, edited by Richard C. Anderson and David P. Ausubel. New York: Holt, Rinehart & Winston, 1965.

————. *On Knowing*. Cambridge: Harvard University Press, 1962.

————. *Toward a Theory of Instruction*. New York: Norton, 1968.

————, Goodnow, J. J., and Austin, G. A. *A Study of Thinking*. New York: John Wiley, 1956.

Burke, Kenneth. *Permanence and Change*. Indianapolis: Bobbs-Merrill, 1965.

Coles, William. *Composing: Writing as a Self-Composing Process*. Rochelle Park, N.J.: Hayden, 1974.

————. *Teaching Composing*. Rochelle Park, N.J.: Hayden, 1974.

Cooper, Charles, and Odell, Lee, eds. *Research on Composing*. Urbana, Ill.: National Council of Teachers of English, 1978.

Craft, Robert. "The Poet and the Rake." *New York Review of Books*, 12 December 1974, pp. 30–31.

deBono, Edward. *Lateral Thinking*. New York: Harper & Row, 1970.

————. *New Think*. New York: Avon Books, 1967.

————. *Po: Beyond Yes and No*. New York: Simon & Schuster, 1972. Reprint. New York: Penguin Books, 1973.

————. *The Use of Lateral Thinking*. London: Jonathan Cape, 1967. Reprint. New York: Penguin Books, 1971.

deCastillejo, Irene Claremont. *Knowing Woman*. New York: Harper & Row, 1973.

Dennett, Daniel C. *Brainstorms: Philosophical Essays on Mind and Psychology*. Montgomery, Vt.: Bradford Books, 1978.

Diamond, Stanley. *In Search of the Primitive: A Critique of Civilization*. New Brunswick, N.J.: Transaction Books, 1974.

Ellmann, Mary. *Thinking about Women*. New York: Harcourt Brace, 1970.

Ellul, Jacques. *The Technological Society.* New York: Vintage Books, 1964.

Emig, Janet. *The Composing Processes of Twelfth Graders.* Urbana, Ill.: National Council of Teachers of English, 1971.

Feyerabend, Paul. *Against Method.* New York: Schocken, 1978.

Fiske, Edward B. "Finding Fault with the Testers." *New York Times Magazine*, 18 November 1979, pp. 152–62.

Flesch, Rudolf. *The Art of Readable Writing.* New York: Collier Books, 1949.

Flower, Linda, and Hayes, John R. "The Cognition of Discovery: Defining a Rhetorical Problem." *College Composition and Communication* 31 (1980): 21–32.

—————. "Writer-Based Prose: A Cognitive Basis for Problems in Writing." *College English* 41 (1979): 19–37.

Foucault, Michel. *The Archaeology of Knowledge and the Discourse on Language.* Translated by A. M. Sheridan Smith. New York: Harper & Row, 1972.

Frantz, Charles. *The Student Anthropologist's Handbook.* Cambridge: Schenkman, 1972.

Ghiselin, Brewster, ed. *The Creative Process.* New York: Mentor Books, 1972.

Goffman, Erving. *Frame Analysis: An Essay on the Organization of Experience.* Cambridge: Harvard University Press, 1974.

Goldstein, Kurt. *Human Nature in the Light of Psychopathology.* Cambridge: Harvard University Press, 1940.

Gordon, William J. J. *The Metaphorical Way of Learning and Knowing: Applying Synectics to Sensitivity and Learning Situations.* Cambridge: Porpoise Books, 1966.

—————. *Synectics: The Development of Creative Capacity.* New York: Macmillan Collier Books, 1961.

Gould, Stephen Jay. "Darwin's Middle Road." *Natural History*, vol. 88, no. 12 (December 1979): 27–31.

—————. *Ever Since Darwin.* New York: W. W. Norton, 1977.

Greer, Germaine. *The Female Eunuch.* New York: McGraw-Hill, 1971.

Hadamard, Jacques. *The Psychology of Invention in the Mathematical Field.* Princeton: Princeton University Press, 1945. Reprint. New York: Dover, 1954.

Halliday, M.A.K., and Hassan, Ruqaiya. *Cohesion in English.* New York: Longman, 1976.

Hanson, Norwood Russell. *Patterns of Discovery.* Cambridge: Cambridge University Press, 1958.

Henry, William A., 3rd. "Still Quacking after All These Years." *Boston Globe,* 22 February 1980.

Herschberger, Ruth. *Adam's Rib.* New York: Harper & Row, 1948.

Hirsch, E. D., Jr. *The Philosophy of Composition.* Chicago: University of Chicago Press, 1977.

Hoffer, Eric. "Works and Days." *Harper's,* October 1978, pp. 73–75.

Hofstadter, Richard. *Anti-Intellectualism in American Life.* New York: Knopf, 1963.

Horgan, Paul. *Approaches to Writing: Reflections and Notes on the Art of Writing from a Career of Half a Century.* New York: Farrar, Strauss & Giroux, 1968.

James, William. *The Principles of Psychology.* 1890. Reprint. New York: Dover, 1950.

Kinneavy, James. *A Theory of Discourse.* New York: Norton, 1971.

Koestler, Arthur. *The Act of Creation: A Study of the Conscious and Unconscious in Science and Art.* New York: Dell, 1967.

Kuhn, Thomas S. *The Structure of Scientific Revolutions.* 2d ed., enlarged. Chicago: University of Chicago Press, 1970.

Langer, Susanne. *Philosophy in a New Key.* Cambridge: Harvard University Press, 1942.

Lapote, Phillip. "Helping Children Start to Write." In *Research on Composing.* Urbana, Ill.: National Council of Teachers of English, 1978.

Lessing, Doris. *Particularly Cats.* New York: Simon & Schuster, 1967.

Lewis, C. S. *An Experiment in Criticism.* Cambridge: Cambridge University Press, 1961.

Luria, A. R. *Cognitive Development: Its Cultural and Social Foundations.* Translated by Martin Lopez-Morillas and Lynn Solotaroff. Edited by Michael Cole. Cambridge: Harvard University Press, 1976.

McKeller, Peter. *Imagination and Thinking: A Psychological Analysis.* London: Cohen & West, 1957.

McNeill, C. G. "A Memory of Malcolm Lowry." In *American Review 17.* New York: Bantam Books, 1973, pp. 35–39.

McNeill, William H. *Plagues and People*. New York: Doubleday Anchor Books, 1976.

Maimon, Elaine P. "Talking to Strangers." *College Composition and Communication* 30 (1979): 364–69.

Maritain, Jacques. *Creative Intuition in Art and Poetry*. Princeton: Princeton University Press, 1977.

Martin, Harold; Ohmann, Richard M.; and Wheatley, James H. *The Logic and Rhetoric of Exposition*. New York: Holt, Rinehart & Winston, 1963.

Mead, Margaret. *Coming of Age in Samoa*. New York: William Morrow, 1928.

Mencken, H. L. "The Sahara of the Bozart." Reprinted in *A Mencken Chrestomathy*. Edited and annotated by H. L. Mencken. New York: Alfred A. Knopf, 1949.

Miller, George A. "The Magical Number Seven, Plus or Minus Two: Some Limits on Our Capacity for Processing Information." In *Readings in the Psychology of Cognition*, edited by Richard C. Anderson and David P. Ausubel. New York: Holt, Rinehart & Winston, 1965.

———. *The Psychology of Communication*. London: Harmondsworth, 1970.

Murdoch, Iris. *The Sovereignty of Good*. New York: Schocken Books, 1971.

Nettler, Gwynn. *Explanations*. New York: McGraw Hill, 1970.

Olson, David R. "From Utterance to Text: The Bias of Language in Speech and Writing." *Harvard Educational Review* 47 (1977): 257–81.

Ong, Walter J., S.J., *Interfaces of the Word*. Ithaca: Cornell University Press, 1977.

———. "Literacy and Orality in Our Times," in *Profession '79*. Selected Articles from the "Bulletins of the Association of Departments of English." MLA, 1979, 1–7.

———. *The Presence of the Word*. New Haven: Yale University Press, 1967.

Ornstein, Robert T. *The Psychology of Consciousness*. New York: Penguin Books, 1972.

Park, Douglas. "Theories and Expectations: On Conceiving Composition and Rhetoric as a Discipline." *College English* 41 (1979): 47–56.

Piaget, Jean. *The Language and Thought of the Child*. New York: Harcourt Brace & World, 1932.

Poincaré, Henri. *Science and Hypothesis*. New York: Dover, 1952.

Polanyi, Michael. *Meaning*. Chicago: University of Chicago Press, 1971.

———. *The Tacit Dimension*. New York: Doubleday, 1967.

Popper, Karl. *The Logic of Scientific Discovery*. New York: Harper & Row, 1959.

Prince, George M. *The Practice of Creativity*. New York: Collier Books, 1970.

Richards, I. A. *The Philosophy of Rhetoric*. New York: Oxford University Press, 1965.

Roth, Philip. "I Always Wanted You to Admire My Fasting: Or, Looking at Kafka." In *American Review 17*. New York: Bantam Books, 1973, p. 17.

Rugg, Harold. *Imagination*. New York: Harper & Row, 1963.

Ryle, Gilbert. *The Concept of Mind*. New York: Barnes & Noble, 1949.

Sheed, Wilfred. Review of *W. C. Fields by Himself*, with commentary by Ronald Fields. *New York Review of Books*, 31 October 1974, p. 26.

Spencer, Herbert. *An Autobiography*, 2 vols. New York: D. Appleton, 1904.

Taylor, Daniel M. *Explanation and Meaning*. Cambridge: Cambridge University Press, 1970.

Thomas, Lewis. *The Lives of a Cell: Notes of a Biology Watcher*. New York: Bantam Books, 1974.

Vidal, Gore. "The Great World and Louis Auchincloss." *New York Review of Books*, 18 July 1974, pp. 10–15. Reprinted in *Matters of Fact and Fiction: Essays 1973–76*. New York: Random House, 1977.

Vivas, Eliseo. *Creation and Discovery*. Chicago: Gateway Press, 1955.

Vygotsky, Lev S. *Mind in Society*. Edited by Michael Cole, Vera John-Steiner, Sylvia Scribner, and Ellen Souberman. Cambridge: Harvard University Press, 1978.

———. *Thought and Language*. Edited and translated by Eugenia Hanfmann and Gertrude Vakar. Cambridge: MIT Press, 1962.

Warnock, Mary. *Imagination*. Berkeley and Los Angeles: University of California Press, 1976.

Westcott, Malcolm R. *Toward a Contemporary Psychology of Intuition*. New York: Holt, Rinehart & Winston, 1968.

White, E. B. "Here Is New York." In *Great Essays,* edited by Houston Peterson. New York: Pocket Books, 1958.

White, Hayden. *Tropics of Discourse.* Baltimore: Johns Hopkins University Press, 1978.

Whitehead, Alfred North. *Modes of Thought.* New York: Macmillan, 1938.

Wilden, Anthony. *System and Structure: Essays in Communication and Exchange.* New York: Methuen, 1980.

Williams, Duncan. *Trousered Apes.* New York: Dell, 1973.

Wilson, John. *Thinking with Concepts.* Cambridge: Cambridge University Press, 1963.

Woodward, C. Vann. Review of *Roll, Jordan Roll,* by Eugene Genovese. *New York Review of Books,* 3 October 1974, pp. 19–21.

Young, Richard. "Invention: A Topographical Survey." In *Teaching Composition,* edited by Gary Tate. Fort Worth: Texas Christian University Press, 1976.

————. "Paradigms and Problems: Needed Research in Rhetorical Invention." In *Research on Composing,* edited by Charles Cooper and Lee Odell. Urbana, Ill.: National Council of Teachers of English, 1978, pp. 29–47.

Index